THE CIVIL JUSTICE PROCESS

A Sequential Model of the Mobilization of Law

STUDIES ON LAW AND SOCIAL CONTROL

DONALD BLACK *Series Editor*

Center for Criminal Justice
Harvard Law School
Cambridge, Massachusetts 02138

P. H. Gulliver. Disputes and Negotiations:
A Cross-Cultural Perspective

Sandra B. Burman and Barbara E. Harrell-Bond (Editors),
The Imposition of Law

Cathie J. Witty. Mediation and Society:
Conflict Management in Lebanon

Francis G. Snyder. Capitalism and Legal Change:
An African Transformation

Allan V. Horwitz. The Social Control of Mental Illness

Richard L. Abel (Editor). The Politics of Informal Justice,
Vol. 1: The American Experience; Vol. 2: Comparative Studies

William M. O'Barr. Linguistic Evidence:
Language, Power, and Strategy in the Courtroom

Donald Black (Editor). Toward a General Theory of Social
Control, Vol. 1: Fundamentals; Vol. 2: Selected Problems

Matthew Silberman. The Civil Justice Process:
A Sequential Model of the Mobilization of Law

THE CIVIL JUSTICE PROCESS

A Sequential Model of the Mobilization of Law

MATTHEW SILBERMAN

Department of Sociology
Bucknell University
Lewisburg, Pennsylvania

1985

ACADEMIC PRESS, INC.

(Harcourt Brace Jovanovich, Publishers)

Orlando San Diego New York London
Toronto Montreal Sydney Tokyo

ACADEMIC PRESS, INC.
Orlando, Florida 32887

United Kingdom Edition published by
ACADEMIC PRESS INC. (LONDON) LTD.
24–28 Oval Road, London NW1 7DX

LIBRARY OF CONGRESS CATALOGING IN PUBLICATION DATA

Silberman, Matthew.
The civil justice process.

Bibliography: p.
Includes index.
1. Dispute resolution (Law)—Michigan—Detroit.
2. Justice, Administration of—Michigan—Detroit.
3. Lawyers—Michigan—Detroit. I. Title.
KFX1384.1.J83S53 1985 347.774'34 85-7537
ISBN 0-12-643350-X (alk. paper) 347.77434

PRINTED IN THE UNITED STATES OF AMERICA

85 86 87 88 9 8 7 6 5 4 3 2 1

To
Sharon
Eric and Diana

CONTENTS

4

SITUATIONAL FACTORS IN THE MOBILIZATION OF LAW

5

STRUCTURAL FACTORS IN THE MOBILIZATION OF LAW

6

OPPORTUNITY STRUCTURES AND ACCESS TO LAW

7

DISPUTES AS SOCIAL ACTS

8

CONCLUSION

APPENDIX A

THE LOG-LINEAR APPROACH TO THE ANALYSIS OF LEGAL PROCESS

APPENDIX B

PREFACE

This book is about the transformation of everyday disputes into legal claims. It is a study of the process by which citizens decide to contact an attorney for assistance in situations in which legal remedies are not usually sought. These situations included consumer problems, disputes between neighbors, and other problems that arise during the course of everyday living. The findings are based on a survey of 780 Detroit metropolitan area residents conducted in 1967 by the Detroit Area Study (DAS) at the University of Michigan.

As a teaching fellow for the original Detroit Area Study in 1967, I became quite familiar with all aspects of the project. I participated in the construction of the survey instrument, interviewed respondents, helped construct codes for the open-ended questions, and assisted in the supervision of graduate student coders and the professional coding staff at the Institute for Social Research. My familiarity with the original project enabled me to interpret with confidence and, where necessary, to recode some of the variables for the analysis presented in this book.

The survey instrument used in the 1967 Detroit Area Study is ideally suited to the purpose of this volume, the development of a sequential model of the mobilization of law. Each interview consisted of a questionnaire that included incident schedules designed to solicit case histories of disputes. These incident schedules were organized to develop information about the sequence of events involved in settling disputes. After some introductory questions about hypothetical situations in which disputes might arise, respondents were asked to indicate which of 23 specific disputes they had actually experienced. These involved disputes between neighbors, landlord–tenant disputes, consumer problems, disputes with public organizations, and discrimination (principally in housing and employment). In-depth case histories were then obtained on the two most serious disputes reported by each respondent.

For sociologists, political scientists, economists, and legal scholars, this book provides a framework for the evaluation of process models of legal behavior. By employing log-linear models that take into account the conditional nature of the relationships between stages of the civil dispute process, it becomes possible to quantify aspects of legal process that have heretofore been treated only in qualitative terms. The analysis of the transformation of disputes into legal claims reveals that this process has two distinct phases, one "primary" and the other "secondary." Consistent with a value-added model of legal process, these two phases are explained independently, the former by the situational context of the initial dispute and the latter by structural determinants of access to legal resources.

The study evaluates the implications of mobilization theory and opportunity theory for explaining the use of lawyers in everyday life. It also elaborates Donald Black's theory of legal behavior by specifying some of the conditions under which the propositions of the theory are and are not supported.

The findings reported in the following chapters also have important practical implications for those who analyze or administer social–legal programs. America has become a litigious society; its citizens are increasingly prone to seek legal counsel even for the most minor matters. By examining the distribution of economic and legal resources in different communities within the Detroit metropolitan area, we find that the use of legal services is predominantly a middle-class phenomenon, even for matters unrelated to property. The more impersonal relationships among the middle class and the concentration of wealth in middle-class communities create a predisposition to seek legal remedies instead of settling disputes through direct negotiation or through informal mediation by third parties. But participation in the organizational life of the community plays a key role in determining the course of everyday disputes by providing alternative mechanisms for their settlement as well as facilitating access to legal resources should such alternatives fail. This suggests that participation in voluntary associations encourages disputants to settle disputes outside the legal arena while increasing access to legal remedies should the need arise.

In the first chapter, I develop a sequential model of the civil dispute process. I describe the method by which I propose to quantify models of social process and present the theoretical assumptions that guide the present work. Distinguishing between primary and secondary aspects of legal process, I describe the basic elements of a value-added model of the mobilization of law. In Chapter 2, I describe the setting and the design of the study. The year this survey was conducted, 1967, was significant for two reasons. First, it was the year of the Detroit riot, a period of great turmoil in America in general, and in Detroit in particular. It was also prior to the effective institutionalization of government-sponsored free legal services for the poor. Now, in the mid-1980s, when there is strong pressure from conservative politicians to eliminate this government program, we can learn what the impact of its elimination might be from an examination of the delivery of legal services at a time when such a program was not available. In Chapter 3,

I describe the distribution of disputes in the Detroit metropolitan area as a function of the social-class characteristics of its population and continue with selected case histories of serious disputes that did and did not involve legal contacts.

The findings of this study are presented in Chapters 4 through 7. Chapter 4 presents the results of the analysis of the effects of situational factors on the dispute-transformation process. Chapter 5 presents the results of the analysis of the effects of structural factors on the mobilization of lawyers in settling disputes. Chapter 6 assesses the effects of the distribution of economic and legal resources on access to law. Chapter 7 describes the process by which structural factors affect the outcomes of disputes when treated as legal categories. The final chapter summarizes the findings, discusses their theoretical implications, and considers the prospects for future research on legal process. Details of the log-linear model are given in Appendix A and the DAS Incident Schedules in Appendix B.

ACKNOWLEDGMENTS

The list of individuals who have contributed in various capacities to the completion of this work is indeed a long one. Leon Mayhew and Albert J. Reiss, Jr., principal investigators of the DAS survey, made the present effort possible. Howard Schuman, Director of the DAS, Wolfgang Grichting and James House, DAS teaching fellows, and about 30 graduate students enrolled in the DAS training program all contributed to the final product.

I am grateful to Bucknell University's Department of Psychology for making available two of its ablest graduate students to work as research assistants on my project. Robert Crowling and Charles Bur assisted in the management and analysis of the data. Mr. Crowling's extensive knowledge of computer hardware and software played an especially important role throughout the study.

My special thanks go to Yvonne Wetzel, who patiently typed and retyped each of the many drafts the following chapters have gone through. I am especially grateful to Joyce Khoury, a person of enormous energy, whose performance in her multiple roles as research assistant, clerk, and typist was invaluable. Ms. Khoury coded the census data, did basic recode operations on the computer, ran analysis programs, and did most of the typing on the research project.

A number of people have commented on portions of this work in its earlier version as a series of papers presented at the annual meetings of the American Sociological Association and the Law and Society Association. Among these are Amitai Etzioni, John Kendrick, Richard Lempert, and H. Laurence Ross. While I have not always agreed with the comments, they sharpened my awareness of the issues and how best to address them.

I cannot say enough about the importance of Clifford Clogg's contribution, as teacher and consultant, to my understanding of the techniques and principles underlying log-linear analysis. My first exposure to this approach to data analysis was a seminar given by Professor Clogg. It was then that I realized the potential that this approach had for contributing to our knowledge of legal process. As consultant on this project, his ability to transmit his knowledge of the log-linear approach to the analysis of qualitative data was essential to its success.

This study was supported by Grant SOC78–09921 from the Law and Social Sciences Program of the National Science Foundation.

1

INTRODUCTION

This book is about disputes. It is a study of their transformation from disjunctive events in the lives of ordinary citizens to civil legal matters. Disputing is a social process that begins with the disruption of normal routines in everyday life and, under certain conditions, ends with the active involvement of agents of governmental social control as dispute settlers or norm enforcers. Disputes may be avoided, negotiated directly between the disputing parties, settled through mediation by third parties, or resolved in court through the enforcement of norms backed by the coercive apparatus of the state. Disputes become legal matters when agents of governmental social control are mobilized on behalf of one or more parties to the dispute.

This book also concerns lawyers. It is about the role that attorneys play in the transformation of disputes into legal claims. For civil matters, contact with an attorney is usually the event that brings disputes from the public domain into the legal arena (Miller and Sarat, 1981). Consequently, attorneys play more than a gatekeeper's role regarding access to the law; they provide a central link between society and the law, at least in a democratically organized society. Attorneys often interpret existing legal rights and duties to citizens who, in turn, may seek to transform socially defined expectations into new legal rights and duties.

The mobilization of lawyers in civil disputes occurs primarily in response to requests for assistance from the community. The mobilization of law is considered proactive when agents of governmental social control initiate dispute-settlement or law-enforcement mechanisms; it is considered reactive when citizens themselves initiate legal activity of one form or another (see Black, 1973). The focus of the present study is exclusively on the reactive mobilization of lawyers in civil matters. It is a study of the conditions under which citizens decide to seek the advice of an attorney when faced with everyday disputes with their neighbors, landlords, employers, or representatives of large private and public organizations with whom they routinely come into contact.

There is a tendency in the dispute-processing literature to treat law and society as analytically and empirically distinct phenomena, rather than seeing disputing as a single social process (see Sarat and Grossman, 1975;

Miller and Sarat, 1981; Felstiner, Abel, and Sarat, 1981). As a result, prelegal aspects of disputing are analyzed separately from legal factors, and different theoretical frameworks are used to account for each. In this book, I treat disputing as a single social process in which the social organization of contacts with lawyers plays a central role (Mayhew and Reiss, 1969; Felstiner, 1974). My objective is to develop an analytical framework suitable for quantitative analysis such that the dispute-transformation process can be represented symbolically and mathematically from beginning to end in a single causal model.

THE DISPUTE AS PROCESS

Analytically speaking, the unit of analysis for this study is the *dispute*. Although the individual is the sampling unit in the original survey on which this study is based, interviewees were treated as informants regarding disputes that they had experienced. More is said later about this type of cluster sampling. The present study is unique in developing a methodology for the direct sampling of disputes. Previous research on disputing fails to make the distinction between the sampling unit and the object of analysis. Despite disclaimers (see Miller and Sarat, 1981:533), research on disputes largely remains research on disputants. This explains the failure of such research to identify the relevant characteristics of disputes that account for variation in dispute processing (see Miller and Sarat, 1981:561).

In this book, a dispute is situationally defined as any disruption in daily or other routines produced through violations of normative expectations by some person, group, or organization. I use this term in the broadest possible sense, encompassing all situations in which disagreements stem from normative violations (cf. Gulliver, 1979:74). Whether disputes are resolved through immediate negotiation (e.g., a landlord fixes a faucet after persistent complaints, followed by threats by a tenant to withhold rent) or through mediation by a third party (e.g., a couple is reconciled following marital counseling), to distinguish between disputes that are resolved and those that are not begs the question that is central to this research: What are the conditions under which disputes are or are not resolved by the parties themselves, by third parties, or ultimately by the courts?

Disputes are often treated as criminal matters. For example, acts of vandalism by neighborhood teenagers often become police matters. And disputes between landlords and tenants are frequently the result of housing code violations. Nevertheless, even when criminal charges can be pressed, they rarely are (see Black, 1980:109–192). The police are infrequently called to handle disputes, and, when they are, it is unusual for them to respond by arresting someone. In fact, there are civil legal remedies for many situations in which the police are called (Black, 1980:167). For example, damage to property is recoverable under tort law. In many cases, disputes between neighbors erupt in actions that generate criminal complaints, although the root of the problem is in some sort of interpersonal conflict (see Merry, 1979). The act of calling the police is itself a form of social control, whether or not a crime has been committed. The object of the present analysis is to study the process by which disputes are transformed into civil legal matters, regardless of whether or not they could have been treated as criminal. The purpose of this research is to study the conditions that lead citizens to seek civil legal remedies for their disputes, not the possible existence of such remedies or the possibility that the state could impose criminal penalties on one of the disputants.

The literature is replete with debate about appropriate labels for each stage of the dispute process (Fitzgerald and Dickins, 1981:702–705). Even those studies that purport to be based on the same research (e.g., the Civil Litigation Research Project, see Kritzer, 1981; Miller and Sarat, 1981; Felstiner, Abel, and Sarat, 1981) employ inconsistent and contradictory labels for different stages of the dispute-transformation process. For some, the case is the basic unit of analysis (see Black, 1973; Kritzer, 1981; Silbey, 1981). This approach defines disputes in terms of existing civil legal categories. Consequently, the research using this strategy (e.g., the CLRP, or the American Bar Foundation's survey, *The Legal Needs of the Public;* Curran, 1977) is biased conservatively in favor of disputes for which legal remedies already exist (see Marks, 1976:195). Still other studies focus only on the last stage of dispute processing, when a dispute has become a case in court or has come before some administrative agency (Merry, 1979; Silbey, 1981).

Miller and Sarat (1981) distinguish between grievances, claims, and disputes, reserving the last category for "rejected claims." On the other hand, Gulliver (1979:75) defines disputes as unresolved disagreements that enter the public domain. A grievance is an entitlement, which if pursued becomes a claim. But entitlements when claimed may or may not become disputes, not because a grievance has been assuaged, but because most such situations do not involve normative violations in the first place. This situation explains why torts are unlikely to become disputes when, say, a personal injury, as in an auto accident, is routinely handled by claims to insurance companies whose more or less favorable responses are accepted as legitimate. When this happens, is there really a "grievance"? Felstiner, Abel, and Sarat (1981) complicate matters further by distinguishing between "naming," "blaming," and "claiming" stages of the dispute-transformation process. A dispute exists when a claim is made (Felstiner, Abel, and Sarat, 1981:631); a grievance exists when another party is blamed, and unperceived injurious experiences become perceived injurious experiences (Miller and Sarat's "grievance") when they can be named or identified. There is little empirical evidence to support the validity of the analytic distinction between naming and blaming. Furthermore, there is no reason to believe that the cognitive and evaluative aspects of such events are separable. In fact, the very essence of disputing involves simultaneously the recognition of a normative violation and an attribution of responsibility. If an appliance fails to function because its parts have worn out after 20 years of heavy use, there is no injury, no grievance, and no dispute. But to identify (name) an injury, say a defective part in a relatively new appliance, is to blame somebody, even when uncertain as to who is responsible. Whether or not we do something about the problem may depend more on our ability to clearly identify who is to blame than on our decision to blame somebody.

Disputes are variously defined as potential legal matters or civil cases, rejected claims or persistent disagreements, claims for redress of perceived injuries, and disagreements. Following phenomenological and interactionist traditions, I consider the universe of disputes to include only situations defined as normative violations by those who experience them. Disputes cannot be "unperceived," since the recognition of disputes is culturally defined. So, for example, leaking water faucets in deteriorated slums will not be seen as a problem by residents who take such conditions for granted. The middle-class apartment dweller, however, will see such a situation as warranting repair. This situation is then defined as a dispute only when the landlord fails to fix the leak or delays in doing so. Disputing begins with the violation of socially defined expectations.

Rather than continuing the endless debate on what labels to apply to each stage of the dispute process, I prefer to employ descriptive terms for each stage of the process. Disputes begin when we become aware that our daily routines have been disrupted by some person, group, or organization. At this point, we *recognize* the existence of a dispute. When a dispute becomes *serious* enough, we feel that something ought to be done, either through direct negotiation or by seeking help from someone else, say an attorney. If someone *contacts an attorney*, a dispute may be handled in a more or less routine manner, or it may become a *serious legal matter*. Such matters often end up *in court*. The language I have used is meant to convey the continuous flow of social process, with *stages* being analytic distinctions that correspond more or less to identifiable empirical events. This approach avoids the reification of the stages of disputing that is created by the legalistic labels currently in use.

THE SEQUENTIAL MODEL OF LEGAL PROCESS

In this chapter, I introduce the disparate theoretical elements that constitute the process model developed in the book. The next chapter is devoted to a full elaboration of the model as it applies to the mobilization of lawyers in the processing of everyday disputes. My objective is to develop a formal model of social process in general and of legal process in particular. I seek to bridge the gap between abstract theoretical approaches to the study of social process and atheoretical empirical accounts of the correlates of particular processes. Ralph Turner's (1953) work, "The Quest for Universals in Sociological Research," provides the conceptualization that makes it possible to bridge the gap between structural functionalist (Smelser, 1962) and symbolic interactionist theories (Becker, 1963; Lofland and Stark, 1965) of social process and quantitative analyses (multivariate or not) of disputing and other legal processes.

A formal model of social process can be presented in diagrammatic or propositional form (Costner and Leik, 1964). Consequently, the distinction between qualitative and quantitative theory and the distinction between theory and research disappear. I agree with Glaser and Strauss (1967) that theory must be well grounded, rooted in generalizations from observable events. Qualitative assumptions about the world are much closer to our experience of social reality, but scientific models of the world tend to be quantitative. We do not experience the world as a series of discrete events, but as a continuous stream of impressions, thoughts, and sensations. Yet as everyday observers of reality (including our own experience) we impose crude cognitive categories on our observations in order to give our experience meaning, to make future action and interaction possible. Thus, we impose structure on experience, defining situations and events according to the dictates of the social units we are part of (Thomas, 1923:41–44). Events occur or they do not occur, objects fit into categories or they do not, and the world appears to be more or less ordered. Nominal scales, based on nominal categories, are closer than any other form of measurement to social reality.

Fortunately, Leo Goodman (1978) has provided us with a mathematical formulation for the analysis of "qualitative/categorical data" that makes more sophisticated techniques based on higher-order levels of measurement no longer necessary. Goodman's log-linear approach to the study of dichotomous and polytomous variables is the mathematical breakthrough that makes the scientific study of social process possible (see Appendix A).

Models of social process are sequential; that is, they are mathematically recursive. Events occur serially, one following the other. Particular steps or stages of a process can be identified and explained. Sequential models differ to the extent that they assume that each stage of a process must be explained independently or that a social process can be explained in its entirety within a single framework.

The Value-Added Model of Social Process

A value-added model is a *strong* version of a sequential model in which each stage of a given social process is explained independently of each succeeding stage, and the independent variables are activated in sequence (see Lofland and Stark, 1965). Social process, from this point of view, can be seen as a series of stages by which a given social phenomenon is altered in such a way as to "allow for progressively fewer outcomes" (Smelser, 1962:14). As each new contingency is introduced, the probability of a given outcome is altered, perhaps favorably (a positive relationship), perhaps not (a negative relationship), depending on the contingency introduced.

A value-added model describes a set of necessary conditions (causes) that, taken together, constitute a sufficient condition for a final outcome. In his study of collective behavior, Smelser (1962:12–21) sees such behavior as the outcome of a series of preconditions (e.g., structural strain) and precipitating factors (e.g., a black family moving into a white neighborhood) that, when combined in a certain way, create an outburst of collective behavior (e.g., a race riot). The value-added approach does not describe a natural history of events, but a critical sequence in which the relevant conditions are activated. Temporal priority and causal priority are clearly distinguished from one another. According to Smelser (1962:14), "every stage in the value-added process, therefore, is a necessary condition for the appropriate and effective addition of value in the next stage." Each subsequent stage represents an increment of value, but the final product or outcome emerges only when all the previous conditions are combined "according to a definite pattern."

Disputing is a social process with analytically distinct stages, from the initial recognition of a dispute to litigation in a court of law. Each stage depends on the existence of previous conditions; for example, the decision to go to court is predicated on the existence of some grievance for which some remedy, legal or otherwise, has been sought unsuccessfully. The strong version of the value-added model assumes that the explanation of each stage of the dispute process is independent of each subsequent stage. Consequently, the variables that account for prelegal stages of disputing (before one contacts an attorney) are not expected to account for legal contacts or other legal variables. Nor are those variables that explain legal contacts expected to explain prelegal aspects of disputing. The failure to make the distinction between explanations of prelegal and legal aspects of the dispute process has led to a considerable amount of confusion. Miller and Sarat (1981), for example, rely on variables designed to account for litigation and other legal variables when they try, without success, to explain prelegal aspects of the dispute process. Explaining disputing is fundamentally different from explaining the mobilization of law. Explanations of the former are situational; explanations of the latter, structural.

Just as there is a structural version of the value-added approach (Smelser, 1962), so there is a situational version rooted in the symbolic interactionist perspective on deviance (see, especially, Becker, 1963; Lofland and Stark, 1965). The symbolic interactionist sees social identity as the product of an ongoing process of increasing commitments. Loosely defined steps in the transformation of individuals into deviant actors can be identified (Becker, 1963:41–58). Labeling theory, derived from this perspective, views the acquisition of roles, and the self implied in each role, in terms of "careers" that depend on a series of contingencies, each of which narrows the field of choices a person has (see Gibbons, 1977:214–221). These contingencies, taken together, constitute a "constellationally-sufficient condition" for deviant conduct (Lofland and Stark, 1965:874). Contingencies may be predispositional (when, for example, a person undergoes an identity crisis), situational (an opportunity for deviant conduct presents itself), or systemic (there are structurally based incentives to engage in deviance). But the most critical sort of contingency is the negative sanction imposed by defining agencies, especially agencies of social control (e.g., mental hospitals, courts, etc.). The assignment of formal labels (e.g., criminal) to individuals transforms "primary" deviance into "secondary" deviance. Secondary deviance is a product of the societal reaction to the initial deviance (Lemert, 1967:40–64).

One of the best examples of an interactionist construction of a value-added model of the deviance process is Lofland and Stark's (1965) description of conversion to a deviant religious perspective. The convert ultimately becomes a "deployable agent," a person totally committed to action on behalf of the religious cult to which he or she has converted. We find such converts soliciting contributions in a variety of public settings, and of course proselytizing their new faith. Before becoming deployable agents, they must experience a personal crisis (e.g., disruption in a close personal relationship), define the world in religious terms (i.e., an active member of a legitimate religious organization is more likely to join a deviant one than a practicing agnostic), and become emotionally attached to members of the cult (Lofland and Stark, 1965:874). These events, like those precipitating collective behavior, need not happen sequentially over time, but must occur in a particular sequence, or "constellation."

Situational theories of deviance are all implicitly instances of value-added, sequential models of deviant behavior. Matza's (1964) notion that delinquents "drift" into and out of delinquency in response to a set of life conditions associated with adolescence illustrates the primary aspects of the deviance process. Theories of deviant careers and labeling in general (Becker, 1960; Cohen, 1966; Glaser, 1971) illustrate secondary aspects of the deviance process. Howard S. Becker (1963) provides the clearest example of a sequential model of deviance in his landmark book, *The Outsiders*. Becker (1963:22–39) describes a sequential model of "deviant careers" in terms of "career contingencies," in which each step in a deviant career is explained separately from each succeeding step and "each explanation constitutes a necessary cause of the behavior." Becoming deviant consists of a series of steps, the end product of which is acquiring a deviant role. Although not made explicit, this is a value-added model of the process by which individuals come to engage in marijuana use. Whereas each step of the process follows a natural history, or sequence, Becker makes no assertion regarding the order of natural occurrence of the situational conditions explaining the occurrence of each step. Becoming a marijuana user follows a logical, natural sequence from "first try" to "regular user," but the conditions explaining why a person may or may not become a regular user, such as moral constraints, are historically and theoretically independent of those situational pressures that lead the person to first try the drug. The process of becoming a marijuana user comprises a set of *dependent* events. The explanations of these events constitute a set of *independent* events that are activated in sequence as they "cause" each dependent event to occur.

Symbolic Representation of the Value-Added Model

The value-added model is an ideal-typical conceptualization of the relationships among several independent and dependent variables. It provides a parsimonious method for organizing a large amount of data in a limited number of equations, propositions, or diagrams. As a strong version of the sequential model, the value-added approach assumes that the explanations of each stage of the process are independent. If we treat each stage as a dependent variable (D_i) in the model, then the explanation of each consists of a mutually exclusive subset (I_j) of the independent variables (I_n), such that the sum of the subsets equals the entire set [$\Sigma\ (I_j) = I_n$]. The value-added model can then be written as a set of sequentially ordered equations of the general form (see Wonnacott and Wonnacott, 1970:193–195):

$$D_i = f(I_j|D_{i-1}),$$

where I_j represents mutually exclusive subsets of I_n. The above set of equations describes the usual path analysis based on standardized regression

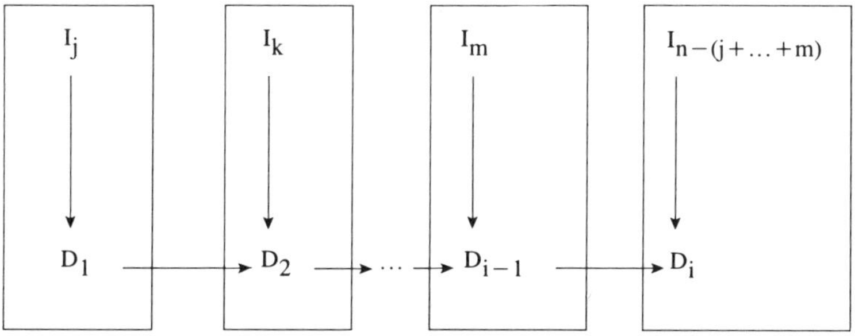

FIGURE 1.1 A value-added model of social process.

equations (Duncan, 1966) or the modified approach to regression analysis using logit (log-linear regression) models for dichotomous variables (Goodman, 1972a), when the restrictive assumption regarding mutual exclusivity is removed. The independent variables are exogenous and the dependent variables endogenous in the recursive system that results. Path analysis is a weak version of the sequential model since it makes no assumptions regarding the independence or order among the exogenous variables; in path analysis, the independent variables may affect any or all of the dependent variables in the model. The dependent variables remain sequentially ordered.

Figure 1.1 is a bloc diagram depicting a value-added model of social process. Each bloc represents a unique explanation of a given stage of the process. Yet the explanation of each dependent variable depends on the explanation of all preceding variables. The independent variables are activated sequentially and, taken together, make up the conditions sufficient for the final outcome of the process. The value-added model differs from the usual path model in which arrows may flow from any I_n to any D_i. Path analysis is ideally suited for determining the extent to which empirical reality corresponds to the theoretical ideal of the value-added model.

The Quantification of Process Models

The conventional approach to process models in sociology has, heretofore, been primarily qualitative in nature. An early formulation of this approach was Lindesmith's (1947) application of Znaniecki's (1934) method of "analytic induction" to the study of opiate addiction. Addiction is "caused" by a prior series of events, including drug use and withdrawal symptoms that characterize the addiction process. By definition, the absence of at least one of these events implies the absence of addiction. Each event is a necessary condition, and an essential characteristic of addiction.

Smelser's (1962) value-added approach to describing the determinants of collective behavior is similar to the method of analytic induction, but differs from it in two important respects. Although the value-added model is also sequential, it specifies the sequence in which events are "activated" rather than their temporal order. And it offers structural, instead of social-psychological, explanations. Although Smelser (1962:19) claims to offer an explanation of collective behavior, the value-added model as such does not explain; it describes.

Becker's (1963:22–39) formulation of a sequential model of the process by which people become regular marijuana users improves upon previous approaches by distinguishing between the stages of the process (the deviant's "career") and the conditions associated with moving from one stage of the career to the next ("career contingencies"). Each stage in a deviant career is explained independently, and "each explanation constitutes a necessary cause of the behavior." First-time marijuana use occurs prior to, and is a necessary condition of, regular use. However, the explanation of why someone would first try marijuana must be considered separately from the explanation of why someone would become a regular user.

In his seminal article, "The Quest for Universals in Sociological Research," Turner (1953) points out that analytic induction is a method for specifying cause-and-effect relations in all-or-none terms. This set of relations constitutes a closed system that "is not capable of activation from within, but only by factors coming from outside the system." Turner adds (1953:610), "Empirical prediction always requires some statistical or probablility statements, because there is some uncertainty . . . in the *way* in which intrusive [external] factors will activate the causal system." Turner concludes, "It is through conceiving the 'essential' conditions in a closed system as the avenues through which correlated factors can operate as causes, that generalizations about closed systems can escape their self-containment, and probability associations may be organized into meaningful patterns." In other words, the explanation of a given social process lies in a quantitative strategy designed to predict how that process operates. In contemporary terms, the external, "intrusive" factors become exogenous variables in a particular statistical model, and the stages of the process become its endogenous variables. Consequently, the quantitative explanation of how a process operates becomes distinct from its qualitative description.

Although the criminal justice system has been conceptualized as sequential in nature (see Kaplan, 1973:65–79), most empirical studies have described the correlates of only one stage of the process by which events and persons are defined as criminal. Some focus on the correlates of arrest, others the correlates of conviction, and still others the correlates of imprisonment. One notable study (Bernstein *et al.*, 1977) employed an explicitly sequential model of the societal reaction to criminal defendants. Three endogenous variables or stages in the processing of criminal defendants were identified: the decision to prosecute, to convict, and to sentence. Each stage was analyzed independently, given the occurrence of preceding stages. However, statistical techniques have been developed that make it possible to include both the exogenous and endogenous variables within a single recursive model employing a set of sequential, rather than simultaneous, equations (Duncan, 1966; Wonnacott and Wonnacott, 1970:193–195).

Most of the research on dispute processing remains qualitative. Empirical studies emphasize mapping the dispute process from grievance to civil litigation, or at best they describe a few correlates of each stage of the transformation process (see Mayhew and Reiss, 1969; Mayhew, 1975; Curran, 1977; Miller and Sarat, 1981; Bumiller, 1981; McIntosh, 1981). Still other studies constitute purely qualitative descriptions of disputing in limited contexts (see Baumgartner, 1980, 1981; Silbey, 1981). A good deal of the work in this field is conceptual, with the greatest amount of attention being paid to labeling different aspects of the process (Kritzer, 1981; Felstiner, Abel, and Sarat, 1981; Coates and Penrod, 1981; Mather and Yngvesson, 1981). Indeed, there still remains a strong degree of skepticism in this field regarding the application of scientific methodology to the understanding of disputing (Sarat, 1983).

A major purpose of this book is to demonstrate the feasibility of creating quantitative models of legal process. The quantification of process models was made possible by the development of logit analysis in the 1970s. Goodman's (1972a, 1972b, 1973a) approach to the log-linear analysis of qualitative variables has proven to be especially useful. Process models differ from traditional path models because of what Turner (1953) refers to as the all-or-none characteristic of the relationships among the endogenous variables in these models. In other words, process models have structural zeros, or logically defined empty cells, in cross-tabulations involving two or more of the endogenous variables. By taking into account the existence of structural zeros (see Bishop, Feinberg, and Holland, 1975:217–218), it is possible to specify a single mathematical model based on a recursive system of equations to describe an entire social process (see Appendix A). This, in my estimation, is a major breakthrough in the analysis of social process in general, and dispute processing in particular, since all previous analyses of process variables have been limited to considering such process one stage at a time. This approach makes it possible to evaluate the independence of the explanations of the dependent variables at each of the different stages of a given process. By controlling for the effects of the independent variables on the dependent variable at one stage of the process, it is possible to determine whether or not any or all of these variables also account for variation in any of the other dependent variables. Consequently, it becomes possible for the first time to evaluate the fit between the data and various sequential models of legal process.

Elements of Process Analysis in Black's *The Behavior of Law*

Donald Black (1972, 1976, 1979) has proposed what he calls a pure sociology of law. The theory is quantitative, propositional, and structural. Law, conceptualized as a quantitative variable, is explained by a variety of aspects of social life (1976:1), stratification, morphology, culture, organization, and social control. The theory constitutes a "pure" sociology since its propositions cannot be reduced or explained by motivational aspects of individual behavior or personality. The theory is structural in the sense that legal behavior is explained by its location in time and space. But it is structural in another sense: All of its propositions are formulated in a static form. There are no explicit propositions about process or social change. Although dynamic propositions can be derived from these propositions, it does not necessarily follow that if, say, "law varies directly with stratification" (1976:13), then the redistribution of wealth reduces the amount of law, since the change itself may produce an increase in conflicts, disputes, and litigation.

The elements of process analysis are, nevertheless, contained in Black's theory of legal behavior. Since "law is governmental social control" (Black, 1972:1096; 1976:2), the quantity of law increases with any kind of legal action by government officials. Black makes this clear:

> A complaint to a legal official . . . is more law than no complaint, whether it is a call to the police, a visit to a regulatory agency, or a lawsuit. Each is an increase in the quantity of law. . . . In criminal matters, an arrest is more law than no arrest. . . . Any initiation, invocation, or application of law increases its quantity. (1976:3)

Moreover, the quantity of law increases with each increment in the extent of involvement by official agents of governmental social control. Black adds:

> Detention before trial is more law than release, a bail bond more than none, and a higher bail bond more than one that is lower. . . . A decision in behalf of the plaintiff is more law than a decision in behalf of the defendant, and conviction is more than acquittal. . . . If a decision is against the plaintiff and he appeals, this is more law. . . . More generally, the quantity of law is known by the number and scope of prohibitions, obligations, and other standards to which people are subject, and by the rate of legislation, litigation, and adjudication. (1976:3)

From the above summary of Black's description of law as a quantitative variable, the value-added nature of his theory becomes evident. With each incremental increase in the amount of law, we find either an increase in its extensiveness (the number of social units to which it applies) or its intensiveness (the scope of involvement of legal officials in the given situation). It is the latter notion that applies most clearly to the value-added perspective. The more involved the state becomes in regulating behavior through its agents, the greater the quantity or value of law invoked. A static, structural approach to the analysis of legal behavior is consistent with treating the intensity of law as a single quantitative variable in which each increment in legality is represented by a higher point on an ordinal, or even higher-level, scale (Horwitz, 1983). A dynamic process orientation to the analysis of legal behavior converts a single quantitative variable into a series of nominal variables in which each increment in legality represents an identifiable sequence in the development of more intense legal behavior. From this perspective, law is a set of endogenous, dependent variables in a sequential model of legal process.

Black's theory of law is a weak version of the value-added model of legal process. In his theory, Black assumes that all aspects of social life (the independent variables) predict the quantity of law equally well. Since he makes no distinction between increments in law at earlier or later stages of legality, this should not be surprising. Yet it is quite conceivable that variables that affect one stage of legal process may not affect another.

MOBILIZATION THEORY AND LEGAL PROCESS

Legal process involves the mobilization of agents of governmental social control in the interests of particular individuals or collectivities (e.g., social strata, organizations, or society as a whole). These agents may act in the interests of others, but they also act in terms of their own individual or collective interests. An important analytic distinction is made between regulation initiated by individual citizens or groups and by agents of social control themselves. The former has been called the *reactive* and the latter the *proactive* mobilization of law (Black, 1973).

Legal process in the United States is predominantly reactive in nature (see Reiss, 1971; Black, 1973). There have been several studies describing the proactive mobilization of police (see Skolnick, 1966; Chevigny, 1969; Lundman, 1974, 1979; Pastor, 1978). However, there is ample evidence that most police action depends on citizen mobilization (see Reiss and Bordua, 1967; Reiss, 1971).

In the vast majority of lawyer–client contacts, citizens initiate legal action by virtue of some complaint, dispute, or property transaction that warrants the assistance of an attorney (Mayhew and Reiss, 1969; Mayhew, 1975). Lawyers may be contacted after the initiation of legal action by another agent (e.g., an arrest by the police), but rarely do lawyers initiate legal action. In fact, such initiation has been prohibited historically in the United States. However, change in the American Bar Association's Code of Professional Responsibility permitting advertising by lawyers has fostered an indirect proactive approach in law firms that creates business by informing the public of the services they can provide. In fact, many legal-services organizations are relatively aggressive in generating business.

The mobilization of lawyers is predominantly reactive because most legal action taken by attorneys is within the realm of private law, law that by definition excludes acts initiated by formal agencies of social control. The enforcement of contracts, torts, and property law cannot, in principle, be initiated by official agents of social control in the United States (Black, 1973:128). These are the areas of law in which citizen mobilization of lawyers predominates (Mayhew and Reiss, 1969).

Richard Lempert (1976) has put forth a somewhat different conceptualization of the mobilization of law. Lempert (1976:3) conceives of the mobilization of law as "the process by which legal norms are invoked to regulate behavior." Consequently, legal action may occur without the actual bringing of a case to court. Lempert criticizes Black's position, which conceptualizes mobilization of law as "the process by which a legal system acquires its case" (Black, 1973:126). Black treats as problematic the conditions under which a potential legal problem will end up as a case. This is the position that I take here. Lempert argues that the very existence of legal decisions acts as a constraint upon action by lawyers or nonlawyers (e.g., insurance agents) when they settle out of court (see Ross, 1971). As I see it, the positions are complementary rather than contradictory. The invocation of legality can also be incorporated within a sequential model as a step within the mobilization process logically prior to the actual mobilization of lawyers. When citizens recognize that legal remedies exist, they are likely to call a lawyer. They also may resolve their disputes without contacting lawyers in light of potential legal remedies. Attorneys, too, may invoke legal norms by taking out-of-court action to resolve a dispute. The invocation of legal norms is only a part, albeit an important part, of the total mobilization process.

Private law is exemplified by the law of contracts. Corbin (1952:5) defines a contract as "a promise enforceable at law directly or indirectly." Within limits, two or more individuals or collectivities are free to make an agreement that establishes a legal duty or obligation for one party and corollary rights for the other(s). The law of contracts does not generally state which promises are or are not permissible, but recognizes an appropriate set of procedures by which it is generally understood that an agreement has been reached. Regulations that are enforced under contract law are procedural rather than substantive.

The enforcement of contractual relations depends, in part, on working definitions of what constitutes an agreement in the public domain. Thus, legal norms and public norms are mutually embedded and indistinguishable in many cases. The norms governing agreements in everyday life and the norms of contract law are indeed very similar (Lempert, 1972). The actual or potential enforcement of contract law can be seen as a vital part of the processes of social control that regulate societal relations in general.

The invocation of a specific legal norm may or may not lead to further legal action. However, the act of contacting a lawyer incorporates the notion that legality has been invoked at least in a general sense. The client, by his or her action, has communicated a belief that a legal remedy ought to exist. Clients may also mobilize attorneys in order to benefit from procedural rules rather than any particular substantive legal norm (Yale Law Journal, 1973).

Unlike many studies of governmental social control, this is not a study of the mobilization of the police in criminal matters (Reiss and Bordua, 1967; Reiss, 1971; Baumgartner, 1980), but a study of citizen mobilization of lawyers in the resolving of everyday disputes between citizens and their neighbors, landlords, governmental agencies, business firms, employers, and others. The exercise of legal power is usually assumed to be a prerogative of the powerful (see Quinney, 1970, 1974; Chambliss and Seidman, 1971; Etzioni, 1975; Black, 1976); the likelihood of legal power being exercised in one's behalf is a function of one's social position in a hierarchically organized society. Mobilization theory (see Black, 1973) is concerned with specifying the conditions associated with the use of legal power by subordinates as well as superordinates. The purpose of this work is to specify those conditions of legal mobilization that are structural in origin, and those that reflect the situational context in which disputes occur. The study of the mobilization of lawyers is best suited to such an enterprise since lawyers are the agents of social control most frequently used in settling everyday disputes, except for those between neighbors (see Chapter 4).

Coercion is lawful when it involves the legitimate use or threatened use of force by the state. Agents of governmental social control behave in ways that represent instances of coercive power by acts of arrest, the issuance of injunctions, or finding for the plaintiff in a civil suit. Such acts are legitimate to the extent that no one acts informally or formally to prohibit them. Consequently, an arrest is lawful to the extent that someone is taken into custody and the arresting officer is not sanctioned negatively for doing so. Similarly, a lawyer who advises a client to sue is acting lawfully to the extent that his or her behavior is not found to be unethical by a review board.

Contacting an attorney in civil matters is analogous to calling the police in criminal matters. In fact, most studies of the mobilization of law describe the process by which the police are asked to handle criminal matters (see Reiss and Bordua, 1967; Reiss, 1971; Baumgartner, 1980). Whether citizens call the police or contact an attorney, they are attempting to mobilize state power to assist them in protecting themselves or their property. Just as the police officer is expected to both interpret and enforce criminal law, the attorney, as an officer of the court, is expected to interpret and enforce civil law (Ehrlich, 1981).[1]

Intervention by the police defines an act as criminal. To the extent that there is some probability that a given act will lead to the loss of liberty, the intervention by state authority defines that act as criminal. This intervention—taking into custody (arrest)—is the essence of police action. When the state intervenes by means other than the immediate loss of liberty, the conduct so regulated is defined as noncriminal, or civil. However, even here, the ultimate sanction for failure to obey the dictates of legal officials is the loss of liberty. In this sense, legal power, both criminal and civil, public and private, is the legitimate deployment of the coercive power of the state or other politically organized entity (Hoebel, 1954:28).

For the most part, the mobilization of attorneys reflects the mobilization of civil law, law "concerned with civil or private rights and remedies" (Black, 1979:223). This is not to say that police do not sometimes mediate disputes and that lawyers do not on occasion enforce criminal statutes (e.g., the attorney of a victim of consumer fraud who seeks to invoke criminal penalties in the process of securing redress for the losses incurred). *Policing* and *lawyering* represent analytically distinct ideal-typical extremes in modes of legality. The manner of legal regulation is structurally determined. Those who have few economic resources, who are socially marginal, and who have little social influence are subject to social control through action by the police, which defines their conduct as criminal (see Black, 1983). In contrast, those who have economic resources, who are socially integrated, and who are relatively influential are subject to mechanisms of social control that treat their disputes as private matters. In this sense, lawyers are called upon to regulate the behavior of the middle class, whereas the police are engaged in regulating lower-class conduct.

Once an attorney has been contacted, any lawful action taken by that attorney constitutes legal action. Even refusal to give legal advice implies an interpretation in fact, if not in principle, of rules of law that govern a particular situation. As gatekeepers of the law, attorneys employ a variety of strategies to inform potential clients that they have no legal rights in a given matter. When the probability of success is low, and the matter is handled tactfully, the potential client has been successfully "cooled out." To the extent that the chance of success is related to one's ability to pursue the

[1]Attorneys admitted to practice in Michigan are automatically considered members of the state bar association (Jacob, 1978:48). As bar association members, in 1967, lawyers were subject to rules of conduct embodied in the American Bar Association Canons of Professional Ethics, later changed to the Code of Professional Responsibility (see Countryman and Finman, 1966:885–897). The canons, which govern the relationships between attorneys and clients, have the force of law since those who violate them can be disciplined by the courts.

matter, that is, to one's "legal competence" (Carlin *et al.*, 1966:70), then legality varies with social position. In other words, once an attorney has been contacted, social position predicts the quality and quantity of legal action pursued, which also depends, in part, on the capabilities of the attorney contacted (Carlin and Howard, 1965:384). Nevertheless, contact with an attorney by plaintiffs or complainants constitutes more law than no contact a all (see Black, 1980:212). Consequently, in this study, the quantity of law is measured in terms of the likelihood that such contact will occur.

The study of the mobilization of police leading to arrest and the study of the mobilization of lawyers leading up to some form of legal action, in or out of court, raise similar theoretical and methodological issues. The relationship between these two processes is more than mere analogy. Both police and lawyers are legal officials, agents of governmental social control. As officials with the power to arrest, the police employ or threaten to employ the coercive power of the state to enforce norms. When lawyers go to court or threaten to go to court, they act as agents of the court in enforcing a normative order that is noncriminal in nature.

The analytic distinction between reactive and proactive mobilization of law applies to both criminal and civil law (see Reiss, 1971; Black, 1973). Some studies see the civil legal process as being distinctly private, based on reactive mobilization by citizens themselves (see Lempert, 1976). Yet others have pointed out that in American society, the criminal law is also predominantly reactive (see Reiss, 1971). Whereas the police act upon their own initiative on occasion, they depend heavily on citizen initiative for most of their cases. In principle, criminal law is public, yet in reality it has a strongly private character. Increasingly, in matters that do not relate to the enforcement of criminal law, government agencies are proactive in enforcing a variety of regulations. This book, however, focuses on the *reactive* mobilization of lawyers for *civil* matters; civil law is the dependent variable.

A SEQUENTIAL MODEL OF THE MOBILIZATION OF LAWYERS

There are two analytically and empirically distinct phases in the process by which disputes are transformed into legal claims, the first characterized by situational and the second by structural determinants. The former is *primary* in the sense that it involves all noninstitutional, prelegal stages of disputing prior to the actual mobilization of attorneys. The second phase begins with the decision to contact an attorney or other legal official. It is *secondary* in the sense that it involves legal institutions in the dispute process. The secondary phase includes all those stages of the dispute process in which attorneys, or other legal agents, become involved. At this point, what happens to the dispute depends on the societal reaction to it. It is here that the structural location of the dispute in the political economy of the community and the social organization of legal institutions play a role in determining what will happen to a given dispute. I consider the invocation of legal norms essentially a prelegal aspect of the transformation process. Only those disputes that actually go to law are considered secondary, or legal, in nature.

This conceptualization of secondary legal process is analogous to Bohannan's (1980:7) notion that "the law rests on the basis of . . . *double institutionalization*" (italics added). To the extent that social behavior is regulated by both custom and law, within the contexts of nonlegal and legal institutions, respectively, law is based on the secondary (double) institutionalization of customary behavior. Legal norms reflect social norms, reinforce normative sanctions through legal sanctions, and on occasion create new social realities by transforming society's primary social institutions. Many legal norms have their origin in customary behavior, but they also exist within the context of secondary legal institutions that cannot be reduced to the social institutions out of which they emerge. Similarly, secondary legal process grows out of the primary process of disputing, yet is explained in institutional terms that are independent of the situational origins of primary process.

A third aspect of the dispute-transformation process is, paradoxically, not part of the process itself, but is its outcome. Outcomes of social process have both objective and subjective components. The former reflect the neutral observer's assessment of the relationship between the initial definition of the situation and the final result of the process. When goals or objectives are formally announced, outcomes can be measured in terms of their relationship to the initial objective. In the case of disputing, we compare the initial self-reported expectations of those experiencing a given problem with what actually transpires at the end of the process. Outcomes may be favorable or unfavorable; those involved in a dispute may be satisfied or dissatisfied with its outcome. While we generally expect favorable outcomes to produce satisfactory results, this is clearly not always the case. According to the title of one publication, "The Process is the Punishment" (Feeley, 1979); there are costs, both economic and personal, involved in seeing a civil dispute to its final conclusion, costs that may leave disputants dissatisfied despite their apparent successes. This is similar to the ironic situation in which the doctor announces to a patient's family that the operation was a success, but the patient died.

Primary and Secondary Aspects of Legal Process

Secondary legal process and double institutionalization are conceptualizations that have their origins in H.L.A. Hart's (1961:77–96) distinction between primary and secondary rules of law.[2] Primary rules are those for which there is a moral obligation to obey. This obligation is manifest in terms of a reasonable prediction that they will be supported and enforced by the community in general. Secondary rules of law are procedural rules supported and enforced by the legal community.

Morality is expressed, more or less, by primary rules or substantive law; legality is expressed, more or less, by secondary rules or procedural law. Primary rules of law, such as those that prohibit theft, are often rooted in society's moral and religious traditions. But primary rules can also be generated by political authority, and may help to change public attitudes and morality, as in race relations. Legality is the reasonable prediction that government officials will adhere to a set of procedural rules (e.g., the exclusionary rule prohibiting the admission of illegally obtained evidence in a criminal trial) when enforcing the law. Morality and legality are variable characteristics of legal rules. Morality reflects the probability of the normative regulation of social conduct, legality the probability of enforcement by government officials. So defined, morality and legality are empirically correlated qualities of legal rules (Silberman, 1976; 1979).

Primary legal process is embedded in socially defined situations. Disputes are processed according to normative expectations, characteristics of the dispute, and the situation itself. At this stage of the dispute process, the course of the dispute is determined by such features as the relational distance between disputants, the relative visibility of the dispute, and the role of third parties as intermediaries. In other words, primary legal process is rooted in nonlegal aspects of disputing.

As Hart (1961:91) puts it, the movement from primary rules of obligation to the use of secondary rules is "a step from the pre-legal into the legal world." Secondary legal process is embedded in the structure of legal relations in society as a whole. Economic, political, and social institutions are the fundamental determinants of the superstructure called the legal system (Bohannan, 1980:6). Primary legal process is logically prior to secondary legal process; the former is a necessary condition of the latter. In this sense, secondary process grows out of primary process in the same way that secondary rules of law are built on primary rules; institutional processes develop from situational processes. Neither the nature of the dispute nor the situation in which it is embedded, however, determines attorney participation in the dispute process. The political and economic structure of the community in which disputes occur and the social organization of its legal institutions are the actual determinants of attorney participation. Although a dispute between neighbors may be visible and persistent, and attempts at third-party

[2]For the sake of efficiency, I refer throughout this section to primary and secondary aspects of legal process as primary legal process and secondary legal process, respectively.

mediation may have failed, the dispute will not go to law unless the social circumstances of the disputants make it appropriate and attorneys are accessible to the community.

When socially defined rights and obligations are at issue in a legal dispute, we have an instance of primary legal process. This process is prelegal and situational in origin. When an act, dispute, or event becomes organized in the context of a legal rule in response to, or in relationship with, legal officials, we have an instance of secondary legal process. As soon as a citizen contacts an attorney, a dispute shifts from one that is merely subject to socially defined obligations to one that is *also* subject to legally defined rights and duties. At this point, the citizen becomes a *complainant* who may be told whether or not he or she has a legal claim in this matter. Whereas primary legal process is situationally determined, secondary legal process is affected by structurally generated, differential access to legal roles.

Stages in the Mobilization of Law

In the sequential model of legal process, the mobilization of law is viewed as a series of stages representing the process by which disputes come to be defined as legal events with particular legal outcomes. The nine stages identified and discussed below are an exhaustive, but not mutually exclusive, set of categories defining the dispute process. The set is exhaustive since it consists of categories designed to describe the process from beginning to end. The categories are not mutually exclusive since, by definition, each stage is a necessary condition for the next one; consequently, each succeeding stage logically entails or incorporates the preceding one. For example, lawyers must be contacted before they can take a case to court.

The stages of the mobilization process are endogenous variables in a causal analysis of the determinants of the transformation of disputes into legal claims. Each stage is defined as a dichotomous dependent variable, making the analysis ideally suited to Goodman's (1973b) log-linear approach to causal modeling using path analysis. That each stage of the process is dichotomous and that each is a necessary condition for the next are matters of definition within a value-added theoretical framework. Whether or not the value-added model of the mobilization of law corresponds to social reality is a matter of empirical verification. Although exceptions may arise in specific cases, it is unlikely that a citizen would attempt to try a case in a court (other than small claims) without the assistance of counsel, nor would he or she be permitted to do so in most situations. There are times when stages collapse within a single empirical event; for example, a disputant chats informally with a neighbor, an attorney, who suggests that he or she might have a good case and asks the disputant to drop by the office in the morning. The stages of the mobilization process are analytically, but not always empirically, distinct categories. The analysis presented in this book enables us to disaggregate the effects on each distinct stage. Another advantage of the value-added approach is that its assumptions hold for any subset of the model. This is especially useful when data are inadequate or not available for some aspects of the process or when the constraints imposed by sample size and other methodological considerations make it impractical to incorporate every stage of the process in a single causal model.

Primary Legal Process

Primary legal process consists of the five prelegal stages of the dispute process. The first stage (D_1) begins with the recognition that a dispute is in progress. Once it has been determined that a dispute has occurred, the second stage of the process begins when a party to the dispute comes to the conclusion that something should be done about it (D_2). Those who do not reach this stage take a totally passive response to the problem, choosing to avoid doing anything at all about it. The third stage (D_3) occurs when a party to a dispute defines it as a relatively serious matter. At this point, the dispute has moved from a relatively innocuous annoyance to one that requires some sort of definite action, whether directly or indirectly through a third party. Some disputes are relatively serious from their inception ($D_1 = D_2 = D_3$), whereas others do not become serious until later in the process, when certain situational contingencies arise, as when disputes become persistent. The fourth stage (D_4) occurs when third parties are contacted inadvertently or deliberately as advice givers, dispute mediators, or referral sources. Third parties act in this capacity as agents or representatives of the community in further defining the dispute, giving legitimacy to further attempts at resolution, or suggesting that the problem was not so serious in the first place. Third parties are unique in their position in the dispute process since they are both part of the process and external to it. The final prelegal stage (D_5) of the mobilization process occurs when legal norms are invoked, usually by third parties such as insurance agents or counselors. This is the point at which disputants are told that they should contact an attorney. Whether or not they do so depends on the institutional forces affecting secondary legal process.

Although primary legal process is rooted in subjective experience, its determinants can be objectively defined and measured. This approach is entirely consistent with the symbolic interactionist tradition, especially when it is expressed in a value-added framework (see Lofland and Stark, 1965). The purpose of this approach is to produce an objective, quantitative analysis of a subjective, qualitative process. This is possible only if we assume that the way in which people experience events is patterned and predictable.

Secondary Legal Process

Secondary legal process consists of four stages, beginning with contact with a legal official (e.g., an attorney) and ending with some sort of legal action taken. The first legal stage (D_6) of the mobilization process is contacting an attorney. Attorneys may give advice, write letters, file a claim, negotiate, go to court, or do nothing at all. No matter what action is or is not taken, the lawyer's reaction defines, in effect, whether a claimant does or does not have available a legal remedy. Taking some sort of legal action (e.g., routine filing of papers or going to court), which is more law than doing nothing or merely giving advice, represents the next stage (D_7) of the mobilization process. Some legal matters are trivial or routine. Others may represent difficult legal questions or special difficulties for claimants. Difficult legal matters constitute the subset of legal actions defined as serious (stage D_8). The last legal stage of the mobilization process (D_9) involves taking a case to court. Not all serious legal matters end up in a court battle, but by definition, any case that ends up in court is serious.

Outcomes

Although not technically a stage of the mobilization process, the conclusion of each event provides a relatively successful or unsuccessful outcome. Outcomes are represented by a dichotomous, dependent variable (D_{10}) indicating whether the outcome was objectively favorable or unfavorable in light of the initial dispute. The outcome is not strictly part of the sequential model since each dispute has some sort of outcome, regardless of whether it goes through the entire mobilization process or exits at an earlier stage.

The last dichotomous, dependent variable (D_{11}) in the analysis of the mobilization of lawyers is the subjective evaluation by claimants as to the satisfactory or unsatisfactory nature of the outcome of the process. These two outcome variables can be treated as part of the total process if we restrict the analysis to legal disputes. To the extent that some sort of legal action is taken by an attorney on behalf of a client, a case has an outcome within the context of the secondary legal mobilization process, whether the case involves litigation or not. If we assume further that the failure of an attorney to act on behalf of a client implies a negative outcome and an unsatisfactory result for the client who hoped or expected the attorney to do something on his or her behalf, then the outcome variables constitute the final stages of the secondary process by which lawyers are mobilized.

The Social Organization of Legal Process

It is possible to distinguish analytically and empirically between the part of legal action that is situationally determined and the part that is based on structurally determined, differential access to institutionalized roles. In principle, contingencies associated with situationally determined action are independent of those associated with institutionalized action. The first five primary stages of the mobilization process are, in theory, situationally determined. Situational factors are expected to affect all stages of the process up to and including the invoking of legal norms. Institutional factors are only expected to affect the secondary legal stages of the mobilization process and their outcomes.

There are at least six different situational contingencies of legal process that reflect the variable nature of the problems people experience and the social situations in which these problems occur. First, problems vary according to their relative persistence over time; problems may be short lived, or they may represent a more persistent nuisance. The network of relationships in which problems are embedded suggests three additional variables: the relational distance between disputants, the relative power of those experiencing disputes, and patterns of differential association that provide information about the availability of legal remedies. The structure of situations in which problems occur adds two more variables: the relative visibility of the problem and the availability of alternative arrangements for dispute settlement. These six situational variables affect the way in which problems are defined and acted upon, up to and including the invoking of legal norms.

Contingencies of secondary legal process reflect differential access to economic, political, and social resources. Six nonlegal institutional variables can be identified. Three of these measure the quantity of economic, political, and social resources at the disposal of those experiencing legal problems; three measure participation in economic, political, and social institutions. The possession of private property as a measure of participation in economic institutions can be distinguished from income as a measure of economic resources, although these variables are obviously correlated. Similarly, involvement in party politics can be distinguished from measures of political efficacy, and membership in voluntary associations as a measure of participation in social institutions can be distinguished from levels of education, occupation, and ethnicity as measures of social resources.

The six nonlegal institutional variables are derived from the "resources theory" of legal process (see Mayhew and Reiss, 1969:311–312). This theory argues that those who have more economic, social, and political resources are more likely to perceive the need for and be able to afford legal assistance. However, it is just as reasonable to assume that those with more resources are more likely to be able to avoid the activation of formal mechanisms of social control in solving their problems because they are able to find alternative solutions. The upper-income person who makes a large purchase is more likely to receive immediate satisfaction when experiencing a consumer problem (because of future potential business) than the lower-income person. In general, the embeddedness of the upper-status person in institutional structures makes it less necessary for him or her to rely upon the legal system to resolve problems.

How, then, can we explain the fact that upper-income people are more likely to use attorneys than lower-income people (Carlin and Howard, 1965)? Mayhew and Reiss (1969) argue that persons with greater income are constrained to use attorneys because they are more involved in the institution of private property. Theoretically, were we to hold constant home ownership and other forms of involvement in the institution of private property, the linear positive relationship between income and use of attorneys should be attenuated. In fact, the above argument leads us to expect a residual curvilinear relationship between income and other measures of resources and use of attorneys. Individuals with the greatest quantity of resources solve their problems through direct action, or can afford to ignore them, rather than incurring the social costs of relying on an attorney for assistance.

For problems other than those related to private property, Mayhew and Reiss (1969:314) find that those with more resources are more likely to use attorneys than those with fewer resources. This suggests that those with more resources not only use attorneys for matters pertaining to private property, but for other areas as well. The presence of economic resources, when associated with the possession of private property, leads to the use of attorneys; this then increases the probability that attorneys will be used again for other matters besides property. More generally, the possession of any resource, when associated with particular interests (economic, political, or social) that constrain legal action in one area, increases the probability of the use of attorneys in other areas.

A visual representation of the sequential model of the mobilization of lawyers is presented in Figure 1.2. The model begins with all disagreements, whether they are defined as disputes or not. At each stage or step of the process, various contingencies operate to channel disputes further along the process to the next step of else filter them out. Situational contingencies (C_i) are theoretically expected to play a role only at the beginning of the dispute process, up through and including the fifth step, whereas institutional contingencies (C_j) are theoretically expected to play a role in the mobilization of lawyers and subsequent steps in the transformation of disputes into legal cases. As we can see, this is a weak version of the process model to the extent that there is no a priori basis for predicting different effects of the institutional contingencies on each of the secondary legal stages of the mobilization process. But it is a strong version of the process model to the extent that the explanations of the two distinct phases of legal process, primary and secondary, are expected to be completely independent of one another.

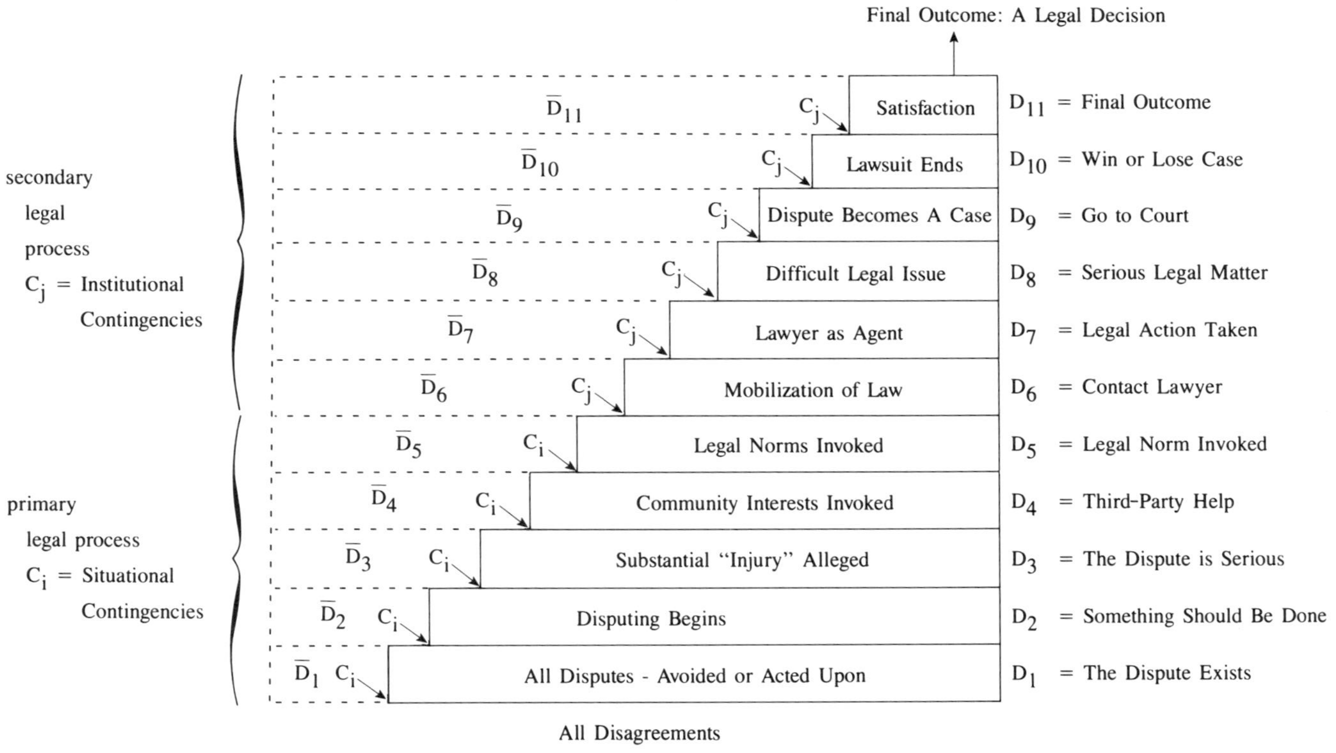

FIGURE 1.2 A step-by-step, value-added model of the mobilization of lawyers.

2

SETTING AND METHODS

THE SETTING

Detroit, founded in 1701 by the French, is one of the oldest communities in the Midwest. By 1958, it was a cosmopolitan city with a diverse ethnic population; 19% of the population in the metropolitan area was of British descent, blacks made up 17%, and only 4% was of French background (see Lenski, 1961:28). Two years later, blacks constituted 29% of the population within the city limits of Detroit (U.S. Bureau of the Census, 1972a:22). By 1970, 44% of Detroit's population was black, and by 1980, 63% of the residents of Detroit, clearly a majority, were black.

The survey conducted by the 1967 Detroit Area Study (DAS) estimated that 17% of the population of the greater metropolitan Detroit area was black, indicating little change in the overall racial composition of the Detroit area since Lenski's study in 1958. Within the city limits of Detroit, however, 33% of the sample was black. But if we were to assume linear growth in the black population between 1960 and 1970, according to the U.S. Census we would expect about 39% of Detroit's residents to be black. This suggests that the DAS systematically underrepresented blacks, especially black males, in its sampling procedures. In any case, there is evidence that the overall racial composition of the Detroit metropolitan area had not changed, but that there had been an increasing concentration of black residents within the inner city.

The 1967 DAS study identified 43 towns and cities in the Detroit Standard Metropolitan Statistical Area's (SMSA) three counties and 49 subcommunities within the city of Detroit. These subcommunities have an average size of approximately 25,000 residents (United Community Services [UCS], 1970:2). United Community Services (formerly the Red Feather agency) first established in 1951 that there were 48 natural subcommunities in the city of Detroit. By 1960, one more had apparently been added, and in 1970, in consultation with the Mayor's Committee for Community Renewal and the City Planning Commission, UCS revised the total to 60 subcommunities, largely in response to residential growth on the outskirts of the city. Subcommunities took into account the economic characteristics of the area, including housing and income, physical barriers, land-use patterns, and cultural identity. The present study employs the 1960 designations since these correspond best to the political and economic reality of the time. Resources for both public and private social services were allocated on the basis of these designations by an umbrella organization of services provided by the private sector.

The importance of the UCS organization in the Detroit metropolitan area cannot be overemphasized. Detroit was the foundation of the United Way movement in America, beginning as it did with the establishment of the first Red Feather Agency in the country. Although UCS was the central coordinating agency for the collection and distribution of funds for a variety of social services, many UCS programs were controlled by local elites and served middle-class needs (Locke, 1969:65). But in response to the difficulties created by the aftermath of the 1967 civil disorder, the UCS provided special programs for the displaced and those in need. The Research Department of UCS, "representing private social agencies" (Locke, 1969:64), and the Planning Department of the City of Detroit, representing public social agencies, worked together in a strongly cooperative relationship. In 1974, using data furnished by the U.S. Census Bureau, the Planning Department prepared a demographic analysis of the City of Detroit, "A Profile of Detroit—1970," according to the subcommunities established by UCS. Thus, it is evident that these subcommunities have meaningful identities within the political and economic context of Detroit.

At the time of the survey, Detroit was an economically prosperous community with the auto industry as its main source of strength. Detroit has always been heavily unionized (Lenski, 1961:29; Meier and Rudwick, 1979). Black participation in the auto industry and in the UAW had been irregular and discriminatory over several decades. Racial conflicts occurred within the auto industry, especially in the context of strikebreaking, as well as more broadly in Detroit as a whole. In 1943, Detroit exploded in racial violence with gangs of white youth preying on blacks who were alone and vulnerable (Lee and Humphrey, 1943). Blacks, too, engaged in violent assaults and property destruction. Despite the city's growing prosperity and its "attempts to make racial integration and social progress a matter of public policy" (Locke, 1969:17), Detroit erupted once again in violence in 1967.

Unlike the racial clashes between blacks and whites in 1943, the civil disorder in 1967 involved large-scale looting, arson, and vandalism. There were several incidents of sniper attacks on police and at least one well-publicized occurrence of retaliatory action by the police in the so-called Algiers Motel incident. In this case, white police officers were accused of execution-style killings of black suspects. In fact, the precipitating incident involved a routine raid by the police on a "blind pig," or after hours bar, in the heart of the Twelfth Street ghetto (Locke, 1969:26).

By the time the so-called riot began on July 23, 1967, over 98% of the interviews for the present survey had been completed. Consequently, there is very little contamination of these data by this event. But it is important to note the social and legal context in which this survey occurred, a context that triggered what one prominent local poverty lawyer described in a personal interview as a "civil rebellion." Despite the Gideon decision several years earlier granting the right to an attorney to all indigent defendants in felony matters, Detroit had not yet established a public defender system. At that time, in Michigan, court appointed counsel were usually young, inexperienced attorneys who were uninterested in criminal work as a lifetime career.

Several months prior to the "rebellion," the City of Detroit had begun its Neighborhood Legal Services (NLS) program as part of President Johnson's War on Poverty. This program, funded by the Office of Economic Opportunity (OEO), provided free legal services for the poor in civil matters (Finman, 1971). But it was relatively new, most of the neighborhood offices had only recently opened, and Detroiters were still unfamiliar with the legal services it could provide. Nevertheless, the Twelfth Street office of the NLS was left unharmed during the eight days of civil disorder!

Within two days after the disorders began, NLS began representing accused defendants in bail hearings for misdemeanor charges related to the disturbances (Locke, 1969:77). Police conducted mass arrests, prosecutors brought large numbers of defendants to court simultaneously, and Recorder's Court Judges set unusually high bail (Michigan Law Review, 1968). Law enforcement officials set up mass detention facilities to hold thousands of blacks in order to contain the riot. These activities and the actions taken by the NLS helped to legitimate the NLS in the eyes of the city's poor, especially those who were black. Yet few additional NLS offices were established throughout the metropolitan area. As a result, many of the poor who lived outside the pockets of poverty in the inner city were left unserved by the OEO-funded legal-services program. One thing remains unequivocally clear: The nature of legal services for the poor changed dramatically after the 1967 situation. Consequently, the present study is relatively uncontaminated by the existence of government-sponsored legal services for the poor. This lack of contamination has important implications today, especially in light of attempts by conservative politicians (including President Reagan) to abolish this type of program.

In light of the subsequent, albeit precarious, institutionalization of free legal services to the poor, we may well wonder to what extent the Detroit area findings can be generalized to the United States as a whole. Moreover, given different cultural and legal contexts across the country, it can be argued that the present findings are unique to one specific community at one point in time. It is for this reason that I have incorporated a limited amount of data from the American Bar Foundation's 1974 national survey of the legal needs of the public (Curran and Spaulding, 1974; Curran, 1977). As we shall see, the basic *structure* of legal relations has not changed since the institutionalization of free legal services for the poor. Although the effect of income on access to lawyers has been weakened somewhat, it remains a significant parameter in the explanation of the mobilization of lawyers. Again, a comparison of the Detroit area and the nation as a whole reveals that the structure of legal relations is fundamentally the same, although Detroiters are somewhat more litigious on the average than other Americans. In Lenski's study of religiosity in the Detroit area, he points out that, by 1958, the nation was "becoming a political, economic, religious, and social unit" (Lenski, 1961:31). With large-scale social mobility and mass communications, Detroiters were no longer a provincial lot. Nearly two-thirds were born elsewhere, and more than two-thirds of these were born outside Michigan. Lenski concludes (1961:31) that the "constant turnover in population also prevents the development of regional peculiarities, and promotes the homogeneity of the national population."

DESIGN OF THE STUDY

The Sample Survey

A weighted random sample of 780 residents of the Detroit metropolitan area were interviewed in 1967 about their disputes with neighbors, landlords, and public and private organizations, and their legal experiences while living in the Detroit area (see Mayhew and Reiss, 1969:309; Mayhew, 1975:402,n.1). Case histories were collected on each respondent's two most serious disputes, with the proviso that these not come from the same general category of disputes. A total of 23 types of disputes were identified and grouped into five categories: disputes with neighbors, landlords, or government agencies, consumer problems, and discrimination. The respondents were then asked if they had ever contacted an attorney, and if they had, brief case histories were collected for the matter that gave them the most difficulty.

The sampling unit was the household, with households inside the city limits of Detroit (Wayne County) sampled at twice the rate (1:785) of those in two adjacent suburban counties, Macomb and Oakland (1:1570). All three counties form the Detroit metropolitan area, according to the U.S. Bureau of the Census. Two independently incorporated communities, Hamtramck and Highland Park, are fully surrounded by the city of Detroit and their households were treated as inner-city households in the sampling design. The purpose of this stratified sample was to "insure inclusion of more Negro citizens" in the analysis (Mayhew and Reiss, 1969:309). There were 173 black and 349 white respondents in the inner city, 3 black and 255 white respondents in the suburbs.

In order to ensure adequate representation of adult (age 18 or over) males and females, interviews alternated between husbands and wives when the head of the household was married. Otherwise, the person defined as head of the household by its residents was interviewed. This procedure tends to overrepresent female heads of households, especially those who are black. Consequently, Mayhew and Reiss' report (1969:310) that females are less likely than males to seek advice from an attorney is somewhat biased. Once relevant controls are taken into account, systematic sex differences in the way in which disputes are resolved disappear. For this reason, sex is not treated as a control variable for most of the analysis in this book.

The sex of the respondent is not a relevant variable in the study of dispute processing because the situational context for the generation of everyday disputes was the household, not the individual. Consequently, even though the respondents were asked about their own experiences, they usually responded as informants about disputes they and their families had had with others. When there were problems with neighborhood children, it was often their own children who had been involved. When the plumbing was faulty, the whole family suffered. When an appliance, say a refrigerator, did not work properly, the entire household suffered the loss of its services. Some problems were personal, such as the denial of a job opportunity because of one's race or age (rarely did the respondents report experiencing any kind of sex discrimination). Yet even such personal problems can have an impact on an entire household. Since these problems were not perceived to be sex linked, the way in which they were handled did not depend on the sex of the respondent.

The original sample consisted of 957 households in the Detroit SMSA with a completion rate of 82%, or 780 interviews (Mayhew and Reiss, 1969:309). Only 12% refused to be interviewed; an additional 6% could not be located after at least three attempts to do so. The sample proved to be representative of the general population since there were few identifiable differences between those who refused to be interviewed and those who complied. One notable exception to this rule was the slight underrepresentation of residents from the most affluent suburbs.

It has been the practice in research on the dispute process to report the raw data in terms of the weighted sample (see Mayhew and Reiss, 1969; Mayhew, 1975; Miller and Sarat, 1981). In the present study, the weighted sample consists of 1038 residents of the Detroit metropolitan area; suburban cases were double weighted in order to achieve a representative sample of the entire Detroit SMSA population. This practice tends to inflate the substantive significance of the findings, especially when supported by tests of statistical significance.

To avoid this problem, all the statistics in this book are adjusted for the weight factor w as follows:

$$w = \frac{\text{original sample size}}{\text{weighted sample size}} = \frac{780}{1038} = 0.7514$$

All chi-square values are multiplied by $w = 0.7514$. This yields the "true" value of chi-square based on the original size of the sample. Log-linear effect parameters (β's) are not affected by sample size, so no adjustment is necessary here, but the standard errors of the estimates of these parameters must be adjusted by $\sqrt{w} = 0.8668$ in order for these estimates to be unbiased.

The survey was part of a graduate training program in survey research conducted by the Department of Sociology at the University of Michigan. This program, the Detroit Area Study (DAS), had been run on an annual basis since 1951. Some of its most notable products have been Miller and Swanson's (1958) book *The Changing American Parent,* Lenski's (1961) book *The Religious Factor,* and Laumann's (1966) book, *Prestige and Association in an Urban Community*. In 1967, the director of the DAS was Howard Schuman. Its two principal investigators were Leon Mayhew and Albert J. Reiss, Jr. There were three research assistants, officially called "DAS Teaching Fellows," Wolfgang Grichting, James House, and the present author. With the assistance of approximately 30 graduate students, the survey instrument was designed and implemented, and open-ended codes were constructed. The students conducted about half the interviews and did about half the coding. The remaining work was performed by the interviewing and coding staffs of the Survey Research Center of the Institute for Social Research (ISR) at the University of Michigan.

Units of Analysis

Four separate data sets were prepared for the analysis, each based on a different unit of analysis: (1) individuals with problems, (2) disputes, (3) legal problems, and (4) types of disputes. The first set of data corresponds to the usual approach to survey analysis. The sampling unit and the unit of analysis are the same. In this case, the analysis is based on the weighted random sample of 1038 residents of the Detroit area. Characteristics of the individual respondents are seen as determining whether or not a person experienced a given problem, what he or she did about it, and so on. This traditional approach is not suited to taking into account the characteristics of disputes or the situations in which they are embedded in explaining the dispute process.

In the second data set, the dispute is the unit of analysis. There were 2778 everyday disputes reported by the weighted random sample of 1038 householders in the Detroit metropolitan area. Respondents were asked whether they had experienced any of 23 types of problems, grouped into five general categories: disputes with neighbors, landlords, or government agencies, consumer problems, and discrimination in a variety of settings. Within each general category, the respondents were permitted to choose residual "other" types of problems. These unidentified disputes make up 11% of the total sample. The remainder, 2463 disputes, constitute the operating sample for most of the analysis of disputing.

The survey instrument becomes a device for sampling events; that is, the respondents become informants, reporting those events that they have experienced and recall. We have here a kind of area sample in which individual households are used as locations in social space. All events in these locations become part of the sample. This approach combines the anthropologist's technique of using a selected number of informants to describe disputing in a given community with the sample survey technique to produce a large number of representative dispute events. For the first time, it becomes possible to generalize about the dispute process in an entire community without the sample bias produced by more primitive approaches to data collection.

The survey technique sacrifices some degree of depth when interviewing informants about their total life experience. But since we are interested in the life histories of disputes, not disputants, the DAS approach is ideal. We are then able to assess the effects of the characteristics of disputes, and the situations in which they are embedded, on the dispute process.

Case histories were obtained for the two most serious disputes, although selecting for seriousness was limited by the constraint that no two problems be chosen from the same general category. There were 1302 disputes defined as serious by our informants (see Mayhew, 1975:413), but in only 1145 cases was enough information available to code them according to their situational contexts. Only 12% of the serious disputes could not be classified as one of the 23 major types of disputes. Since this proportion corresponds very closely to the proportion of the total sample that could not be classified, there appears to be little systematic difference between the serious and nonserious disputes with respect to missing data.

The third data set treats the individual with legal problems as the unit of analysis ($N = 1038$). Of the weighted sample, 69% have contacted an attorney at some time in their lives. The object of analysis is the legal contact, with the determinants of contact based on measures of individual characteristics, including location along structural dimensions. These data are an important source of information about structurally generated opportunities to contact an attorney in everyday disputes that do not ordinarily go to law.

The final data set is based on the aggregation of 2463 everyday disputes into 23 types of civil disputes with aggregate measures on each of seven endogenous variables (see Nie *et al.*, 1975:203–217). Sample disputes included noisy neighbors, clamoring creditors, and age discrimination in seeking employment. Respondents who experienced each type of dispute were coded "1" (variable characteristic present) or "0" (variable characteristic absent) on each of the seven variables: (1) something should be done, (2) sought third-party help, (3) invoked legal norms (e.g., "ought to see a lawyer"), (4) saw a lawyer, (5) legal action taken by attorney (e.g., "he took it to court"), (6) outcome (objective measure of the respondent's success in getting what he or she initially expected), and (7) expressed satisfaction with the results. For each type of dispute, the proportion who scored "1" for each of the seven endogenous variables was obtained. The aggregate analysis is based on a total of 23 types of civil disputes.

The unit of analysis here is the type of dispute rather than the dispute event. Miller and Sarat (1981:554–555) report that problem-specific characteristics of disputes explain most of the variance in the early stages of the dispute process. In fact, little, if any, of the variance is explained by structural factors (Miller and Sarat's "claimants' capacities"). The purpose of the aggregate analysis is to identify the characteristics of events or social acts in and of themselves and the roles they play in social process. As I have demonstrated elsewhere (Silberman, 1976), individual and aggregate analyses can yield very different results when trying to explain criminal behavior in terms of the deterrent effect of threatened punishment. Whereas the deterrence literature is replete with ecological fallacies, the dispute literature nowhere recognizes the relevance of aggregate phenomena for understanding social process. This lack of recognition occurs because it is more difficult to see the unity of a social category such as "credit problems" than that of "robbery" since the latter exists as a clearly defined legal category and the former does not. Yet the former is a clearly defined social category with potential legal consequences as the evidence presented in this book shows.

Statistical Analysis

The study employs statistical techniques suited to the different levels of analysis and measurement involved. Log-linear and linear statistical models are employed where appropriate, the former where dichotomous and polytomous variables are used, and the latter where higher-order levels of measurement are employed (see Duncan, 1966; Goodman, 1972a, 1972b, 1973a, 1973b).

At the individual-problem level of analysis, all the dependent variables are dichotomous. Problems occur or do not occur; lawyers are contacted or they are not. Such data are ideally suited to the use of log-linear models. The log-linear approach permits the testing of a variety of models, searching for that model which best fits the data. Main and interaction effects are identified, causal models tested, and related path diagrams described. Consequently, the independent explanation of each step of the sequential model described in this monograph can be tested and alternative explanatory models that may fit the data can be better evaluated. (See Appendix A for an expanded discussion of the use of log-linear analysis in the study of legal process.)

When we change the unit of analysis to the *type* of problem (or type of legal problem), the dependent variables become ratio scales in which each type of problem is described in terms of the proportion of problems that move through each stage of the mobilization process. Sarat and Grossman (1975:1208) propose that a "use-dispute index," the ratio between the number of court contacts and the number of disputes, be used in the study of the mobilization of adjudication. This type of index can be constructed for each stage of the mobilization process. Linear regression methods are best suited to the analysis of aggregate data (see Silberman, 1976).

In varying the levels of analysis, levels of measurement, and statistical models, we can determine to what extent the findings at one level can be generalized to the other. Furthermore, certain kinds of relationships can be explored only with certain kinds of data. For example, when the problem or individual experiencing the problem is the unit of analysis, the structure of the relationships between the dependent variables is fixed by the way in which the sequential model is defined. However, when the data are analyzed in the aggregate, the structure of the relationships among the dependent variables is not predetermined. It is conceivable that problems most likely to produce nonlegal action are least likely to invoke legal norms. For example, a person having a problem with noisy neighbors may be more likely to do something about it (e.g., attempting to get the noise stopped by talking to the landlord about it) than someone with a credit problem. However, a person with a credit problem, once having done something to solve the problem (e.g., talking to a credit bureau about one's credit rating) may be more likely to consider taking legal action than someone whose neighbors continue to be noisy. With this strategy for analyzing the mobilization process, it is possible to determine whether the likelihood of moving through one stage of the mobilization process affects the likelihood of moving through succeeding stages.

METHODOLOGICAL ISSUES

Data Collection Strategies

There are three established data collection strategies employed in the study of the use of lawyers: (1) the *legal problems* strategy, (2) the *everyday problems* strategy, and (3) the *serious problems* strategy.

The Legal Problems Strategy. Using this strategy, respondents are asked whether or not they have ever experienced a particular type of *legal* problem and whether or not they ever consulted a lawyer about it. Problems are selected because of their preconceived legal character, thus limiting such studies to areas where legal rights are already established (see Mayhew and Reiss, 1969). Marks (1976:195) calls this the "static problem list," and argues that a more effective research strategy is, in an open-ended fashion, to ask people about contacts they have had with lawyers and about the kinds of things they would like to have seen a lawyer about, but did not (see Marks *et al.*, 1974). While this solves the problem of getting a complete list and description of lawyer contacts, we still have a static list of legally defined problems.

The fundamental problem with this strategy is that information is collected about already existing patterns of legal action. At best, the type of research question that can be asked is: What are the correlates of the existing distribution of legal services, given the nature of legal rights as they are defined at the time the data are gathered? It is not possible to ask a far more interesting and important theoretical and empirical question: How do socially valid claims come to be defined as legally valid claims? This question can be answered only when we begin our analysis with disputes or problems in general, regardless of their apparent legal character, and determine the process by which they come to be defined as legal. For example, in the case of insurance claims, we are interested in the process by which one party or the other comes to define the dispute as requiring a legal remedy, the conditions producing the dispute, and the conditions associated with the decision to seek legal counsel. Unless we explore the total process by which legal services are mobilized, it is impossible to determine whether those with higher incomes are more likely to seek legal assistance in making such claims (see Mayhew and Reiss, 1969:314) because they have greater access to legal services or because they experience more of the kinds of problems that produce such disputes. Once we employ a strategy designed to analyze this process, it becomes possible to ask another important theoretical and empirical question: How does the process by which socially valid claims come to be defined as legally valid claims change over time; that is, how is law created?

The Everyday Problems Strategy. This strategy represents an attempt to overcome the limitations imposed by the legal problems strategy. It begins with a list of common disputes or problems experienced by a randomly selected group of citizens, whether or not these problems are initially perceived to be legally relevant (e.g., disputes with neighbors, inadequate street repairs, or a new appliance that does not work properly). These problems are not selected because of their legal relevance, but because citizens experience them as problems without apparent regard to whether or not they represent violations of the citizens' legal rights. The problem for analysis, then, is to specify those conditions under which such disputes or problems come to be defined as legal in nature and those that lead to the use of alternative mechanisms of dispute resolution. The existence of legal remedies becomes only one of several variables that determine whether citizens will contact an attorney.

The 1974 national survey sponsored by the American Bar Foundation, "Everyday Problems," represents a mixed case of an everyday problems strategy and a legal problems strategy (see Curran and Spalding, 1974; Curran, 1977). The form of the questions is an everyday one, but the questions asked are legally oriented and are posed in legalistic language. For example, the Detroit study asks about neighborhood disputes, whereas the Bar Foundation study does not. In the Detroit study, respondents are asked specifically about being "badly overcharged" for a series of items, receiving goods that were "broken or didn't work," whereas the Bar Foundation study asks about the "quality or condition of the goods purchased, or other promises made in connection with these goods." In the area of marital problems, the Bar Foundation study inquires about divorce and separation and problems associated with divorce and legal separation, but not marital disputes as such. Although entitled "Everyday Problems," this study departs significantly from the everyday problems strategy as defined here. By restricting questions to problems that are already defined as legally relevant, the issue of how problems come to be so defined is ignored.

In avoiding the static list problem, another problem is generated, that of the decreasing *N*. In the DAS, case histories were obtained for 1302 incidents defined as the respondents' most important and difficult disputes or problems. Information on whether or not legal action was taken was available for only 1263 of these. Respondents saw a lawyer or wanted to see a lawyer, or took some legal action (e.g., "go to court") in 200, or 16% of these problems. Respondents actually saw an attorney 9% of the time and went to court in only 1% of the 1263 disputes for which information was available. Unfortunately, by the end of the process, there are relatively few cases to study. That 9% of these cases went to attorneys can be compared with the 31% figure reported in the American Bar Foundation's study of the use of lawyers (Curran, 1977:147). This difference is explained by the legal orientation of the questions asked in the American Bar Foundation study.

The Serious Problems Strategy. The 1967 DAS study still represents the only study to use this strategy by developing case histories for the two most serious and difficult everyday problems encountered by those interviewed. Leon Mayhew and Albert J. Reiss, Jr. devised this strategy in order to overcome the problem caused by the relatively small number of cases that would yield legal action.

Serious problems are not as likely to produce legal encounters as are more routine matters involving property transactions, estates, or family dissolution. Had a wider range of problems been incorporated in the survey, including less serious, more routine problems (those that have a higher probability of requiring legal assistance), there would have been a greater number of cases involving attorneys and going to court.

A strategy for collecting data on the mobilization of lawyers that overcomes the problems associated with the three approaches described above has yet to be developed. Such a strategy should be based on sampling types of disputes that vary in their legal relevance such that the probability of using a lawyer varies greatly among dispute categories. To develop theoretical explanations of the mobilization process, it is not necessary to sample every conceivable type of dispute. Instead, it makes sense to study a limited number of types, including common everyday disputes, serious problems, and those that represent routine and nonroutine legal matters. Consequently, *legality* becomes a variable characteristic of disputes, measured in terms of the extent to which lawyers are mobilized to resolve the disputes. The central research question becomes: What are the determinants of the legality of disputes? Such a strategy would avoid some of the pitfalls of the three approaches discussed above.

Validity Issues

The study of the mobilization of lawyers involves the survey of events, rather than the attitudes and orientations of individuals. Moreover, these events are legal in nature. Methodological problems associated with this approach are comparable to those associated with surveys of self-reported criminality (see Waldo and Chiricos, 1972; Silberman, 1976) and criminal victimization (see Wolfgang, 1967; Biderman, 1975). These surveys focus on the criminal act rather than the civil dispute, but both represent legal or potentially legal events. Whether we are studying criminal acts or civil disputes, these studies rely upon nonexpert informants to describe their legal experiences. Consequently, public definitions of crime or disputes are used instead of those of legal experts.

This approach raises several validity issues that require some attention. The first is the problem of accuracy when the average citizen is expected to report on the nature of his or her legal problem, criminal behavior, or victimization. To the extent that citizens are asked whether they have had a specific legal problem, committed a specific crime, or been the victim of a specific crime, we are relying upon the accuracy of public definitions of events that may or may not be legal in nature. In fact, it is part of the role of lawyers and other functionaries of the legal system to evaluate the legality of a particular event. At issue, in part, is the nature of the relationship between public definitions and legal definitions, their correspondence and transformation. For example, a husband striking a wife can be variously defined as a criminal assault, grounds for divorce, or a noncriminal family dispute. How such an act is legally defined depends on existing statutes and judicial and police practices in the community in which it occurs. Whether or not a husband or wife define such an act as an assault may depend on the court's willingness to define it as such. The solution to this problem depends on our ability to obtain reliable descriptions of disputes regardless of whether or not the disputants define the events as legally relevant. These events can then be categorized using a framework that is independent of preconceived legal categories.

The second major validity problem in the survey of events is the general accuracy of recall problem. When individuals are asked to reconstruct histories of past events, inaccurate recall of these events may be due in part to the problem of "retrospective interpretation" (Kitsuse, 1964). Should a dispute be defined as a legal matter at a given point in time, respondents may reconstruct the history of that dispute in order to provide a consistent justification for taking legal action. One possible result may be a tendency to exaggerate the seriousness of the initial dispute. Should legal action *not* have been taken in a given matter, respondents may minimize the seriousness of the dispute. In other words, we can expect some degree of dissonance reduction after a decision has been made to pursue or not to pursue a legal remedy. For all practical purposes, this problem is not one that can be easily solved. A panel design in which data are collected initially on ongoing disputes or problems, with follow-ups on steps taken to solve these disputes, would avoid the retrospective interpretation problem, but would present problems of its own. Interviewer effects would be particularly great with such an approach, and the relative increase in costs would not be worth what would probably be only a slight increase in validity.

The relative seriousness of a dispute is of central concern in the literature (see Sarat, 1977). Serious disputes are less likely to produce avoidance responses and more likely to produce efforts to solve the dispute. Defining seriousness in terms of the likelihood that something will be done presents a third validity problem when measuring the impact of seriousness on actions taken. Allowing respondents to define which problems are their most serious still presents the same tautological problem, since the respondents are more likely to retrospectively define as serious those problems in which more serious (e.g., legal) action was taken. A more objective method of measuring relative seriousness must be designed, one that is clearly independent of subjective judgments and courses of action actually taken. One such method is to order problems in terms of their relative frequency in the community. The relationship of such ordering to seriousness is evident when comparing criminal offenses (see Silberman, 1976); that is, relatively serious crimes (e.g., assault) are less likely to occur than less serious ones (e.g., marijuana use). In other words, seriousness is operationally defined in terms of relative frequency. This approach has a certain amount of face validity; it makes sense intuitively to assume that offenses that are publicly defined as more serious will not occur as frequently as those considered to be less serious.

The fourth and last major validity problem concerns a major conceptualization in the literature on the legal profession—access. Although central to the study of institutions of legal representation, this concept has never been adequately measured independently of actual use of legal services (e.g., Mayhew, 1975). Access is conceived, in the abstract, in terms of opportunities to use lawyers. It is difficult to measure access independently of its determinants (the available supply of attorneys, financial resources, etc.) or its consequences (the actual use of attorneys). Although somewhat of a departure from the original intent of such a concept, it is possible to measure access in terms of patterns of use of lawyers for certain types of disputes in order to predict the likelihood that individuals will seek legal action for other types of disputes. The access principle predicts that those who have used lawyers in, say, personal injury cases are more likely to use lawyers in disputes with their neighbors. There is some evidence, however, that prior legal experience tends to make people avoid subsequent legal encounters (see Hunting and Neuwirth, 1962). Actual access (experience) to the legal system deters, rather than encourages, further contact with lawyers.

3

DISPUTES IN THE DETROIT AREA

In this chapter, I give the reader as clear a picture as possible of the kinds of disputes Detroiters experience in their everyday lives. First, the chapter reports the frequencies of disputes by type of problem: neighborhood, landlord–tenant, consumer, public organizations, and discrimination. Then it breaks down the frequencies of types of problems and the incidence of specific disputes by socioeconomic status. Similarly, the chapter describes the incidence of the most serious disputes by type of problem, breaking down the latter according to socioeconomic status. It also describes the incidence of legal contacts among the different status groups. The final section illustrates the dispute-resolution process through case histories of the most serious everyday disputes. In this way, I hope to bring to life otherwise sterile statistical data.

The concept of dispute is a sensitizing one designed to turn our attention to everyday conflicts for which legal remedies may or may not exist. We are interested in knowing something about problems people have with their neighbors, with their landlords, when they purchase expensive consumer goods, when they deal with public officials, or when they experience discrimination in housing or employment. These problems are interpersonal in the sense that they are defined as conflicts between individuals, or between individuals and representatives of organizations. Once we turn our attention to legal problems, we are no longer discussing matters that are purely interpersonal. Legal problems often address larger issues that go beyond the present situational context. Indeed, legal matters often reflect the structure of political, economic, and social relations in the community in which they occur.[1]

EVERYDAY DISPUTES

Everyday disputes were grouped into five general areas in the original survey: neighborhood, landlord–tenant, expensive purchase (consumer),

[1] For a discussion of the distinction between the concept of dispute and the concept of law, see Cain and Kulscár, 1982.

public organization, and discrimination. Neighborhood and consumer problems were reported most frequently. An estimated half of all Detroit area residents had experienced at least one neighborhood or consumer problem over the previous 10 years (see Table 3.1). Approximately one-third of all Detroit area residents had a dispute with a government agency. And, finally, about one out of six residents had a dispute with their landlord. Similarly, one out of six experienced some sort of discrimination in housing, employment, or other areas. While all Detroit residents are eligible to have neighborhood, consumer, and governmental problems, not all are eligible for disputes with landlords and discrimination. These estimates represent the incidence of such problems in the sample as a whole. Consequently, we are underestimating the actual incidence of disputes in relation to those at risk.

In the aggregate, it appears that the frequency distribution of perceived injuries (disputes), is a function of social class position measured in terms of income, but not property ownership (see Tables 3.2 and 3.3).[2] The effect is a curvilinear one, with lower-middle and upper-middle income groups reporting a significantly higher probability of experiencing disputes than either the lowest or highest groups. Disaggregating disputes into the five main categories, we find great variability in the relationship between the frequency distribution and measures of social class. Variability is even more evident when particular types of problems within each category are further isolated. This suggests that the curvilinear effect of income is not a systematic one, but an artifact of the variable distributions among the different types of specific disputes within each general category.

At first glance, it appears that the curvilinear relationship between the incidence of everyday disputes and income might account for the curvilinear association between income and legal contacts, but this is not the case. As we can see from Table 3.2, the likelihood of legal contacts significantly increases with income for those who report experiencing everyday problems. In addition, Table 3.3 shows that those who own their own homes are more likely than renters to contact an attorney although they are not more likely to experience everyday problems. The association between class and legal contacts cannot be reduced to class effects on perceived injuries. In other words, the socially and economically privileged are *not* more likely to go to law because they are more likely to perceive injuries. The explanation of the former is independent of the explanation of the latter.

Problems with neighbors occur frequently among all income groups. Income does not have a significant effect on the reported frequency of neigh-

[2]Social class is measured in terms of total family income in 1966. Income groups are categorized as follows: lower < \$7000; lower-middle = \$7000–14,999; upper-middle = \$15,000–\$24,999; upper ≥ \$25,000. Property ownership is measured in terms of home ownership at the time of the survey (1967).

TABLE 3.1
Incidence of Everyday Disputes in the Detroit Area

Type of problem	Number of persons reporting problems	Percentage reporting each type of problem	Percentage of total sample reporting problems[a]
Neighborhood	550	100.0	53.1
Kids	336	61.1	32.4
Noisy neighbors	218	39.6	21.1
Busybodies	136	24.7	13.2
Undesirable neighbors	62	11.3	6.0
Messy neighbors	208	37.8	20.2
Other	103	18.7	10.1
Landlord–Tenant	169	100.0	16.3
Poor repairs	126	74.6	12.2
Undesirable tenants	36	21.3	3.5
Property damage	26	15.4	2.5
Owed money	21	12.4	2.0
Other	31	18.3	3.0
Consumer	491	100.0	47.3
Overcharged	124	25.3	12.0
Broken	262	53.4	25.3
Guarantee	218	44.4	21.0
Credit	108	22.0	10.5
Other	55	11.2	5.4
Public organizations	357	100.0	34.5
Soc. Sec./Vet. Admin.	64	17.9	6.2
Welfare	29	8.1	2.8
IRS	106	29.7	10.2
Property tax	37	10.4	3.6
City services	123	34.5	11.9
Police	86	24.1	8.3
Other	46	12.9	4.5
Discrimination	164	100.0	15.8
Employment	87	53.0	8.4
Joining a club	5	3.0	0.5
Housing	53	32.3	5.1
Services	27	16.5	2.6
Other discrimination	45	27.4	4.4
Discrimination based on:			
Age	64	39.0	6.2
Sex	5	3.0	0.5
Race	39	23.8	3.8
Religion	7	4.3	0.7
Nationality	6	3.7	0.6
Beliefs	6	3.7	0.6
Total (persons reporting problems)	807		77.7

[a] Percentages are based on the weighted sample (N = 1038), excluding missing data cases.

TABLE 3.2
Incidence of Everyday Problems and Legal Contacts by Income (in Percentages)[a]

	Income				
	Lower	Lower-middle	Upper-middle	Upper	Likelihood ratio χ^{2b}
Type of problem					
Neighborhood	49.0	56.6	55.0	41.2	5.27
	(341)	(530)	(100)	(34)	
Landlord–Tenant	19.4	16.4	6.9	11.8	8.09*
	(341)	(530)	(101)	(34)	
Consumer	39.0	54.3	44.1	41.2	15.71**
	(341)	(530)	(102)	(34)	
Public organizations	28.8	35.7	38.2	41.2	4.78
	(340)	(530)	(102)	(34)	
Discrimination	18.6	15.5	7.8	8.8	6.82
	(339)	(530)	(102)	(34)	
Aggregate measure of everyday problems[c]	71.2	81.7	82.4	64.7	12.98**
	(340)	(530)	(102)	(34)	
Legal contact					
Ever see a lawyer	55.1	73.8	85.3	70.6	36.86***
	(341)	(530)	(102)	(34)	
Saw a lawyer for everyday problem (respondents with problems)	9.1	12.0	21.4	27.3	8.67*
	(242)	(433)	(84)	(22)	

[a] Figures in parentheses are sample sizes for corresponding percentages.
[b] Adjusted for weight factor.
[c] Indicates respondent experienced at least one everyday problem.
* $p < .05$; ** $p < .01$; *** $p < .001$ ($df = 3$).

borhood disputes (see Table 3.2), but there is a tendency for middle-class Detroiters to report experiencing such problems more frequently, a tendency that reflects a greater willingness to do something about the problems they experience. They report being troubled by many different kinds of disputes with their neighbors, but messy (read "lower-class") neighbors concern the middle class most (see Table 3.4).

The proportion of homeowners and renters who indicate that they have experienced neighborhood disputes are virtually identical (Table 3.3). However, by disaggregating neighborhood disputes, we find that renters (who reside primarily in apartment houses) are significantly more likely than homeowners to express their anger at noisy neighbors and those who cannot mind their own business (see Table 3.4).

The effects of income and ownership on the distribution of neighborhood disputes are independent of one another. Middle-class individuals are more

TABLE 3.3

Incidence of Everyday Problems and Legal Contacts by Home Ownership (in Percentages)[a]

	Rents	Owns	Likelihood ratio χ_2[b]
Type of problem			
Neighborhood	53.4 (283)	53.1 (749)	0.00
Landlord–Tenant	36.0 (283)	8.8 (751)	75.66***
Consumer	44.7 (284)	48.5 (751)	0.87
Public organizations	32.7 (284)	35.1 (750)	0.37
Discrimination	24.0 (283)	12.7 (750)	14.02***
Aggregate measure of everyday problems	78.9 (284)	77.5 (750)	0.18
Legal contact			
Ever see a lawyer	50.7 (284)	75.2 (751)	41.51***
Saw a lawyer for everyday problem	8.5 (224)	15.1 (581)	5.06*

[a] Figures in parentheses are sample sizes for corresponding percentages.
[b] Adjusted for weight factor.
* $p < .05$; *** $p < .001$ ($df = 1$).

TABLE 3.4

The Effects of Income and Home Ownership on the Incidence of Neighborhood Disputes (in Percentages)[a]

Type of dispute	Income: Lower	Lower-middle	Upper-middle	Upper	Likelihood ratio χ^{2b} ($df = 3$)	Rents	Owns	Likelihood ratio χ^{2b} ($df = 1$)
Kids	29.6	34.0	34.0	38.2	1.81	31.0	33.0	0.41
	(341)	(530)	(100)	(34)		(284)	(749)	
Noisy	22.4	22.4	14.0	14.7	3.82	26.1	19.2	4.20*
	(340)	(526)	(100)	(34)		(284)	(744)	
Busybodies	13.2	13.4	19.0	2.9	5.19	18.7	11.1	7.22**
	(340)	(528)	(100)	(34)		(284)	(746)	
Undesirables	4.4	7.0	6.0	5.9	1.95	5.3	6.3	0.29
	(340)	(527)	(100)	(34)		(284)	(745)	
Messy	15.2	22.9	26.0	14.7	7.87*	16.3	21.6	2.77
	(341)	(524)	(100)	(34)		(282)	(745)	
Other	9.2	10.2	15.3	11.8	2.16	8.8	10.6	0.55
	(337)	(521)	(98)	(34)		(283)	(735)	

[a] Figures in parentheses are sample sizes for corresponding percentages.
[b] Adjusted for weight factor.
* $p < .05$; ** $p < .01$.

likely to report disputes with their neighbors, regardless of whether they own their homes or rent. Conversely, homeowners and renters are equally likely to complain about their neighbors, regardless of their class position. Renters are more likely than homeowners to be troubled by noisy neighbors, whether they live in expensive high-rise apartments or tenements.

There is a statistically significant correlation between income and the incidence of landlord–tenant disputes. Lower- and lower-middle-income individuals are more than twice as likely as those with upper-middle and upper income to have had such difficulty while living in the Detroit area (see Table 3.2). This correlation, however, appears to be an artifact of the very strong correlation between renting and disputing with landlords (see Table 3.3). (These disputes are viewed from the perspective of the tenant.) Controlling for home ownership, the correlation between income and disputes with landlords disappears. In other words, once dispute eligibility is accounted for in terms of the individual's status as renter, lower-income individuals are no more likely to experience problems with their landlords than upper-income individuals. In general, the lower classes are more likely to experience disputes with landlords because they are more likely to rent their homes or apartments.

Of course, it is quite conceivable that the kinds of problems the lower and upper income groups experience are different. Lower-income renters are more likely to have difficulty getting the landlord to maintain the property in adequate condition and to keep undesirable persons out of the building (see Table 3.5). Upper-income renters are more likely to dispute with their landlords over monetary matters, such as deductions from rent for repairs made by tenants. Controlling for ownership status, we find that both low- and high-income renters have difficulty getting repairs and services, although there is a tendency for lower income groups to have more trouble than the others. One problem appears to be unique to lower income groups. The presence of "undesirable" tenants or others in their buildings is a special problem for lower- and lower-middle-income renters.

Income is a correlate of consumer problems (Table 3.2). The lower-middle class is significantly more likely to report such problems than either the poor or upper income groups. In general, it appears that the "poor pay more" (see Caplovitz, 1963), but the poorest among us are either less likely to recognize these "little injustices" (Nader, 1980:4) or are not in a position to enter into relationships that produce them.

Breaking down consumer problems into specific types of situations, we find that lower and lower-middle income groups are considerably more likely than upper-middle and upper income groups to report being overcharged (see Table 3.6); the poor, indeed, do pay more. The poor are not able to purchase expensive consumer items and consequently are less frequently in

TABLE 3.5

The Effects of Income and Home Ownership on the Incidence of Landlord–Tenant Disputes (in Percentages)[a]

Type of dispute	Income: Lower	Income: Lower-middle	Income: Upper-middle	Income: Upper	Likelihood ratio χ^{2b} (df = 3)	Rents	Owns	Likelihood ratio χ^{2b} (df = 1)
Poor repairs	14.7	12.1	5.0	5.9	7.22[c]	29.0	5.9	68.3***
	(340)	(529)	(101)	(34)		(283)	(750)	
Undesirables	5.9	2.7	0.0	2.9	9.91*	9.2	1.2	25.97***
	(341)	(529)	(101)	(34)		(283)	(750)	
Damages	2.6	2.8	2.0	0.0	1.56	3.9	2.0	2.05
	(341)	(528)	(101)	(34)		(283)	(749)	
Money owed	2.1	1.9	2.0	5.9	1.30	3.5	1.5	2.98
	(341)	(529)	(101)	(34)		(283)	(750)	
Other	1.8	3.6	4.0	2.9	2.26	4.6	2.3	2.74
	(340)	(526)	(101)	(34)		(281)	(748)	

[a] Figures in parentheses are sample sizes for corresponding percentages.
[b] Adjusted for weight factor.
[c] The β coefficient for the effect of *lower* income on the likelihood of having difficulty with repairs is significant at the .05 level.
* $p < .05$; *** $p < .001$.

TABLE 3.6

The Effects of Income and Home Ownership on the Incidence of Consumer Complaints (in Percentages)[a]

Type of dispute	Income: Lower	Income: Lower-middle	Income: Upper-middle	Income: Upper	Likelihood ratio χ^{2b} (df = 3)	Rents	Owns	Likelihood ratio χ^{2b} (df = 1)
Overcharged	12.3	14.9	2.9	0.0	17.70***	13.7	11.5	0.26
	(341)	(523)	(102)	(34)		(278)	(750)	
Broken	17.7	29.5	28.4	32.4	13.14**	24.0	25.9	0.28
	(340)	(529)	(102)	(34)		(283)	(750)	
Guarantee	13.8	26.5	19.6	11.8	17.23***	13.0	24.1	12.36***
	(341)	(529)	(102)	(34)		(284)	(750)	
Credit	8.8	11.4	15.7	5.9	3.66	15.2	8.7	6.57*
	(339)	(526)	(102)	(34)		(282)	(747)	
Other	4.2	7.2	2.0	0.0	8.08*	5.4	5.5	0.73
	(334)	(514)	(102)	(33)		(278)	(733)	

[a] Figures in parentheses are sample sizes for corresponding percentages.
[b] Adjusted for weight factor.
* $p < .05$; ** $p < .01$; *** $p < .001$.

a position to complain about purchasing goods that do not work or about the failure of the manufacturer to honor a guarantee. Furthermore, the poor report fewer problems getting or maintaining credit than either the lower-middle or upper-middle income groups. This supports the notion that participation in the consumer society is limited to those who can afford to do so. Among those who participate through the purchase of expensive consumer goods, regardless of their income, consumer problems occur frequently; but it is the lower-middle class that is most likely to be faced with consumer problems generally. Although immune from most mundane consumer problems such as credit, guarantees, and overpaying, the upper income group is not immune from receiving defective merchandise. Fully one-third of the most affluent residents in the sample reported a major expenditure in which the object (e.g., car, furniture, or appliances) did not work properly or was broken.

Home ownership is unrelated to the incidence of consumer problems (Table 3.3). Nor does controlling for income affect the association between home ownership and the incidence of problems involving expensive purchases. Maintaining credit, however, is more of a problem for renters than for homeowners, whereas homeowners have greater difficulty getting servicemen and contractors to honor their guarantees.

The effects of income and ownership on problems with guarantees are independent and additive. Almost one-third (29%) of the lower-middle-income homeowners experienced such problems in contrast with less than one-tenth (9%) of the lower-income renters reporting this kind of problem. The effects of income and ownership on credit problems are also independent and additive, but the direction is reversed and the effect of income approaches, but does not achieve, statistical significance. Lower-middle-income renters have the greatest difficulty maintaining good credit relationships with banks and other sources of credit. Almost one in five (19%) reported experiencing such a problem over the past 10 years. At the other extreme, only 5% of lower-income homeowners and 6% of upper-income homeowners reported having problems securing and maintaining good credit. It appears that the ownership of property, including home ownership, facilitates securing and maintaining credit, regardless of one's current income.

There is a tendency for the incidence of disputes with public organizations to increase with income, but the effect of income is modest (see Table 3.2). Of greater interest is the way in which the kind of dispute with the government depends on income (see Table 3.7). Disputing with the IRS is primarily a middle-class phenomenon. Collecting money from entitlement programs [such as those provided by the Social Security and Veterans Administrations] is a major problem for the poor. Paradoxically, all income groups

TABLE 3.7

The Effects of Income and Home Ownership on the Incidence of Disputes with Public Organizations (in Percentages)[a]

Type of dispute	Income: Lower	Lower-middle	Upper-middle	Upper	Likelihood ratio χ^{2b} ($df = 3$)	Rents	Owns	Likelihood ratio χ^{2b} ($df = 1$)
Soc. Sec./VA	10.0	4.3	2.0	0.0	14.34**	4.2	6.9	2.10
	(340)	(530)	(102)	(34)		(284)	(750)	
Welfare	2.1	2.6	2.9	2.9	0.32	4.6	2.1	3.09
	(340)	(530)	(102)	(34)		(284)	(750)	
Income tax	4.4	12.6	14.9	8.8	15.64**	7.1	11.3	3.29
	(340)	(530)	(101)	(34)		(283)	(750)	
Property tax	2.6	3.0	6.9	8.8	4.48	1.8	4.3	3.18
	(340)	(529)	(101)	(34)		(282)	(750)	
City service	8.6	13.8	14.9	5.9	5.85	11.3	12.1	0.10
	(338)	(530)	(101)	(34)		(282)	(749)	
Police	6.2	8.5	7.8	23.5	7.08	10.6	7.5	1.82
	(339)	(528)	(102)	(34)		(284)	(747)	
Other	3.6	5.8	4.0	0.0	4.16	3.2	5.1	0.15
	(335)	(517)	(101)	(32)		(278)	(732)	

[a] Figures in parentheses are sample sizes for corresponding percentages.
[b] Adjusted for weight factor.
** $p < .01$.

are equally unlikely to report problems with public welfare agencies. It seems that it is more difficult to collect earned benefits such as pensions, medical care or government-sponsored loans than welfare payments. Home ownership is uncorrelated with the incidence of disputes with government agencies. Homeowners and renters are equally likely to report problems with government agencies in general (see Table 3.3). Moreover, there are no systematic differences between homeowners and renters in the kinds of government disputes they experience (see Table 3.7).

Discrimination, especially age discrimination, varies inversely with income (see Table 3.8). The oldest low-income residents experience special difficulty in securing employment, housing, and adequate services. But, age discrimination is less a function of low income than it is of rental status. Renters are more likely than owners to experience discrimination in employment. Renters are also more likely to receive inadequate services because of their age. In housing, age discrimination occurs only among renters, whose incomes tend to be lower on the average than homeowners. Racial discrimination occurs in securing employment, housing, and adequate services, regardless of ownership or income status.

TABLE 3.8

The Effects of Income and Home Ownership on the Incidence of Discrimination (in Percentages)[a]

	Income: Lower	Income: Lower-middle	Income: Upper-middle	Income: Upper	Likelihood ratio χ^{2b} ($df = 3$)	Rents	Owns	Likelihood ratio χ^{2b} ($df = 1$)
Type of discrimination								
Job	10.6	7.7	3.9	5.9	4.41	12.0	6.9	4.86*
	(339)	(530)	(102)	(34)		(283)	(749)	
Club	0.3	0.4	0.0	5.9	5.88	0.4	0.5	0.12
	(339)	(530)	(101)	(34)		(284)	(750)	
Housing	7.1	4.0	4.0	5.9	3.33	12.7	2.3	29.97***
	(337)	(530)	(101)	(34)		(283)	(748)	
Service	3.9	2.1	1.0	0.0	4.19	4.3	2.0	2.79
	(337)	(530)	(102)	(34)		(282)	(749)	
Other	2.9	5.7	1.0	5.9	5.94	4.6	4.3	0.04
	(339)	(528)	(100)	(34)		(282)	(747)	
Discrimination based on								
Age	8.6	5.8	2.0	0.0	8.72*	10.6	4.5	8.87**
	(339)	(530)	(102)	(34)		(283)	(750)	
Sex	0.6	0.6	0.0	0.0	1.10	1.1	0.3	1.75
	(339)	(530)	(102)	(34)		(283)	(750)	
Race	4.7	3.6	2.0	2.9	1.51	6.0	2.9	3.67[c]
	(339)	(530)	(102)	(34)		(283)	(750)	
Religion	0.3	0.8	0.0	2.9	2.77	0.4	0.8	0.52
	(339)	(530)	(102)	(34)		(283)	(750)	
Nationality	0.6	0.4	2.0	0.0	2.18	1.4	0.3	3.03
	(339)	(530)	(102)	(34)		(283)	(750)	
Beliefs	0.3	0.6	0.0	0.0	1.14	0.0	0.8	2.90
	(339)	(530)	(102)	(34)		(283)	(750)	

[a] Figures in parentheses are sample sizes for corresponding percentages.
[b] Adjusted for weight factor.
[c] Pearson $\chi_2 = 4.01$, $p < .05$; $\beta = -.37$, $p < .05$.
* $p < .05$; ** $p < .01$; *** $p < .001$.

Renters are about twice as likely as homeowners to report incidents of discrimination of all kinds. This relationship holds for all income groups and is particularly significant for the young, the old, and blacks. The ownership of property insulates individuals from discriminatory practices. Upper-middle- and upper-income individuals are virtually immune from discrimination because they are likely to own property, not because of their income per se. Low-income renters are especially likely to experience discrimination. In fact, low income and rental status interact to enhance the likelihood of experiencing discrimination on the basis of both age and race.

Fully one-sixth of the respondents reported experiencing discrimination of one sort or another while living in the Detroit metropolitan area. Half of these (see Table 3.1) reported difficulties in securing employment, one-third in housing, and one-sixth in receiving adequate services. An insignificant number complained about membership in private clubs or associations, although many did report miscellaneous "other" discriminatory experiences. Most of the respondents—two out of five, in fact—reported that their discriminatory experiences had been on the basis of age. Half as many, about one in four or five, reported experiencing racial discrimination. Few reported being discriminated against on the basis of sex, religion, nationality, or beliefs they held.

Of the 64 respondents who reported incidents of age discrimination, half of these (31) were in employment, one-third (20) were in housing, and only 9 were for receiving inadequate services. Similarly, of the 39 respondents who reported incidents of racial discrimination, three-fourths (29) were in employment, one-third (14) were in housing, and only 9 reported receiving inadequate services. Employment clearly ranked first as the area in which discrimination was reported; it was especially of concern among those who reported discrimination on the basis of race. Most of the respondents who reported experiencing racial discrimination only experienced problems in seeking employment, or they experienced difficulty in employment and in at least one other area, usually housing (see Table 3.9). Rarely (only 6 times) did respondents report racial discrimination as their only problem in housing, service, or some other area. In contrast, respondents frequently (30 times, or 47%) reported age discrimination in housing, service, or other areas as their only problem.

Everyday disputes are a common occurrence in all strata of the Detroit population. The recognition or identification of such disputes is more likely to occur among middle-income groups than at either of the extremes. There is no correlation between property ownership and problem identification in general, but the reporting of certain problems does depend on whether Detroiters own their own homes or rent. The distribution of contacts with attorneys for everyday disputes does not depend on the distribution of the disputes themselves. As a result, the explanation of the former does not depend on the explanation of the latter. The likelihood of contacting an attorney for everyday disputes increases with income and ownership. But individuals who are in the upper-middle-income group are most likely to contact a lawyer at some time during their lives. In part, this is because the relationship between income and contacting a lawyer for nonproperty matters is curvilinear (see Chapter 4). In other words, the effects of income aside, going to see a lawyer about non–property-related disputes is a middle-class phenomenon. Not only are members of the middle class most likely to

TABLE 3.9
Incidence of Discrimination by Age and Race (in Percentages)[a]

Area of discrimination	Age	Race
Only one area reported		
Employment	31.3 (20)	46.2 (18)
Housing	18.8 (12)	7.7 (3)
Services	9.4 (6)	2.6 (1)
Other	18.8 (12)	5.1 (2)
Multiple areas reported		
Employment & other(s)	17.2 (11)	28.2 (11)
Not employment, but others	4.7 (3)	10.3 (4)
	100.2[b] (64)	100.1[b] (39)

[a] Figures in parentheses are sample sizes for corresponding percentages.
[b] Rounding error.

experience everyday disputes, but they are also most likely to contact an attorney when they do, especially when the dispute is not about a property matter.

SERIOUS DISPUTES

Serious disputes are identified as those that gave "the most difficulty" to the respondents. This identification was accomplished in two stages. First, each respondent selected the problem that "bothered you most during the last 10 years" within each of the five general categories. Then, with up to five bothersome problems selected, the most difficult and the second most difficult were identified. If the respondent had problems in only one or two areas, the most bothersome in these areas were, by definition, the most difficult. Case histories were then obtained on all disputes defined as serious, that is, as the most difficult and the second most difficult.

A total of 2778 disputes were reported by the weighted sample of 1038 Detroit area residents (see Table 3.10). A plurality of these (38%) involved disputes between neighbors. Consumer problems were next (28%), then problems with government agencies (18%), then disputes with landlords (9%), and, finally, discrimination was least frequently reported (8%).

There is little variation in the likelihood that each type of problem was defined by the respondents as serious (see Table 3.10). About 40 to 50% within each category were so designated. However, when we look more closely at specific types of disputes, we find great variation within each category. Problems with neighborhood children or teenagers ("kids") were

TABLE 3.10
Incidence of Serious Disputes in the Detroit Area

Type of problem	Number of reported problems		Percentage of problems defined as serious[a]
Neighborhood	1063	(38.3%)	41.3
Kids	336		59.8
Noisy neighbors	218		31.2
Busybodies	136		26.5
Undesirable neighbors	62		25.8
Messy neighbors	208		30.8
Other neighborhood problems	103		52.4
Landlord–Tenant	240	(8.6%)	39.6
Poor repairs	126		51.6
Undesirable tenants	36		27.8
Property damage	26		11.5
Owed money	21		33.3
Other landlord problems	31		32.3
Consumer (expensive purchase)	767	(27.6%)	53.7
Overcharged	124		48.4
Broken	262		51.1
Guarantee	218		60.6
Credit	108		54.6
Other consumer problems	55		49.1
Public organizations	491	(17.7%)	53.6
Social Security/Veterans Admin.	64		65.6
Welfare	29		62.1
IRS	106		50.0
Property tax	37		54.1
City services	123		52.8
Police	86		41.9
Other governmental disputes	46		63.0
Discrimination	217	(7.8%)	52.1
Employment	87		62.1
Joining a club	5		—
Housing	53		39.6
Services	27		14.8
Other discrimination	45		48.9
Discrimination based on			
Age	64		67.2
Sex	5		—
Race	39		84.6
Religion	7		—
Nationality	6		—
Beliefs	6		—
	2778	(100.0%)	47.6

[a] Percentages not reported for $N < 10$.

the most frequently reported problems and the problems most likely to be defined as serious. Similarly, inadequate repairs or services were the most frequently reported disputes with landlords and the disputes most likely to be considered serious. It appears that the initial reporting of these disputes depends, in part, on the amount of difficulty they present to the respondents. More serious disputes are reported more frequently. This suggests that there is a threshold of difficulty that affects the recognition of disputes, and this threshold is itself an indication of the seriousness of the dispute. In other words, seriousness is a sufficient condition for the dispute to be recognized and reported. Conversely, the recognition of disputes is necessary for their identification as serious.

There is much less variation in the likelihood of disputes concerning consumer problems and disputes with public organizations being defined as serious. These are relatively unambiguous events and their recognition is less likely to depend on the seriousness of the problem at hand. Either a purchased object is broken or it is not. Either the IRS selected you for an audit or it did not.

Discrimination on the basis of age and race stand out as the two most serious problems from the point of view of those who experience them. In fact, 67% of those who reported being the victim of age discrimination considered this to be their most serious or second most serious problem, and 84% of those who did see it as serious considered it to be the single most important problem they had experienced over the previous 10 years. Similarly, 85% of those who reported being the victim of racial discrimination considered this to be their most important or second most important problem, and 70% of these considered it to be the single most important problem they had experienced over the previous 10 years. Whereas discrimination was the least frequently reported problem, it was an extremely serious matter to those who were its victims. This is consistent with Mayhew's (1975:413) finding that the victims of discrimination are more likely than any other group to demand "justice," that is, vindication of their legal rights.

Not only is there little variation across types of problems in the likelihood that a dispute will be defined as serious, there is little systematic variation across status groups (see Tables 3.11 and 3.12). The proportion of disputes defined as serious for the different income groups is virtually constant. This is, in part, an artifact of the way in which seriousness was measured. Since seriousness was measured in terms of the evaluation of disputes by respondents, there should be roughly the same proportion of disputes defined as serious within each group of respondents, assuming no group has a particularly strong tendency to avoid such definitions. However, there is some idiosyncratic variation when it comes to specific types of problems. The lower-middle-income group is especially unlikely to report disputes with

TABLE 3.11
Incidence of Serious Disputes and Legal Contacts by Income (in Percentages)[a]

	Income				
	Lower	Lower-middle	Upper-middle	Upper	Likelihood ratio χ^{2b}
Type of problem					
Neighborhood	41.3	41.1	40.4	43.3	0.07
	(320)	(579)	(114)	(30)	
Landlord–Tenant	41.3	39.3	23.1	33.3	1.34
	(92)	(122)	(13)	(6)	
Consumer	52.3	52.4	62.9	64.7	2.77
	(193)	(471)	(70)	(17)	
Public organizations	63.8	46.6	59.3	64.7	9.11*
	(127)	(268)	(54)	(17)	
Discrimination	52.4	55.2	50.0	12.5	4.52
	(84)	(105)	(10)	(8)	
All types of everyday problems	48.5	46.3	49.8	48.7	1.33
	(816)	(1545)	(261)	(78)	
Legal contact					
Saw a lawyer for serious dispute	5.7	8.1	17.2	15.8	12.32**
	(385)	(692)	(128)	(38)	

[a] Figures in parentheses are sample sizes for corresponding percentages.
[b] Adjusted for weight factor.
* $p < .05$; ** $p < .01$ ($df = 3$).

TABLE 3.12
Incidence of Serious Disputes and Legal Contacts by Home Ownership (in Percentages)[a]

	Rents	Owns	Likelihood ratio χ^{2b}
Type of problem			
Neighborhood	33.6 (301)	43.2 (759)	3.00
Landlord–Tenant	47.2 (142)	29.2 (96)	5.93*
Consumer	46.3 (201)	56.4 (566)	4.55*
Public organizations	53.7 (121)	53.7 (369)	0.00
Discrimination	45.8 (96)	56.7 (120)	1.89
All types of everyday problems	44.0 (861)	49.3 (1910)	4.94*
Legal contact			
Saw a lawyer for serious dispute	5.7 (367)	10.5 (915)	5.87*

[a] Figures in parentheses are sample sizes for corresponding percentages.
[b] Adjusted for weight factor.
* $p < .05$ ($df = 1$).

government agencies as serious. Perhaps this is because disputes with government agencies are status dependent. The poor have problems with entitlement programs such as Social Security and veterans' benefits. The affluent have tax problems.

Homeowners are more likely than renters to consider their disputes to be serious (see Table 3.12). Homeowners are especially likely to be bothered by neighborhood disputes, consumer complaints, and discrimination in employment and housing, whereas renters are most troubled by problems with landlords. This difference is, of course, an artifact of rental status (although many current homeowners have rented in the past and have had related problems). The tendency for homeowners to take their problems more seriously than renters reflects their greater willingness to do something about their problems, including contacting attorneys.

SELECTED CASE HISTORIES OF SERIOUS DISPUTES

In-depth case histories were collected for all serious disputes. The present analysis is based on a 10% random sample of these case histories. What follows are 10 representative cases designed to illustrate both those that did and those that did not involve contacts with lawyers. Cases from each of the five main categories of disputes are described below.

Discrimination was the most serious type of dispute experienced by residents of the Detroit metropolitan area (see Table 3.13). Nevertheless, Detroiters were relatively unlikely to seek the advice of counsel when discrimination occurred (see Table 3.13). In fact, the modal response to discrimination, whether on the basis of age or race, was to "lump it." Detroiters were also unlikely to contact an attorney when they experienced conflicts with their landlords, but the landlord–tenant disputes were considered to be the least serious type of problem they had. Detroit-area residents were most likely to contact an attorney when it came to consumer affairs and disputes with government agencies; thus, disputes with organizations, both public and private, were most likely to go to law (about one time in eight). Neighborhood disputes were of about average seriousness and were below average in frequency of contacts with lawyers.

Neighborhood Disputes

The typical neighborhood dispute occurred between respondents and neighborhood children, often involving some form of harassment. The victims were people whose characteristics, personal or otherwise, made them

TABLE 3.13

Incidence of Legal Contacts and Degree of Seriousness by Type of Serious Dispute (in Percentages)[a]

	Total serious disputes	Type of serious dispute					Likelihood ratio χ^{2b}
		Neighborhood	Landlord–Tenant	Consumer	Public organization	Discrimination	
Most serious dispute	61.0	62.9	47.4	57.5	62.7	73.5	13.55**
	(1322)	(439)	(95)	(412)	(263)	(113)	
Legal contact	9.1	6.3	4.4	13.0	11.1	5.4	12.90*
	(1284)[c]	(427)	(91)	(401)	(253)	(112)	

[a] Figures in parentheses are sample sizes for corresponding percentages.
[b] Adjusted for weight factor.
[c] Excludes missing data.
* $p < .05$; ** $p < .01$ ($df = 4$).

vulnerable. They were elderly, or they overreacted to an initial act of mischief, leading to retaliatory acts by juveniles. In many of these cases, a relationship that centered around a cycle of harassment and complaint seemed to develop. Other neighborhood complaints concerned particular families identified as "troublemakers" because of persistent drunkenness, "obscene" language directed at children, loud quarreling between spouses late into the night, and loud parties.

A typical neighborhood dispute that was *not* resolved through legal means involved a 70-year-old black woman living in a city housing project. Mrs. A was poor, uneducated, Protestant, and an active churchgoer. She had lived in the project for more than five years and had had problems with fellow tenants from time to time over the years. Mrs. A identified herself as a strong Democrat and a supporter of President Johnson in the 1964 election. She reported:

> We have trouble with children in the halls. There are quite a few of them in this building. They are always knocking on my door annoying me. A lot of times we cannot sit downstairs in peace.

Mrs. A complained to the building manager, who said that the "families with children were to be moved" from this particular building. Aside from talking with the manager, Mrs. A took no other action and the problem persisted.

Although the reader may wonder why Mrs. A would have contacted an attorney under such circumstances, we find several similar instances in which respondents did so. Four neighborhood disputes in which lawyers were contacted showed similar patterns. While it was not clear whether or not legal remedies were available to these complainants at that time, it is evident that they believed that they should have been.[3] Two of these disputes involved complaints against children (teenagers) who fought with the respondent's own children, "hung out" and drank beer, and destroyed property. In one case, in which the complainant was white and the offending teenagers were black, the police were called and the attorney took the case to the city council. In the second case, in which both complainant and the offending children were black, the attorney advised, "You can't do anything about children." Both remaining complaints involved obscene language directed at children or other family members. One attorney recommended calling the police, which resulted in the offender "quieting down." The second recommended securing a "peace bond" and then going to court, but "that took too long," so no further action was taken. The respondent reports that "the neighbor still fights with his wife but it's not as bad."

[3]This is a study of how disputes are defined, including the conditions under which they are defined as civil legal matters. To limit the study to only those disputes for which civil legal remedies already clearly exist would beg the question, since the major determinant of the mobilization of law would be the law itself.

One neighborhood dispute that went to an attorney involved interracial conflict in a predominantly white, ethnic neighborhood. According to Mr. B, a 46-year-old, Roman Catholic, white middle-income homeowner, black teenagers used to "hang around" a house next door. Mr. B reported:

> Called police twice. I saw the officer go in and he, too, was colored. They handed him some beer and that was the end of that. These people who live here and are causing the trouble belong to the NAACP. They all do.

Mr. B further reported that an attorney was contacted, presumably by a group of Mr. B's neighbors, who "took it to council." In the end, the problem was solved since the "neighbors got together and the 'city' burned it [the 'shanty'] down." The reader is reminded that this was during a time of great racial tension in the Detroit area. Mr. B was of Slavic descent, was relatively uneducated (he had completed grade school), and lived in a predominantly white, ethnic, suburban community (bordering on the city of Detroit) that has resisted racial integration, even to this date. While it appears that an attorney was contacted in this matter, direct action by someone in the community helped solve the problem, at least from Mr. B's point of view.

Landlord–Tenant Disputes

The typical dispute between tenant and landlord concerned the failure to make repairs. Most of these complaints appear to be of a minor sort, such as leaky faucets or malfunctioning speakers (to see who is buzzing at the door). More serious disputes erupted when landlord and tenant "just didn't get along." In one case, a tenant was evicted on some pretext when she made too many requests for repairs. The tenant moved without a fight.

Routine repair problems did not involve legal assistance. Mrs. C was a young (age 28) high school graduate. She was a white, Roman Catholic housewife whose annual family income was close to the median at the time. She reported that the landlord

> Doesn't keep up repairs—very lax. [Probe] He is a nice man—too busy. [Probe] Bathroom needed repair since we've moved in, but he hasn't gotten around to it. He doesn't even keep up his own place.

Although the problem apparently lasted for some time and provided considerable inconvenience to Mrs. C, she did nothing about it. Eventually the landlord got around to making the repairs.

In only four disputes between landlords and tenants did the latter seek the advice of counsel. In view of the role subsequently played by OEO-funded legal-services programs in protecting and even creating tenants' rights, this is a remarkable statistic. Unfortunately, no case in which a lawyer was contacted was selected in the 10% sample. The closest situation involved an uncontested eviction of a 32-year-old, Irish Catholic divorcee. Mrs. D, a high school graduate with income less than $5000 per annum, and a Goldwater supporter in the 1964 presidential election, had difficulty getting along with her neighbors and her landlady. She reported:

> People snooping through garbage to see what you ate, listening at the door. [The neighbors] were too forward, asking how much you made. . . . They wanted to know all about you. . . . I lived in a home upstairs and [the landlady] lived downstairs. [Probe] She was waiting for something to happen. When the window came loose and fell out, she had me evicted. It was an emotional thing. We just didn't get along.

Mrs. D, despite all apparent hostility, did little to fight the eviction. She was upset by the eviction, which "made me look bad. I'd had liked to prove she was wrong just to balance the record," she said. Mrs. D further expressed her hostility to the small-claims court when she added:

> You're not given time to tell the story. It's a kangaroo court. You're not even heard. They don't listen to you. . . . They won't even listen to [your] story. It's over.

In the end, Mrs. D did not hire an attorney or even go to court. In her own words, she just "moved out." Mrs. D had never been to court and reports satisfactory experiences with attorneys. Her avoidance of pursuing a legal remedy in what to her was obviously an important matter was not related to her previous legal experience, but to the nature of the dispute itself. In her own words, "When you're living with people and are not wanted, there isn't much you can do. Just get out."

Consumer Compaints

Consumer complaints were frequent and varied. Being overcharged for items purchased, or for services rendered, was not uncommon. Being overcharged for auto repairs is a familiar experience. Similarly, sale prices for furniture are manipulated in ways that appear fraudulent, yet little is done to stop this practice. In one case, a store simply added $56 to the agreed upon price. The customer persisted in confronting the store several times until the "error" was corrected. On another occasion, a store owner delivered a mattress that was more expensive than the one that was originally ordered. Of course, the bill reflected the price of the higher-priced item. Despite this switch, and despite the fact that the customer was upset enough by this to consider this his most serious problem, he did nothing about it—he just paid the bill. In still another case, a man whose wife had just had a baby felt that a doctor's bill was unreasonably high. He complained to the doctor, but unfortunately, doctors do not negotiate their fees. The doctor quickly turned the $35 bill over to a collection agency, which then filed in small-claims court, increasing the patient's total cost to $53. In this instance, direct action by the consumer failed. These kinds of complaints appear to occur among the young (early 20s) and the old (60s), and among those with lower incomes.

Consumers complain when they have difficulty obtaining adequate service from plumbers, electricians, and others who do home repairs. In one case, a black woman had difficulty getting a white plumber to return to make good on a $100 furnace-fired hot water tank repair (she felt that race was a relevant issue in this matter). Consumers also complain when they have difficulty establishing credit. This is especially true of young people who have not had the opportunity to develop a good credit rating. One young couple had difficulty establishing credit when purchasing a new bedroom suite. They had to pay half in cash, then pay off the rest.

The typical consumer complaint with regard to overcharging did not end up at the doorstep of an attorney. In the case of the doctor's fee that was collected in small-claims court, the husband was a young, white, high school dropout who could afford to pay the bill (he earned between $7000 and $9999), but felt it was unfair. In the case of the $56 overcharge for furniture, Mrs. E, a 25-year-old black housewife, who took care of teenage siblings in addition to her own children, "took the law into her own hands." Mrs. E, who was a high school graduate, and whose husband, also a high school graduate, was employed at relatively low wages (between $5000 and $6999), reported:

> I went back to the store several times and they finally agreed that they had overcharged me and they took it off my bill. [Probe] After I had brought [the furniture] home, I wanted to take it all back. [Probe] I thought it was against the law [to return the furniture] after they had brought it out and put it up.

Should Mrs. E have consulted an attorney, she might have found out otherwise. Nevertheless, she took direct action and remedied the problem.

In a similar case, a customer paid cash for the complete cost of a carpet, then received further bills. A married 45-year-old, middle-income black woman reported contacting a lawyer on the matter. He advised her to "let him take charge and settle it." She did, and he did.

Typical of the sort of consumer complaint that went to an attorney was the case of Mr. F, a white, male, Protestant high school graduate, and an upper-middle-class homeowner. Mr. F was upset by false claims made by a magazine salesman. Mr. F stated:

> I wouldn't recommend that outfit. Well, I went to the Better Business Bureau, you know, turned him in and they recommended a lawyer. That lawyer cost more than the three years of the magazine. It was the principle of the thing. [Probe] I just got an attorney and paid the attorney. That [was] the end of the deal.

In two ways, Mr. F's case appears to be typical of the use of lawyers in consumer complaints. First, the issue goes beyond the amount of money involved, whether large or small. The consumer feels that he or she has been treated unjustly. Second, winning appears to be less of an issue than being treated fairly. When consumers do not seek the assistance of attorneys, they appear to be content to accept their losses if they are minor, or cut them if they are not. Experience with small-claims courts appears to be one-sided and negative, a finding that is consistent with the literature (see Students of the Columbia Law School, 1969).

Disputes with Government Agencies

Many complaints about government agencies reflected generalized dissatisfaction with either the quality of government services or the performance of government bureaucrats. Property tax assessments were too high, police investigations were incompetent, files got mixed up, and streets were kept in disrepair. Given the generalized nature of these complaints, no specific action was taken. Respondents typically felt that the law should be changed or more competent officials should be employed.

Audits by the IRS appear to be particularly disturbing, especially when a mistake is made, or the citizen's deductions are accepted as legitimate by the IRS once the audit is complete. None of the four disputes with the IRS in the subsample involved attorneys. The most serious case involved an $800 tax bill that Mr. and Mrs. G were unable to pay. The IRS threatened to auction Mr. G's business (trucks) and his house. His wife expressed the desire to pay out the debt in monthly installments. She said:

> They just kept coming out here. I didn't want my house to go. . . . I signed a paper to pay $100 a month with interest to another man until the $800 was paid.

Mr. and Mrs. G were uneducated, low-income, self-employed blacks who, despite their very serious tax problem, never contacted an attorney.

A common complaint was the attitude of public officials who administer entitlement or social welfare programs, particularly when citizens attempt to correct what they perceive to be an error. In one case, the widow of a veteran of World War II and the Korean War was denied benefits by the Veterans Administration. She went to work to support her children because of the meager benefits she felt she was receiving. Unfortunately, because she was working and receiving benefits, she was fined. In another case, a woman initially was denied disability payments by the Social Security Administration. Active pursuit of the matter ended in a satisfactory resolution of this case.

An illustration of the kind of case that goes to a lawyer involved the denial of welfare payments to a 41-year-old woman who was suddenly widowed and had no source of income. Mrs. H, whose husband earned less than $7000 the previous year, had few assets. She had rent to pay, a large family to support, and no independent source of income. Mrs. H was an uneducated (grade school only), white Protestant, of German and British origin. She received the assistance of the West Central Organization, a volunteer community service group that contacted the welfare department. Mrs. H had had little success at first, until the welfare office manager was contacted by the attorney for the organization. In Mrs. H's own words:

> They look at you like you crawled out from under a log—with this terrible tone of voice. It was soon after my husband died. . . . I was in a bad mood—I walked out—West Central Organization stepped in. My sister called them. They [intervened] for me and I had another interview with the [welfare workers]. [Probe] [I was seeing them] to get help. All pay checks were in my husband's name. . . . I needed help for three months because we had no income without these . . . [Probe] I was so upset [at my first interview] though I still wanted some money. [Probe] After I left the worker, my sister or mother, I forget, called West Central Organization. They came to help me . . . [Probe] We [Mrs. H and her attorney] went to the manager in the welfare office and they gave me a new appointment. This time, she wasn't so snotty. That time, they sent me to ADC. No problems there. They were all very nice and I got help. [The lawyer] talked to me at the welfare office, told me to go back, that they'd see me and do the right thing. He told me to answer [their] questions.

The case of Mrs. H's initial denial of ADC is one in which the benefits of both organization and legal assistance are apparent. Mrs. H ended up getting what she needed to survive until she was ready to "stand up on her own two feet."

Discrimination

Typical complaints of discrimination were in jobs and housing on the basis of age and race. Four such cases were selected in the subsample; two involved age discrimination in employment, one involved age discrimination in housing, and the remaining one involved racial discrimination in employment. Only one discrimination case out of the four went to an attorney.

Both cases of age discrimination when seeking employment involved older men who were denied opportunities because of their age. In one case, a 36-year-old white male had been refused a job (after being told he was hired) when company officials realized he was over the official age limit of 34. His response was, "It was the company's policy and I couldn't do anything about it."

In the second case, a 56-year-old white male with some college education found it "hard to compete with younger men." Mr. J stated:

> Discrimination isn't open today. They just let you know [subtly]. I was looking for a certain thing and had trouble. [Probe] Government is trying to deal with the problem. All governments are trying. [Probe] [I'd] like to see all men have some advantages.

Mr. J did contact an attorney in order to seek redress for his mistreatment. In response to the question, "What did [the lawyer] tell you to do, or what did he do?" Mr. J responded briefly, "[The lawyer] just talked." At the time of the interview, Mr. J was unemployed and had been for some time.

The case of housing discrimination involved the young, lower-middle-income family of a white factory worker. They had difficulty finding an apartment to rent because, as the young housewife put it, "When you say you are young with children [two boys], they don't want you." The respondent was 22-years old and was a high school dropout. She had never voted, expressed no political interest, had no religious affiliation, and belonged to no organizations. Her structural alienation was reflected in her passive response, "You have to take what you can get."

The last illustration involves Mr. K, who experienced blatant racial discrimination in employment, but did nothing about it. Mr. K was a 51-year-old unemployed black man, with an annual family income of less than $3000. Mr. K, a Roman Catholic, had completed high school and lived with his wife in an apartment in a two- or three-family house. He defined himself as retired; that is, he was no longer seeking employment. Describing his experience, Mr. K said,

> I tried to get a job. They run an ad in the paper. When I go to apply, they say that the job has been taken. And then a white woman comes right up. They let her in the back room. I asked her later if she got the job. She says she did. My asking her, [and her answer], showed that I was discriminated against. [Probe] I thought that in the constitution you aren't suppose to be discriminated against. You should not discriminate against anybody for race, religion, color, or creed or something like that. [Probe] I believe there should be some kind of way [to fight discrimination]. They shouldn't take my word for it. They should have agents who go out and try to get jobs. Then they will find out more things actually exist. [Probe] I had amind that I wanted to do everything. I couldn't take people to court. Maybe the woman who got the job really needed it. I just got disgusted and came on out of there. [Probe] You've got to have witnesses, so I couldn't take them to court. I couldn't get any witnesses.

4

SITUATIONAL FACTORS IN THE MOBILIZATION OF LAW

This chapter simultaneously pursues several objectives. Its primary purpose is to specify the conditions of legal mobilization that reflect the situational context in which disputes occur. The second objective is to develop a model that takes into account the objective and subjective aspects of the civil dispute process. This development is accomplished by incorporating situational and structural variables in a sequential model that includes both prelegal and legal stages of the process. And, finally, the model describing the process through which everyday disputes are transformed into legally relevant issues is placed within a broader theoretical context. The findings presented in this chapter have important implications for a theory of social control that recognizes the importance of the availability of legal power in the resolution of everyday disputes.

Contacting an attorney is the most frequent form of legal mobilization for everyday disputes between citizens and their landlords, government agencies, business firms, and employers, in short, any everyday dispute except for those between neighbors. Only for disputes between neighbors are the police more likely to be contacted than attorneys. Of the 1284 most serious disputes reported, 323 (25%) involved contact with a lawyer, the police, or some other governmental or quasi-official agency. Of these, 117 (36%) involved contact with an attorney and 128 (40%) involved the police. Lawyers are contacted most frequently in disputes involving citizens in their roles as consumers. In fact, almost half (44%) of all contacts with attorneys concerned such disputes. Police are called most often for assistance in disputes between neighbors (also see Black, 1980:119), with 103 (80%) of the police contacts being the result of neighborhood conflicts.[1] Excluding police calls for neighborhood disputes, contacts with attorneys constitute over half (53%)

[1]The police are also frequently called to handle family disputes (see Black, 1980:121), but these were not included in our survey. Rarely are the police asked to settle disputes that do not involve family members or neighbors.

and police calls only 11% of the remaining contacts with officials of one sort or another. In sum, contact with attorneys is the broadest, most representative mode of legal assistance for everyday disputes other than those between neighbors. Fully one-fourth of the serious disputes go to law in some form or other, and, excluding disputes between neighbors, the majority of these go to lawyers.

THE SITUATIONAL CONTEXT OF LEGAL MOBILIZATION

There is a great body of theoretical and empirical literature on the extralegal factors affecting legal process. Some of this work focuses on the effects of individual differences among enforcement personnel. Much of the remainder centers on the effects of social structure, measured in terms of the race, ethnicity, income, education, and other similar attributes of victims, offenders, or plaintiffs. The published data from existing surveys of lawyer mobilization have been limited to reports of the structural correlates of contacts with lawyers (see Mayhew and Reiss, 1969; Curran, 1977).

Unfortunately, there is less theory and empirical research on situational factors in the mobilization of law. Most of the theory that has a bearing on the present work is interactionist, has been applied to the explanation of deviant behavior, and is qualitative rather than quantitative in its methodological approach. Consequently, the present work is innovative on three counts: It generates theory, explains that which has been previously unexplained, and does so within a complex, quantitative, multivariate framework.

Situational factors are treated as exogenous variables in a recursive model of legal process. Two variables are treated as endogenous; that is, they are explained as part of the mobilization process. These are (1) the decision to seek legal assistance and (2) the seriousness of the dispute. Donald Black (1979:18) notes that the use of seriousness of the offense to account for the mobilization of police is rooted in common sense, a mode of explanation that fails to distinguish between facts and values. Similarly, the evaluation of everyday problems as serious must be considered part of the process by which citizens decide to mobilize lawyers, distinct from the quantitative explanation of that process in terms of facts external to it. Properly conceived, seriousness cannot be analytically separated from the mobilization process itself. By definition, the decision to mobilize agents of social control implies that the event at hand is serious and reflects the valuation of participant or observer, who then explains the decision in these terms. This is what makes such an explanation common sense.

There has been little research on legal process that is explicitly sequential and quantitative (see Bernstein *et al.*, 1977; Nagel, 1980). Typically, the endogenous variables are explained independently by regressing the exogenous variables on each of the endogenous variables, in turn. For example, the factors associated with arrest are usually treated as independent of those associated with conviction, and vice versa. On the face of it, it makes little sense to explain the likelihood of conviction in terms of the likelihood of arrest in other than commonsense terms. People who are arrested are more likely to be convicted than those who are not. Arrest is a necessary condition for conviction, just as seriousness is a necessary condition for the decision to seek legal assistance. And arrest and conviction, like seriousness of the dispute and contacting an attorney, can be included in a sequential model of legal process that treats the explanation of each endogenous variable as dependent on the explanations of those that precede it.

In this chapter, I develop a strategy for analyzing the endogenous variables within a single explanatory model that takes into account the conditional nature of the relationships among them. Relying on Goodman's (1972a, 1972b, 1973a, 1973b) approach to log-linear analysis, I develop a causal model that incorporates all stages of the mobilization process within a single quantitative framework.

The Data

The analysis presented below is based on 2463 everyday disputes reported by the respondents in the Detroit survey (see Mayhew and Reiss, 1969; Mayhew, 1975). Respondents were asked whether they had experienced any of 23 types of problems, grouped into five general categories: disputes with neighbors, landlords, or governmental agencies, problems in the consumer area, and discrimination in a variety of settings. Some specific types of problems were noisy neighbors, failure by a landlord to make repairs, purchasing something that did not work, a dispute with the IRS, and housing discrimination. Case histories were then obtained for the two most serious disputes, although selecting for seriousness was limited by the constraint that no two problems be chosen from the same general category.

The basic unit of analysis is the dispute. Since randomly selected respondents listed all the problems they had experienced while living in the Detroit area, the disputes they reported approximate a random sample of all similar disputes occurring in the Detroit metropolitan area.

The respondents considered 1284 disputes to be their most serious; of these, 139 were excluded from the final analysis because the information available was insufficient to code their situational characteristics. In some situations, case histories were incomplete or not taken at all, making the determination of the seriousness of the dispute problematic. The remainder of the excluded cases consisted of the residual "other" responses in each category (see Appendix B).

Since case histories were available for only the most serious disputes, the situational variables could be coded only on the basis of the most general characteristics described in the incident schedules (see Appendix B). The codes were then validated by a closer examination of those situations for which case histories were available.

The Variables

All five exogenous variables in the model evaluated in this section are situational. I have chosen to limit the present analysis to the situational variables in order to determine whether or not their effects on the mobilization process are entirely prelegal. What I am trying to show is that, by taking into account prelegal stages of the process such as the definition of everyday disputes as serious, we can explain the apparent zero-order relationships between the situational variables and the decision to seek legal assistance.[2] In other words, I hope to determine the extent to which the relative seriousness of disputes explains the effects of situational factors on the use of lawyers.

There are three broad categories of situational variables. First, disputes can be measured in terms of their basic characteristics, such as their relative *persistence*. The greater social costs associated with more persistent problems leads us to expect dispute avoidance to occur more frequently when disputes are less persistent (see Felstiner, 1974). According to Hunting and Neuwirth (1962:10), the economic costs resulting from a personal injury affects the likelihood that someone will make a claim and, if necessary, obtain a lawyer. Similarly, persistence increases the costs, personal or financial, associated with the continuation of disputes. Consequently, we can expect the likelihood of seeking legal assistance to increase with persistence.

The second broad category of situational variables reflects the social situation in which the dispute is embedded. Three situational variables were selected to indicate different aspects of the situation. First, the relative *visibility* of the dispute was measured. Just as the police are more likely to make an arrest if a crime occurs in the public domain (Chambliss and Seidman, 1971:332–336; Chambliss, 1976:157), potential cases may not come to the attention of lawyers unless they are in some sense publicly visible. The public nature of the problem itself may constrain the individual to do something about it. Second, the *relational distance* between disputants is expected

[2]Zero-order relationships are unexplained simple correlations between two variables.

to increase the likelihood of legal mobilization. Donald Black (1970:740–742) originally developed this concept to explain the production of crime rates. Black found that acts were less likely to be defined as criminal if the parties involved were closely related (e.g., relatives, friends, or neighbors). Assaults, thefts, and other wrongful acts were more likely to be defined as criminal when committed by strangers. Third, the *availability of alternative arrangements* for dispute settlement is expected to reduce the likelihood of legal mobilization (see Sarat, 1976). The existence of nonlegal dispute settlers such as ministers, union representatives, and friends tends to diminish the perceived need for an attorney. However, unions, churches, and other voluntary associations provide institutional supports that create access to attorneys. Should available alternatives fail to help solve a given problem, the dispute is likely to be channeled further into the legal arena (see Galanter, 1974).

The final category of situational variables reflects the cultural context in which the dispute occurs. Consequently, different types of communities can be expected to process disputes differently, depending on the level of cultural integration (see Black, 1976:61–83). In this chapter, I use the distinction between urban (within the city limits of Detroit) and suburban *location* to indicate cultural context in the broadest sense.

The effects of the situational variables on the likelihood of seeking legal assistance for everyday disputes are reported in Table 4.1. Disputes in suburban areas, disputes between distant parties, and disputes that occur where alternatives are available are more likely to lead to legal involvement than disputes in the city, between close parties, and where alternatives are not available. Unexpectedly, the kinds of disputes that are less visible and less persistent are more likely to lead to legal contact than those that are visible or persistent. Since seriousness is a necessary condition for seeking legal assistance, the relationship between these two variables is mathematically indeterminate.

Seriousness as a Necessary Condition for Seeking Legal Assistance

That seriousness is a necessary condition for seeking legal assistance is a theoretical assumption derived from our everyday, commonsense understanding of what it means to consider a problem serious enough to warrant contacting an attorney. None of the disputes at hand routinely involve legal help. While it is often the case that relatively serious matters do not go to law, it is assumed that, for the type of matters involved here, going to see an attorney is a sign of the relatively serious nature of the problem. In fact, the original survey instrument was designed to take this relationship into ac-

TABLE 4.1
Odds Pertaining to the Use of Lawyers for Everyday Disputes

Variable	Odds	(N)	β effects[a]
Location			
Suburbs	0.0493	(1234)	+.25*
City	0.0302	(1229)	−.25
Relational distance			
Distant	0.0574	(1309)	+.52***
Close	0.0203	(1154)	−.52
Persistence			
Persistent	0.0317	(1303)	−.22°
Not persistent	0.0488	(1160)	+.22
Visibility			
Visible	0.0276	(1600)	−.41***
Not visible	0.0628	(863)	+.41
Availability			
Help available	0.0657	(308)	+.30*
Not available	0.0361	(2155)	−.30
Seriousness			
Serious	0.0894	(1145)	—
Not serious	0.0000	(1318)	—
Overall odds	0.0397	(2463)	

[a] Structural zero in [not-serious × lawyer] cell makes β indeterminate. Given the one-way distribution of each variable, the two-way association is completely determined; i.e., seriousness is a necessary condition of seeking legal assistance.
° $p < .10$; * $p < .05$; *** $p < .001$ (adjusted for weight factor).

count, since it was assumed that respondents would contact an attorney only for those matters they defined as relatively serious.

Since seriousness is treated as a necessary condition for contacting an attorney, there are no cases in which a problem is not defined as serious and a lawyer is contacted. In the two-way table described below, one cell contains a "structural zero," a zero that is not due to sampling but to the way in which the variables are defined.

	Lawyer	No lawyer	Totals
Serious	94	1051	1145
Not serious	0	1318	1318
	94	2369	2463

In this case, the effect of seriousness on seeking legal assistance is considered to be positive. (See Appendix A for a discussion of the statistical aspects of this relationship.)

The advantages of this approach to the study of legal process are threefold. First, we are able to specify the explanation of each stage of the process independently of each other stage. The explanation of each stage of the process controls for the explanation of each prior stage. Consequently, we can be certain that the explanation of the decision to seek legal assistance is not confounded by the explanation of earlier stages of the process specified in the model. In this case, the explanation of legal contacts is independent of the subjective evaluation of the seriousness of disputes and the explanation of that evaluation.

The second advantage of this approach is that we are able to specify the linkage between stages of legal process in a single model. This enables us to see how the explanations of prior stages of the process affect the explanations of subsequent stages.

And, finally, specifying structural zeros in the relationships among the endogenous variables provides a new strategy for the analysis of social process, one that distinguishes between the conditional relationships among the endogenous variables of a social process and the putative effects of the exogenous variables on that process.

The Explanation of Legal Contacts

In the best-fitting log-linear regression (logit) model of the situational factors affecting the decision to contact a lawyer, the main effect of the availability of alternatives on the use of lawyers is positive, and the main effect of visibility remains negative (see Table 4.2). The main effect of relational distance is positive, but it disappears when holding constant the seriousness of the dispute. Neither location nor persistence has a direct effect on the use of lawyers for everyday disputes.

The availability of alternative dispute-resolution mechanisms reflects two conflicting processes. Indirectly, the existence of alternatives reduces the likelihood of contacts with attorneys by decreasing the perceived seriousness of the dispute. But alternatives also increase the use of lawyers directly by channeling disputes into the legal arena (see Figure 4.1).

I considered those respondents who indicated that they had gone at least once to a voluntary association for help on a legal matter to have an alternative dispute-resolution mechanism available to them. There are, therefore, two components to the alternatives variable, one morphological and the other situational. The former, indicated by organizational membership, is a *structural* property of the dispute-settlement process and has a direct positive effect on the use of lawyers (see Chapter 5 for further analysis and discus-

TABLE 4.2

The Effects of the Situational Variables on the Use of Lawyers in the Best-Fitting Log-Linear Path Models, With and Without Controlling for Seriousness

Best-fitting log-linear path models	Best-fitting logit models	*df*	Likelihood ratio χ^{2a}	*P*	Dependent variable	Parameters in the model[b]	β effect, no control[c]	β effect, control[c]
	H_1	4	2.27	> .60	—	C,A,D[d]	—	—
	H_2	6	4.19	> .60	Persistence	DP	−1.83***	−1.83***
	H_3	4	6.24	> .20	Visibility	CV	−.18*	−.18*
						PV	+.81***	+.81***
						DPV	−.48***	−.48***
						CAPV	−.23**	−.23**
						ADPV	+.28*	+.28*
	H_4	27	27.47	> .40	Seriousness	AS	—	−.26**
						DS	—	+.39***
						DVS	—	−.22*
	H_5	28	35.50	> .10	Lawyer	AL	+.30*	—
						DL	+.43**	—
						VL	−.29*	—
	H_6	32	34.12	> .30	Lawyer	AL	—	+.68***
						VL	—	−.32***
						SL	—	+[e]
Without controlling for seriousness	$[H_1 \cap H_2 \cap H_3 \cap H_5]$	42	48.20	> .20				
Controlling for seriousness	$[H_1 \cap H_2 \cap H_3 \cap H_4 \cap H_6]$	73	74.29	> .40				

[a] Adjusted for weight factor.
[b] C = location; A = availability of alternatives; D = relational distance; P = persistence; V = visibility; S = seriousness; L = saw a lawyer.
[c] Excludes nonsignificant and single variable parameters in order to simplify presentation. These are not excluded in the actual model.
[d] In the best-fitting model, these variables were independent of one another. Consequently, there were no multiway β effects to report.
[e] Structural zeros present in the fitted marginal (SL) makes β indeterminate. That seriousness is a necessary condition of lawyer use means this effect is "positive" and S is logically prior to L. Excluding the SL parameter from the model does not alter the degrees of freedom of χ^2 value in model H_6; i.e., given the distribution of S and the distribution of L, the SL distribution is determined ($df = 0$), S explains none of the variance in L, and the model excluding the SL effect is equivalent to the model including the effect.
* $p < .05$; ** $p < .01$; *** $p < .001$ (adjusted for weight factor).

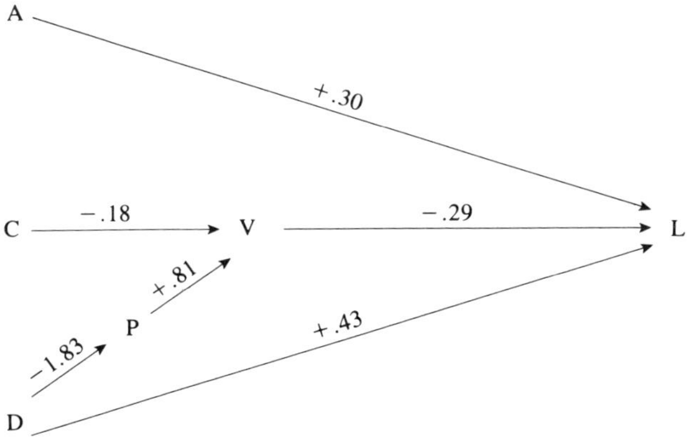

FIGURE 4.1a Path diagram for the best-fitting log-linear path model describing the effects of the situational variables on the use of lawyers (see Table 4.2).

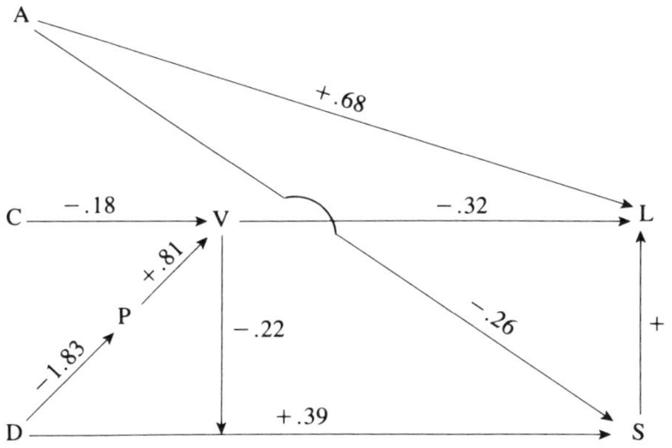

FIGURE 4.1b Path diagram for the best-fitting log-linear path model describing the effects of the situational variables on the use of lawyers, controlling for seriousness (see Table 4.2).

sion). The latter, indicated by the perceived availability of such dispute settlers as ministers, union leaders, or brothers in a fraternal order reflects the *situational* nature of the process. The availability of alternatives reduces the likelihood of legal contacts because disputes are less likely to be situationally defined as serious enough to warrant legal assistance. On the other hand, disputes are more likely to go to law when alternatives are available because greater participation in the organizational life of the community increases access to the legal profession.

The explanation of the unexpected negative effects of persistence and visibility on legal contacts reported in Table 4.1 lies in a multivariate analysis that takes into account the negative interaction between visibility and the ownership of property and its effect on third-party involvement and the use of lawyers for serious everyday disputes. (The statistical model describing this interaction effect is elaborated in the next section.) These disputes become visible to third parties, in part, because of their persistence. Since third parties are likely to refer, to attorneys, disputes that they are unable to settle, the indirect effects of persistence and visibility on legal contacts are, as expected, positive. Since third parties refer the most difficult matters to attorneys, persistent and visible disputes are likely to be handled by an attorney. Moreover, this is the case regardless of the socioeconomic status of the disputant. On the other hand, when disputes are not visible, when they do not occur in the public domain, situational factors play less of a role and structural factors more of a role in determining whether or not third parties (including lawyers) become involved in the dispute process. Since property owners live in situations in which disputes are unlikely to be visible, *less* visible disputes are *more* likely to go to law than one would otherwise expect. As it happens, the negative interaction between visibility and property ownership completely explains the apparent negative effects of persistence and visibility on legal contacts.

Although disputes concerning property matters are less visible than those between neighbors or between landlords and tenants, the negative correlation between visibility and legal contacts cannot be explained by differences in the way in which lawyers handle property and nonproperty matters. None of the disputes in the sample involved property matters. Similarly, legal matters involving property transactions may be less persistent than interpersonal disputes that arise between neighbors, but, once again, none of these disputes are property related.

As a status category, property ownership affects the way in which ordinary, nonproperty disputes are processed. In addition to consulting attorneys about property transactions, property owners are more likely than others to consult attorneys about nonproperty matters as well. For example, homeowners are more likely than renters to ask an attorney for assistance when facing problems with neighborhood children, discovering an overcharge by a storekeeper, or when being denied benefits by a government agency. Renters are especially unlikely to consult an attorney unless constrained to do so, as in situations in which their disputes have become visible to third parties. For example, persistent vandalism by neighborhood children or teenagers, run-down living conditions caused by an unresponsive landlord, or irregular garbage collection by the city may come to the attention of others who may suggest that the complainant contact an attorney.[3] Upper-middle-income renters are more likely to seek legal assistance than lower-income renters. But, for the most part, renters are passive responders to disputes unless pushed to do otherwise.

The most straightforward finding in the analysis of the situational factors affecting the dispute process is the relational-distance effect. Holding constant the perceived seriousness of the dispute, the effect of relational distance on legal contacts disappears. The evaluation of disputes as more or less serious occurs within a situational context in which the relationship between disputants plays a major role. Disputes between strangers are more likely to be defined as serious than otherwise similar disputes between friends or neighbors. Serious disputes are those that, by definition, are more likely to go to law. Thus, disputes between strangers are more likely to go to law than those between intimates because they are more likely to be perceived as serious enough to warrant legal counsel. It is not the nature of the dispute, but the relationship between disputants that determines the seriousness of the dispute. And it is the seriousness of the dispute that leads the disputant to contact an attorney.

Persistence plays an important, but indirect, role in the dispute-resolution process (see the path diagrams in Figure 4.1). Disputes between closely related parties are likely to persist since strangers are able to ignore or avoid unpleasant confrontations. (For a similar argument, see Baumgartner, 1980, for a description of dispute avoidance among affluent suburbanites who are essentially "strangers next door.") Persistent disputes tend to become visible and then involve third parties in the dispute process.

Location, suburban or urban, also plays an indirect role in the dispute process. The positive correlation between location and the use of lawyers (see Table 4.1) is completely explained by the complex interactions between location and the other situational variables. Suburban and urban life differ in a variety of ways. Urban residents experience everyday problems as persistent and serious matters. Suburbanites, especially those who own their own homes, experience less visible disputes, and the lack of visibility, as we have seen before, is consistent with more frequent legal contacts. In general, suburban and urban life are qualitatively different experiences that yield different ways of defining and evaluating otherwise similar events.

[3]This discussion does not imply anything about what attorneys do once contacted. In many of these cases, they advise their clients that there is little that can be done. Nevertheless, this "cooling out" function of the attorney is an important one. The discovery that one has no legal rights in a given matter frequently leads to the avoidance of legal action in subsequent situations.

A comparison of the two path models, with and without controlling for seriousness (see Table 4.2), reveals a considerable improvement in the fit when the evaluation of the seriousness of the dispute is taken into account (also see Figure 4.1). This improvement demonstrates the importance of the evaluative process in the explanation of legality. Note that we are discussing the role of situational variables on the definitional process that is part of the legal process, but nevertheless precedes the actual decision to contact an attorney.

THE ROLE OF THIRD PARTIES

Third-party involvement in the settling of disputes can be treated as exogenous or endogenous in the civil dispute process. Third-party involvement is an exogenous variable to the extent that it represents access to intermediaries, thereby affecting the probabilities associated with one or more stages of the civil legal process.

As an exogenous variable, third-party involvement is similar to the alternatives variable, but it is meant to convey something quite different. Turning to third parties for assistance in handling a dispute is different from taking direct action (self-help) or doing nothing at all (lumping it), and from going to see a lawyer. Of course, one may turn to a lawyer for help as a friend or a neighbor, but this is analytically distinct from the decision to invoke the law by asking for legal advice or demanding some sort of action on the part of an attorney.

In the present analysis, third-party involvement is treated as an endogenous variable, an intermediate stage in the civil legal process lying somewhere between the evaluation of disputes as serious and the decision to contact an attorney. Third parties play an analogous role to lawyers qua lawyers, but are distinguished by the nonlegal character of mediation. Third-party involvement is a prelegal stage of the mobilization process, one that is logically and empirically prior to the mobilization of law itself. Third parties may or may not successfully help resolve disputes. Upon failing to solve the problem at hand, they may or may not channel the dispute further into the legal arena. Alternatively, they may suggest further mediation or "cool out" the disputant in a manner similar to that of an attorney.

Since information on third-party involvement was obtained only through case histories obtained for the most serious disputes, the analysis was necessarily limited to these cases. To further simplify matters, only the single most serious dispute reported by each respondent was included in the analysis, for a total of 712 cases. This excludes 326 respondents who reported experiencing no problems in the five general categories described above. It also excludes the "second most serious problem" reported by many, but not all, who reported at least one problem.

In the incident schedules designed to obtain case histories for their two most serious disputes (see Appendix B), the respondents were asked to describe in an open-ended fashion what they did to have their problem "settled." Responses were coded according to whether they (1) took direct action by turning to someone in an offending organization (e.g., the car dealer, the welfare department, etc.), or negotiated directly with the offending party (e.g., parents of noisy kids, the salesman, etc.), (2) avoided any action altogether, or (3) turned to third parties for help (e.g., public officials, ministers, voluntary associations, etc.). Those who turned to third parties (including legal officials) for help were distinguished from the remainder in order to identify that point in the mobilization process when disputes are removed from a purely personal or interpersonal context to one in which society begins to develop an interest in what happens.

Third-party involvement and going to see a lawyer are analytically, but not empirically, distinct stages of the mobilization process. The third-party variable is contaminated to the extent that it includes some contacts with attorneys who were turned to for help as friends or neighbors. This contamination factor tends to artifactually increase the correlation between third-party involvement and legal contacts.

One of the advantages of logit analysis is that we can simultaneously control for the interactions among the independent variables and their effects on the dependent variables. Consequently, the contamination of the third-party variable by legal contacts is taken into account in a path model that includes the effect of the former on the latter. In such a model, in which third-party involvement is antecedent to contacting a lawyer, the explanation of the latter is independent of the explanation of the former.

The Explanation of Third-Party Involvement

Those who have sought third-party help are five times more likely to contact an attorney for their most serious problems than those who have not done so (see Table 4.3). In fact, the odds are nearly one-in-three that someone who has sought third-party assistance for a given dispute will eventually contact an attorney.

To explain the role of third parties in the mobilization of lawyers, I incorporated both situational and structural variables and prelegal and legal stages of the mobilization process in the same multivariate, log-linear path model. Log-linear path analysis is ideally suited to this problem, but it does have some limits. In particular, there are practical constraints on the number of variables that can be specified in a given log-linear model—seven at most

TABLE 4.3
Odds Pertaining to the Use of Lawyers for Most Serious Everyday Disputes

Variable	Odds	(*N*)	β effects
Home ownership			
Owns	.110	(506)	+.33°
Rents	.056	(206)	−.33
Visibility of the problem			
Visible	.070	(446)	−.34*
Not visible	.137	(266)	+.34
Persistence of the problem			
Persistent	.090	(365)	−.05
Not persistent	.098	(347)	+.05
Third-party help			
Third-party help	.290	(129)	+.80***
No third-party help	.058	(583)	−.80
Overall odds	.094	(712)	

° $p < .10$; * $p < .05$; *** $p < .001$ (adjusted for weight factor).

(see Dixon, 1977:297–336). As the number of cases becomes smaller, cell frequencies may approach zero, making the analysis more difficult to carry out and interpret. In order to minimize the number of problems associated with small cell frequencies, I have chosen to limit the analysis to one representative structural variable (home ownership), two situational variables (persistence and visibility), one prelegal stage (third-party involvement), and one legal stage (contacting a lawyer) of the mobilization process, for a total of five variables (see Tables 4.3 and 4.4 and Figure 4.2).

On theoretical, legal, and empirical grounds, home ownership should be associated with going to law. Although home ownership represents a minimal degree of participation in the economic institution of private property, it is an indicator of at least some participation in "the organized system for the transmission of property" (Mayhew and Reiss, 1969:314). According to Mayhew and Reiss (1969:312), the purchase of legal services is often a necessary part of the transmission of property and its acquisition, maintenance, and increase. Although the private ownership of property itself is a legal concept, property is often transferred, acquired, maintained, and increased without legal assistance. Contrary to popular belief, especially the beliefs of attorneys, the evidence suggests that homes are frequently purchased in the Detroit area without the assistance of counsel, despite advice to the contrary.[4] Citizens are less constrained to go to lawyers in property matters than

[4]In Michigan, real estate is often transferred by means of a "land contract" (see Braun and Page, 1979:96–97), which is not recorded and does not require the formal participation of an

TABLE 4.4
The Effects of Situational and Structural Variables on Third-Party Involvement and the Use of Lawyers in the Best-Fitting Log-Linear Path Model[a]

Best-fitting logit models	*df*	Likelihood ratio χ^{2b}	*P*	Dependent variable in logit model	Parameters included in logit model[c]	β effects
H_1	2	4.88	> .05	Visibility	PV	+.94***
H_2	3	4.82	> .10	Third Party	OT	+.67***
					PT	+.42**
					VT	+.31°
					OVT	−.48**
H_3[d]	12	14.12	> .20	Lawyer	OL	+.46*
					VL	+.05
					TL	+.79***
					OVL	−.60***

[a] In the saturated model for the two-way contingency table [OP], $\beta = -.20$, $p < .05$ ($\chi^2 = 0$, *df* = 0). The likelihood ratio chi-square for the best-fitting path model $[H_1 \cap H_2 \cap H_3] = 23.82$, *df* = 17, $p > .10$.
[b] Adjusted for weight factor.
[c] P = persistence; V = visibility; O = home ownership; T = third-party involvement; L = saw a lawyer.
[d] H_3 approximates the logit model. Since fitting marginal (OPVT) yields a zero cell frequency due to sampling, the log parameter for this term is set at zero.
° $p < .10$; * $p < .05$; ** $p < .01$; *** $p < .001$ (adjusted for weight factor).

lawyers would prefer to believe. Although none of the disputes in this study involved property matters, property ownership generates access to attorneys not otherwise available to those who do not own property. Those who own their homes are more likely than those who do not to contact an attorney, even in matters unrelated to property.

In the multivariate, log-linear regression model, only the main effects of home ownership and third-party involvement on legal contacts remain statistically significant ($\beta = +.46$, $p < .05$ and $\beta = +.79$, $p < .001$, respectively; see Table 4.4). The negative correlation between visibility and legal contacts disappears when the negative interaction between ownership and visibility is taken into account. (The interaction effect of ownership and visibility on legal contacts is quite strong; $\beta = -.60$, $p < .001$.)[5] An examin-

attorney. Little or no down payment is required, interest-only payments can be made, often for as long as 40 years. Full payment is expected at the end of the contract before the deed is actually transferred. This form of home "ownership" is used by those "who would have difficulty qualifying for a bank loan" (ordinary mortgage); e.g., the young, those with low incomes, and members of minority groups.

[5]A test of the nonhierarchical model that excludes the VL effect yields $\chi^2 = 14.14$ ($df = 13$, $p > .30$). The difference between the hierarchical model and the nonhierarchical model, exclud-

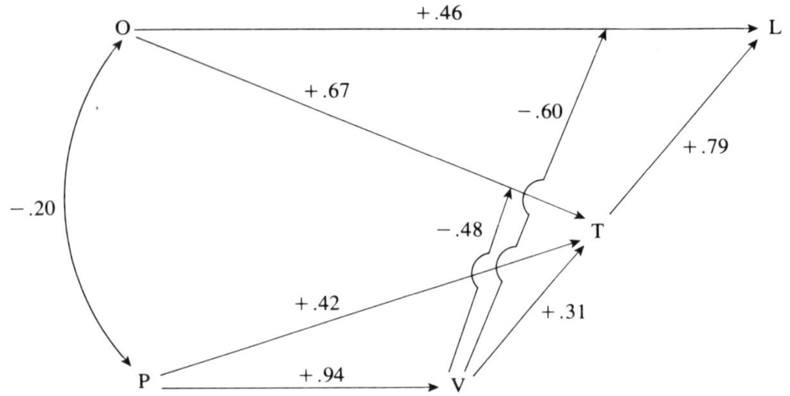

FIGURE 4.2 Path diagram for the best-fitting log-linear model describing the effects of situational and structural variables on third-party involvement and the use of lawyers (see Table 4.4).

ation of the conditional odds associated with third-party involvement (Table 4.5) and the use of lawyers (Table 4.6) helps to explain why. The apparent negative effect of visibility on the use of lawyers is an artifact of the negative interaction of visibility with the effects of ownership on both third-party involvement and the use of lawyers. The effect of ownership on the mobilization process depends on the lack of visibility of everyday problems. When problems are *not* visible to others, namely third parties and lawyers, property owners are significantly more likely than renters to involve third parties and lawyers in their disputes.

The indirect effect of visibility on the mobilization process is positive. Visible disputes are more likely to involve third-party mediation and, when all else fails, lawyers. When disputes become visible to others, they take on a public character that brings third parties into the process. The constraint provided by going public is independent and, indeed, overrides the effect of ownership on the mobilization of both third parties and lawyers. Visible disputes, by bringing third parties into the process, are paradoxically less likely in the end to go to law than those that are less visible. As a result, property owners with less visible disputes are quite likely to turn to third parties (odds = .250) and, if they do, are especially likely to contact an attorney (odds = .538; see Table 4.6), whereas renters who experience

ing the VL term, is 0.02 ($df = 1$, $p > .80$). Consequently, both models fit the data equally well (see Bock and Yates, 1973, for the method for estimating nonhierarchical models). This supports the assumption that the apparent negative effect of visibility on the use of lawyers is spurious.

TABLE 4.5
Conditional Odds Pertaining to Third-Party Involvement for Most Serious Everyday Disputes

Persistence	Visibility	Home ownership	Odds	(*N*)
Persistent	Visible	Owns	.373	(206)
		Rents	.234	(95)
	Not visible	Owns	.345	(39)
		Rents	.000	(25)
Not persistent	Visible	Owns	.099	(100)
		Rents	.098	(45)
	Not visible	Owns	.229	(161)
		Rents	.051	(41)
Overall odds			.221	(712)

similar disputes hardly ever turn to third parties (odds = .031) and are even less likely to turn to lawyers for help (odds = .015).

Situational variables directly affect third-party involvement, but not the likelihood of using lawyers (see Figure 4.2). This is consistent with the assumption that the situational context of the mobilization process is primarily prelegal in nature. Persistent disputes are likely to come to the attention of third parties either because they are more likely to become visible or because their persistence over time makes it inevitable that they become known to others.

Ownership affects third-party involvement and the use of lawyers in quite a similar manner, including the negative interaction between ownership and visibility (see Figure 4.2). The redundant structure of the interaction be-

TABLE 4.6
Conditional Odds Pertaining to Use of Lawyers for Most Serious Everyday Disputes

Visibility	Third-party involvement	Home ownership	Odds	(*N*)
Visible	Third party	Owns	.226	(65)
		Rents	.158	(22)
	No third party	Owns	.030	(241)
		Rents	.063	(118)
Not visible	Third party	Owns	.538	(40)
		Rents	.000	(2)
	No third party	Owns	.119	(160)
		Rents	.016	(64)
Overall odds			.094	(712)

tween ownership and visibility on the mobilization process at two distinct stages suggests that a fundamental process has been identified, one that is embedded in the structural fabric of society.

When third parties become involved in dispute settlement, they often invoke legal norms. In doing so, third parties in effect anticipate outcomes of the judicial process should disputants seek legal remedies. This raises the question as to whether the similarities in the underlying explanations of third-party involvement and the use of lawyers are due to the public nature of disputes, as argued above, or to the implicit legal content in many third-party attempts to settle disputes. Ministers who counsel couples with marital problems often invoke religious and therapeutic norms. But they also invoke legal norms to facilitate reconciliation by reminding couples, for example, that there may be a custody battle over the children. To this extent, ministers anticipate what lawyers will do should they, as clergy, fail to reconcile the disputing couple. It appears that the quasi-legal nature of third-party intervention has important implications for a theory of the social control of everyday disputes.

A CAUSAL MODEL OF THE MOBILIZATION PROCESS

By creating a general causal model based on the path analyses presented above (see Figure 4.3), we can identify an emerging pattern among the effects of the situational and structural variables associated with the mobilization process. Two or three exogenous variables are uniquely associated with each stage of the process and, thus, appear to be characteristic of that stage.

The transformation of everyday problems into serious disputes is a function of the availability of alternative dispute-resolution mechanisms and the relational distance between disputants. When help has been available in the resolution of past disputes through various community organizations, citizens are less likely to define their problems as serious. Additionally, disputes between strangers are more likely to be defined as serious than disputes between closely related parties. Furthermore, the effect of relational distance is amplified through a feedback process that reflects the negative interaction of visibility on the distance effect. Since disputes between distant parties are less likely to become visible and the effect of relational distance is stronger when disputes are less visible, the absence of visibility plays an important role in intensifying the positive effect of relational distance on seriousness.

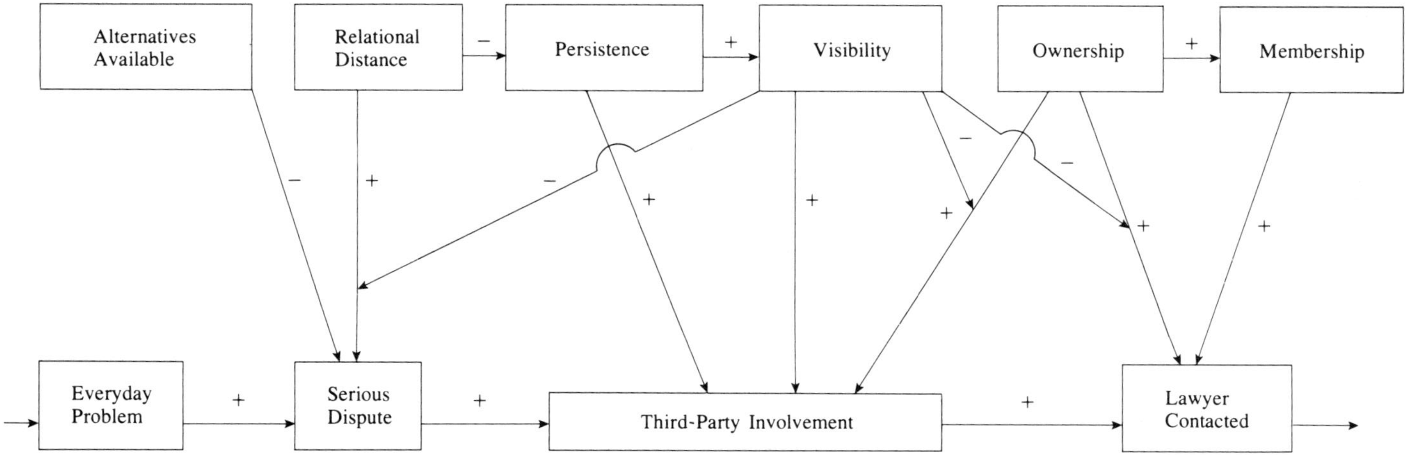

FIGURE 4.3 A causal model of the mobilization process.

The transformation of serious disputes into matters involving third-party intermediaries is affected by the relative persistence and visibility of the dispute and by the ownership of property. As elements of the situational context of disputes, persistence and visibility play a role in bringing disputes out of their personal and interpersonal contexts into the public arena by bringing third parties into the process. Since third parties represent interests other than those of the disputants, the process of social control reflects norms that derive from sources external to the situation at hand; that is, from the wider societal context or from the law itself. The effect of property ownership on third-party involvement reflects the degree to which social stratification affects the way in which interests beyond those of the disputants are introduced into the social control process. The situational visibility of disputes helps to reduce the impact of social structure on social control by reducing the effect of ownership on third-party involvement.

With the mobilization of lawyers, we see the final stage in the transformation of disputes into legal matters. At this point, no situational variables play a direct role. Only the structural variables, ownership and membership (a component of the alternatives measure), directly affect the mobilization of lawyers. Visibility again plays a role in reducing the impact of ownership on the use of lawyers just as it does on third-party involvement. It has no impact on the effect of organizational membership on the use of lawyers. The positive effect of ownership on membership described in Figure 4.3 is derived from findings reported in the next chapter.

One final note on the structure of the relationships among the exogenous variables in Figure 4.3 and the implications of their structure for our understanding of the mobilization process. There is a sharp break in the pattern of causation between the prelegal and legal stages of the process. Strong interrelationships occur among the situational variables and among the structural variables, but not between the two groups. By virtue of the constraints provided by the visibility of disputes in social situations, this situational variable plays an important role in linking the prelegal and legal stages of the mobilization process through its interaction effects. Because of the effects of visibility and property ownership, third-party involvement appears to be a transition stage between the prelegal transformation process and the ultimate decision to contact an attorney. Contacting an attorney invites the application of legal criteria to the definitional process, imposing state-generated norms on the resolution of disputes. Even when an attorney's advice is to do nothing, he or she is thereby employing legally relevant criteria and invoking legal norms in defining the nonlegal character of the dispute. To the extent that third parties invoke legal norms, they facilitate the next stage in the transformation process, the mobilization of lawyers and the recognition of the legal nature of the dispute.

These findings support the notion that the explanation of dispute processing is qualitatively different from the explanation of the social organization of law. The association of situational variables with the former and structural variables with the latter suggests that interactionist theories are more suited to the explanation of the transformation of disputes, whereas structural theories concerned with the distribution of wealth and power in society are more suited to the explanation of the mobilization of law per se.

THE SOCIAL CONTROL OF EVERYDAY DISPUTES

Legal control depends on the ability of "an individual or group possessing the socially recognized privilege" to threaten or actually use coercion (force) in the regulation of normative conduct (Hoebel, 1954:28). Social control is distinguished from legal control by the absence of coercion in the regulation of conduct. Instead of legal norms, social control depends on "implicit community values, compromise, and individualized discretion" occasionally embodied in alternative dispute-resolution mechanisms (Yale Law Journal, 1979:908). These mechanisms involve third parties who may or may not take into account legal norms when attempting to settle disputes (Yale Law Journal, 1979:909).

According to Weber (1954), the involvement of third parties who invoke legal norms is not sufficient to consider regulatory actions legal. Law occurs not only when coercion is implicitly threatened by third parties who invoke legal norms, but when a specialized staff exists for the purpose of coercing conformity (Weber, 1954:5). Lawyers are institutionalized enforcers in the broadest sense—defining, interpreting, and ultimately going to court in some form or other to gain or prevent compliance with legal rules on behalf of their clients, be they individuals, organizations, or the state. Consequently, third-party mediation is a form of social control that shares many of the characteristics of legal control, except a crucial one: the legitimate use of coercion. Akers sharpens the distinction between third-party mediation as a form of social control and legal control with this definition:

> A social norm is law if its breach is met by physical force or the threat of physical force in a socially approved and regular way by a socially authorized third person. (1975, p. 39)

Third-party intervention is further distinguished from other forms of social control by the direct involvement of persons whose interest lies not with one of the parties to the dispute, but with the public's interest in social order, public safety, and the prevention of crime (Nader, 1979:1000–1002).

Contradictory assertions regarding the role of third parties in the social control of everyday disputes reflect either mainstream or critical perspectives on the law and the legal system. The mainstream view is that third parties act as intermediaries who channel potential clients to lawyers (Hunting and Neuwirth, 1962:65–70; Lochner, 1975; Ladinsky, 1976). The higher the status of the intermediary, the more likely it is that potential clients will be referred to attorneys (Lochner, 1975:465). Hunting and Neuwirth (1962:65) refer to these persons as "authority figures," the sort of people others turn to because of their relevant expertise, such as an insurance salesperson in a personal injury matter. Ladinsky (1976:219) reminds us that these intermediaries have high status largely because the disputants who are in contact with them are themselves of high status.

Defining legality in terms of the benefits conferred upon individuals who use the services of attorneys to meet their legal needs, Galanter (1976:225–227) argues that more efficient alternatives can be devised to meet these needs. These alternatives are to be drawn from those high-status intermediaries described above who, if given the authority, may be better at "securing routine gains and protections in recurrent situations" (Galanter, 1976:240).

A special issue on dispute resolution in the Yale Law Journal (1979:906) was devoted to "a critical perspective . . . [on] the goals underlying these alternatives." In this issue, Laura Nader (1979:998–1021) questions the assertion that third parties play a beneficial role in the dispute-settlement process. Third parties often do not resolve disputes, Nader points out, nor do they channel unresolved disputes into the legal arena. Rather, they frequently "cool out" the claimant. This is accomplished by making the complaint process so difficult that people often "lump it" rather than pursue complaints further. Nader adds (1979:1008) that intermediaries "do not compensate for the inequalities that impair the operation of the market system." In fact, they "reinforce those inequalities and respond to interests other than those of individual complainants."

Perhaps it is not surprising that those who see the law and its alternatives as beneficial are sociologists and lawyers who tend to study the structural aspects of legal process and ignore its situational aspect, and that it is an anthropologist who, examining the situational context in which disputes occur, finds that alternatives to legal institutions "dissuade individuals from pursuing relief" (Nader, 1979:1006), reinforcing the "cooling out" role of attorneys. The findings reported here suggest that both arguments are correct, but that each reflects analytically and empirically distinct differences in the roles third parties play as intermediaries in the mobilization process.

Although it is the case that most individuals who turn to third parties for help do not go on to seek the help of an attorney, they are much more likely to do so than if they had not sought third-party help in the first place. Consequently, the evidence supports the notion that intermediaries constitute a facilitating network that increases access to the legal profession. At the same time, we have seen that the situational *availability* of alternative opportunities to resolve disputes, measured in terms of past experience using such alternatives *decreases* the probability of going to see a lawyer because of the reevaluation of disputes as less serious, that is, not warranting legal help. This supports Nader's notion that disputants become discouraged by their experience with alternatives, justifying their avoidance behavior by redefining their situations as less problematic than those of others who have not had such an experience.

5

STRUCTURAL FACTORS IN THE MOBILIZATION OF LAW

This chapter focuses on the structural aspects of the mobilization process and, in so doing, assesses several explicit and implicit propositions found in Donald Black's *The Behavior of Law* (1976). In particular, it evaluates the effects of social structure on the decision to seek legal assistance for serious everyday disputes. As we shall see, three dimensions of social structure explain variation in legal behavior better than others: (1) stratification, the unequal distribution of resources, (2) morphology, the unequal distribution of social involvement, and (3) social control, the unequal distribution of social influence (see Black, 1976, for a complete explication of the role these variables play in the behavior of law). Culture, the symbolic aspect of social life, does not have a direct effect on legal action; the effects of variables reflecting the differential distribution of culture are mediated by the effects of stratification.

THE BEHAVIOR OF LAW

Law, or "governmental social control" (Black, 1972:1096), is the behavior of those who occupy positions of legitimate political authority. One approach to the measurement of law, then, is to determine the rate at which legal behavior occurs (see Black, 1980:213). In this study, we are interested in the rate at which citizens contact attorneys for any reason, whether merely to seek advice or to pursue a particular course of legal action.

Some General Principles

Three principles governing legal relations appear consistently in Black's *The Behavior of Law* (1976): (1) the linear principle, (2) the directional principle, and (3) the distance (curvilinear) principle.[1] The first takes the form

[1]By principle, I mean something more general than the term "proposition" used by Black. These principles refer to the form of the relationships entailed in Black's propositions, which vary in content.

"law varies directly with [*x*]," where *x* is some organizing principle such as stratification, social integration, culture, or organization. The second principle takes the form "law is greater in a direction toward less [*x*] than toward more [*x*]"; law is directed toward lower socioeconomic status, marginal status, unconventionality, and less organization. And, finally, the third principle is that "the relationship between law and [*x*] is curvilinear," where *x* is limited to cultural distance and the morphological dimensions of differentiation and relational distance.

Black does not indicate that the dimensions of stratification or organization have curvilinear relationships with law; very few observers have (see, however, Baumgartner, 1980). If we recognize that we are dealing with a general principle governing the relationships between *distance* and law, we can account for a variety of curvilinear effects on dispute resolution. As Black (1976:41) points out, "Law is inactive among intimates, increasing as the distance between people increases but decreasing as this reaches the point at which people live in entirely separate worlds." Similarly, "Law is less likely at the extremes, where there is little or no cultural diversity, and also where it is great" (Black, 1976:74). If we define economic distance in terms of the relative economic positions of disputants, those in the same strata are *close;* they share similar interests and, among those who are relatively privileged, have a stake in maintaining their position. Economic distance, then, increases with differences between the strata of disputants. As economic distance increases, interests come into conflict. The curvilinear principle predicts that when economic distance is very great or very small, law is least likely to occur. Disputes among the most affluent and among the poor are least likely to go to law. In disputes between the poorest and the wealthiest in society, the poor are powerless to act, and the wealthy have no need to do so. Similarly, disputes between individuals and disputes between organizations are less likely to become legal matters than disputes between individuals and organizations. Organizational distance is defined in terms of the relative size, complexity, and power of the disputants.

Economic distance can be measured in terms of economic inequality. Given the range of circumstances experienced in everyday life studied here, the curvilinear principle predicts that disputes involving affluent complainants are least likely to go to law. Most of the complaints by the affluent are against relatively powerful individuals or organizations, both private and public. As complainants in everyday matters increase in economic status, the economic distance between them and the source of their difficulty diminishes. Disputes among the affluent, then, are least likely to involve legal contacts.

The curvilinear principle predicts that disputes between equally wealthy or equally powerful parties produce less law than disputes between those who are unequal in wealth or power. It is possible to observe disputes among the culturally privileged (Black, 1976:73–79), those who are highly interdependent (Black, 1976:39), and those who are either closely related or total strangers (Black, 1976:40–48), but the anthropologist and sociologist alike find it difficult to observe systematically disputes among the rich and powerful or the highly organized (e.g., major corporations). Macaulay's (1963) study of disputes among businessmen is one of the few efforts in this area; it is clear from his research that, among businessmen, legal remedies are rarely employed in the resolution of disputes. Galanter (1974:110) reports that there is little litigation in disputes between highly organized disputants, especially when these disputes involve business firms. Baumgartner (1980) finds that upper-status suburbanites are less likely to invoke legal remedies for interpersonal disputes than their lower-status counterparts.

If we consider that status similars share common interests and orientations to the world, it is reasonable to expect greater compromise and informal dispute resolution among them. Galanter (1974:113) points out that disputes between "repeat players" and disputes between "one-shotters" (those who rarely initiate or otherwise become involved in litigation) are less likely to be litigated than disputes between repeat players and one-shotters. Disputants may seek alternative dispute-settling mechanisms (e.g., mediation), engage in self-help, or choose to do nothing at all (Galanter, 1974:124–135). Economic inequality implies fundamental conflicts between the interests of different strata. Similarly, organizations and individuals, when engaged in disputes, have conflicting interests in the kinds of legal remedies they seek. The rules of the game favor the more organized interests (Galanter, 1974:123). The wealthy and the well organized are better able to mobilize the coercive power of the state (law) to secure their interests. For those in less favorable positions, the use of coercive power is likely to be defined as illegitimate and to be subject itself to legal regulation (Black, 1983:42).[2]

Two distinctive aspects of social rank must be identified in order to understand how stratification can have both linear and curvilinear effects on the quantity of law. First of all, it is the increased amount of wealth, just as it is the increased amount of social integration and organization, that effects an increase in the quantity of law. But, the relative position of disputants also affects the quantity of law, and it does so independently of the amount of wealth, social integration, or organization. Status similars are less likely to go

[2]Donald Black argues that crime is often a form of social control that involves, as the saying goes, "taking the law into your own hands." "Crime," writes Black (1983:42), "often expresses a grievance. This implies that many crimes belong to the same family as gossip, ridicule, vengeance, punishment, and law itself." Those who resort to crime as social control are more likely to be from lower socioeconomic strata. Thus, the poor are more likely to resort to crime, whereas the affluent are more likely to resort to law as a method of social control.

to law than those who are relatively distant from one another. As a result, society's privileged are less likely to seek legal remedies than one would expect, given the linear effect of stratification alone.

Hunting and Neuwirth (1962:98–99) have found that, in general, there is a positive correlation between socioeconomic status and the employment of an attorney for personal injury matters. However, when one controls for the failure to take any action, a characteristic of the lowest status groups, the relationship is reversed; among those who do something, status is inversely related to going to law. In other words, legal remedies in pursuit of personal injury claims are most likely sought by middle-ranked individuals. Members of the highest status groups are most likely to take direct action in such matters; those of the lowest groups are most likely to take no action at all.

Evidence of Curvilinearity

Most encounters with attorneys during one's lifetime are for more or less routine legal matters involving the transfer of property and business activity. However many legal contacts involve nonproperty matters such as domestic, neighborhood, government, and landlord–tenant disputes, disputes about insurance claims arising from automobile accidents and other personal injuries, and disputes concerning the purchase of goods and services. The overall effect of social class on lifetime legal contacts is curvilinear. Controlling for the type of legal matter, however, we find that the effect of social class on the use of lawyers is linear and positive for legal matters concerning property relations and curvilinear for disputes involving nonproperty matters (see Table 5.1). It seems that the curvilinear effect of social class on the use of lawyers for non–property-related disputes is strong enough to mask its linear effect for property matters (also see Table 3.1).

THE STRUCTURAL CONTEXT OF LEGAL MOBILIZATION

In this section, I focus on legal contacts for a variety of matters, including routine property transactions, in order to discover the structural context of the legal mobilization process. Since legal relations are basically economic in nature, most legal contacts are constrained by the structure of property relations in our society. It is my contention that the structural context generated by property relations determines how and when citizens choose to seek legal assistance in ordinary, everyday disputes. Such disputes do not typically concern property rights, nor are legal remedies readily available to solve them. Once I have established the contours of the structural context for the mobilization of law in general, I examine how that context shapes the transformation of everyday disputes into legal claims.

TABLE 5.1

The Use of Lawyers for Property and Nonproperty Matters by Income[a]

Social Class[b]	Property only β	Nonproperty only β	All matters β	All matters Odds	Number of persons reporting problems
Upper	+.70	−.43	−.13	2.40	34
Upper-middle	+.30	+.33	+.90***	6.69	100
Lower-middle	−.19	+.27	+.03	2.82	516
Lower	−.81	−.16	−.80***	1.23	335
				2.20	985

[a] The β's for property and nonproperty matters are derived from the saturated model, the only model that fits the data. The likelihood ratio χ^2 for the three-way interaction between types of legal matters and income = 12.10 (adjusted), $df = 3$, $p < .01$. The likelihood ratio $\chi^2 = 38.67$ (adjusted), $df = 3$, $p < .001$, for the two-way interaction between total contacts with attorneys and income in the saturated model.

[b] See Chapter 3, n. 2, for the operational definition of income groups.

*** $p < .001$ (adjusted for weight factor).

The Role of Class and Race

Race is not a significant factor in determining whether someone is more or less likely to seek legal assistance. Although whites in the Detroit metropolitan area are more likely than blacks to contact a lawyer (see Table 5.2), once wealth and ownership are taken into account, the association between race and law disappears. In other words, the correlation between race and law reflects the effects of past discrimination on current class position. Blacks are not denied equal access to legal assistance by virtue of current discriminatory practices, but because throughout history they have been denied equal access to the benefits of American society. Controlling for income and home ownership,[3] the amount of variation in the odds pertaining to legal assistance explained by race drops to nearly zero (see Table 5.3). To the extent that race indicates something more than class position, say cultural differences, it has no effect whatsoever on the use of attorneys.

Social class consists of two distinct elements: (1) wealth (here indicated by income), which facilitates the purchase of legal services, and (2) the ownership of property (indicated by home ownership), an economic relation that is

[3]In this analysis and during the remainder of this chapter, income is dichotomized at $7000 annual family income. This is necessary in that there are so few upper-middle- ($15,000 or over) and upper-income ($25,000 or over) blacks in the sample. This renders meaningless an analysis based on these finer distinctions. Dichotomizing variables is generally more convenient in the multivariate analysis of categorical data. Furthermore, for both property and nonproperty matters, this point on the income dimension appears to be most significant in differentiating rates of lawyer usage by social class.

TABLE 5.2
The Use of Lawyers in One's Lifetime

Variable	Ever see a lawyer			β effects
	%	(*N*)	Odds	
Home ownership				
Owns	75.5	(723)	3.08	+.52***
Rents	52.0	(273)	1.08	−.52
Income[a]				
≥$7000	76.0	(659)	3.17	+.47***
<$7000	55.5	(337)	1.25	−.47
Race				
White	71.1	(828)	2.46	+.27**
Black	58.9	(168)	1.43	−.27
Employment status				
Self	77.9	(95)	3.52	+.26°
Other	67.8	(830)	2.11	−.26
Education				
Some college	77.6	(210)	3.47	+.28**
High school or less	66.3	(715)	1.97	−.28
Memberships				
Three or more	83.2	(250)	4.95	+.52***
Two or less	63.6	(675)	1.74	−.52
	69.1	(996)[b]	2.23	

[a] Total family income in 1966.
[b] Overall odds = 2.21, N = 925, excluding missing data cases from the multiway analysis incorporating the latter three variables.
° $p < .10$; ** $p < .01$; *** $p < .001$ (adjusted for weight factor).

defined and maintained through legal action. That wealth affects property ownership is taken into account in the causal analysis of the effects of race and income on the odds pertaining to seeking legal assistance (see Figure 5.1). This analysis follows from the findings presented in Table 5.1. An increase in wealth implies a greater capacity to own property, which increases the likelihood of seeing a lawyer for property matters. By controlling for ownership and income in the causal analysis, it becomes possible to identify the direct and indirect effects of wealth on the purchase of legal services.

Given the period of this study just prior to the institutionalization of government-sponsored legal services for the poor, one might argue that the structure of the relationships described should have since been altered. However, comparison of the effects of ownership and race on the use of legal

TABLE 5.3
Analysis of the Variation in the Odds Pertaining to the Use of Lawyers (L) for Home Ownership, Family Income, and Race

Variation due to	Likelihood ratio χ^{2a}	*df*	p^b
Ownership (O)	23.45	1	< .001
Income (I)	18.75	1	< .001
Race (R)	0.70	1	NS

[a] Adjusted for weight factor.
[b] Significant effects reflect the differences between the best-fitting log-linear regression model [(RIO)(OL)(IL)], $\chi^2 = 2.98$ (adjusted), $df = 5$, $p > .70$, and the model excluding the specified effect. Non-significant effects reflect the differences between the best-fitting log-linear regression model and the model including the specified effect. There are no significant interaction effects.

services in the Detroit area in 1967, and in a national sample survey completed seven years later in 1974,[4] reveals no change in the basic *structure* of legal relations (see Table 5.4 and compare with Table 5.2).[5] In other words, both the direction and magnitude of the effects of race and home ownership on the use of lawyers are virtually identical in both surveys. The role of property relations in the law has not changed. Nor has the relative legal position of blacks vis-à-vis whites improved despite the advent of increased access to the law for the poor. Changes that have occurred in the opportunity for legal assistance among the poor have not affected the relative legal posi-

[4]The data used in this analysis are based on responses recorded on questionnaires from the national survey undertaken by the ABA's Special Committee to Survey the Legal Needs of the Public in collaboration with the American Bar Foundation (see Curran and Spalding, 1974; Curran, 1977). However, the coding of responses for purposes of this book are based on a coding system developed by the author and not the coding system used by the American Bar Foundation in its reports.

[5]Theodorson and Theodorson (1969:395) define social structure as, "The pattern of interrelated statuses and roles found in a society or other groups at a particular time and constituting a relatively stable set of social relations." In the present context, we are interested in the set of social relations that incorporates legal rules as a basic element in its overall structure. The equations that make up the log-linear path models in Figures 5.1 and 5.2 describe a relatively stable social structure in which the relationship between economic and ethnic statuses and legal roles are a central element constituting a relatively stable set of legal relations.

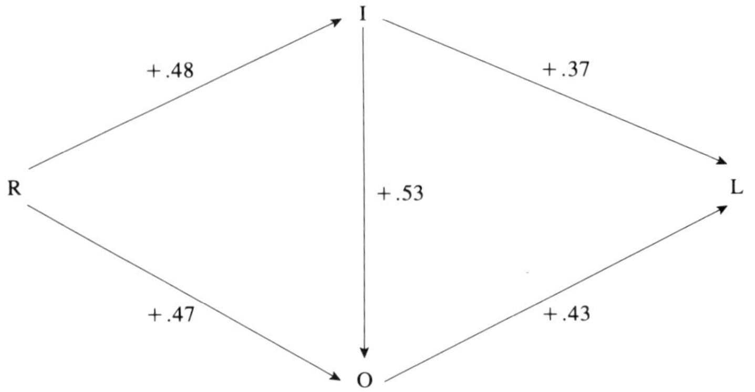

FIGURE 5.1 Path diagram for the causal model describing the effects of home ownership (O), income (I), and race (R) on the odds pertaining to the use of lawyers (L)—Detroit sample.

tion of blacks nor the role of property in governing legal relations. But these changes have virtually eliminated the discrepancy between the frequencies with which the poor and the lower-middle class contact attorneys. This has the net effect of weakening the correlation between income and law. Nevertheless, the upper-middle class was still at an advantage over lower income groups in 1974 (67.5% versus 52.7% had contacted lawyers, $N = 1838$, $\beta = +.31$, $p < .001$; compare Table 5.2). The economic impact on the structure of legal relations remained unchanged betwben 1967 and 1974, except for the relative position of the poor.

Controlling for race, home ownership, and income in both the Detroit and national samples, we find additional evidence that the basic structure of legal

TABLE 5.4
The Use of Lawyers in One's Lifetime by Home Ownership and Race in the National Sample

	Ever see a lawyer			
	%	(*N*)	Odds	β effects
Home ownership				
Owns	66.9	(1369)	2.02	+.58***
Rents	38.6	(616)	0.63	−.58
Race				
White	59.4	(1804)	1.46	+.26**
Black	46.4	(181)	0.87	−.26
	58.1	(1985)	1.39	

** $p < .01$; *** $p < .001$ (adjusted for weight factor).

TABLE 5.5
Conditional Odds Pertaining to the Use of Lawyers by Home Ownership and Race in the Detroit and National Samples

		Detroit		National	
Race	Ownership	Odds	(*N*)	Odds	(*N*)
White	Owns	3.18	(636)	2.06	(1283)
	Rents	1.21	(192)	0.66	(521)
Black	Owns	2.48	(87)	1.69	(86)
	Rents	0.84	(81)	0.46	(95)

relations is essentially equivalent and unchanged by the advent of free legal services for the poor. Limiting the comparison to variables measured in the same way in both studies—race and home ownership—reveals that the relative advantage of being white and a homeowner is the same in both Detroit and the nation as a whole (see Table 5.5). It is important to note that the overall probability of contacting an attorney is higher in Detroit than on the average nationally. This can be explained, in part, by the relatively high rate of home ownership in the Detroit area, which indirectly contributes to the use of lawyers by increasing access to the legal profession. Controlling for income in addition to race and home ownership, we find that the direction and magnitude of the path coefficients in the national sample are roughly equivalent to those in the Detroit sample (compare Figures 5.2 and 5.1).[6] This implies that the findings based on the DAS sample alone can be generalized with some confidence to the nation as a whole. Hence, the analysis of the civil dispute process and the mobilization of law presented in this book describes a process that is not unique to a particular time or place. Indeed, in the final analysis, I believe that I have identified some fundamental dynamics of the dispute process in contemporary society.

Government-sponsored legal services have had little impact on the effect of structural inequality on the civil legal process. The provision of free legal services to the poor has not eliminated the indirect effect of income on racial

[6]The impact of inflation over seven years and the different geographical bases of the samples make it difficult to measure income in precisely the same manner in both studies. The median family income rose nationally from $7436 in 1966 (U.S. Bureau of the Census, 1976:2) to $12,051 in 1973 (U.S. Bureau of the Census, 1975:1). In the Detroit study, income was dichotomized at the $7000 annual (1966) family-income-category level, the closest point to the national median. In the national sample, both the $10,000 and $15,000 levels (1973) were used in the log-linear path analysis with no appreciable difference in the coefficients measuring the effects of race and ownership on the use of legal services. The higher level was chosen for the presentation of the path analysis in order to retain the effect of income in the model.

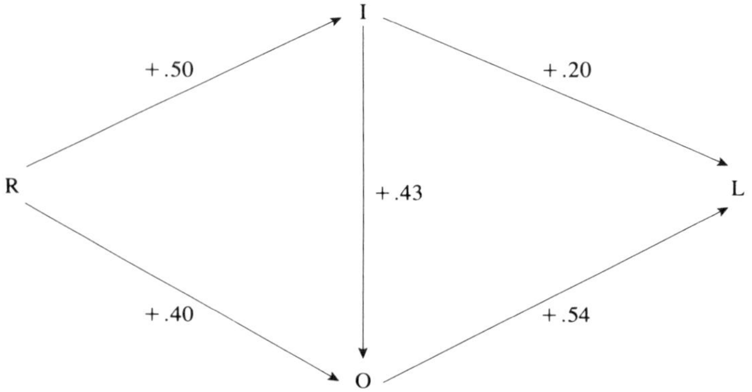

FIGURE 5.2 Path diagram for the causal model describing the effects of home ownership (O), income (I), and race (R) on the odds pertaining to the use of lawyers (L)—national sample.

differences in access to law. The wealthier (but not the wealthiest), who are more likely to be white, are still more likely to secure legal advice and representation than the less wealthy. Since property ownership creates a demand for legal services, and since the use of legal services in general increases with the frequency of legal contacts for property matters, the "haves" are still better off than the "have-nots."

The Effects of Education and Employment Status Explained

In their analysis of the Detroit data, Mayhew and Reiss (1969:310) describe the relationships between employment status, education, and lifetime legal experience. Self-employed individuals are more likely to have contacted an attorney than those who are employed by others; those with some college education are more likely to contact an attorney than those with a high school education or less. However, when we control for the effects of income and home ownership on legal contacts, the effects of employment status and education disappear. In the complete log-linear path model that takes into account the effects of race, participation in voluntary associations, income, and home ownership (see Figure 5.3),[7] we find that the apparent effect of education on legal contacts is mediated by all the variables except

[7]The path model consists of the intersection of the five best-fitting logit models [(RE)(ES) ∩ (SRE)(RI)(EI) ∩ (ISRE)(IO)(SO)(RO) ∩ (IOSE)(IORE)(ISRE)(IOSR)(OM)(EM) ∩ (IOSE)(IORE)(ISRE)(IOSR)(IOEM)(IORM)(OREM)(OSM)(SEM)(ISM)(OL)(IL)(ML)], $\chi^2 = 109.42$ (adjusted for weight factor), $df = 126$, $p > .80$, adjusted for zero cells by fitting the appropriate marginals. The effect (RE) is derived from the saturated model [RE] where $df = 0$ and $\chi^2 = 0$. There are no significant interaction effects.

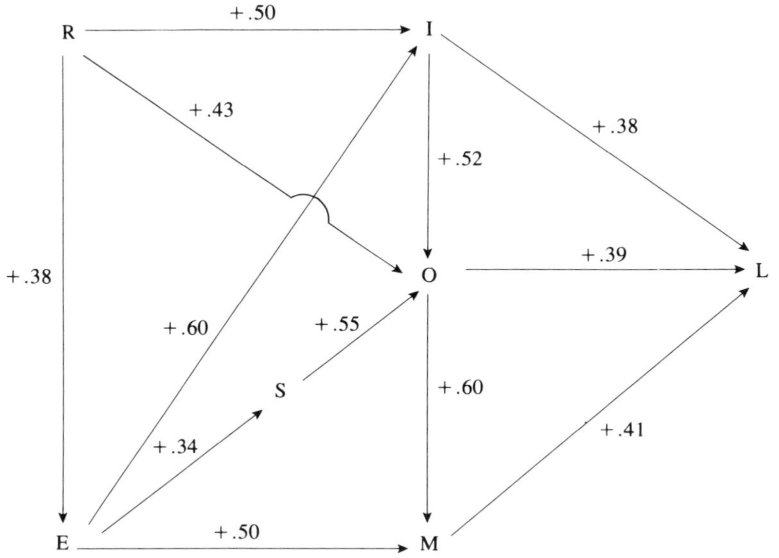

FIGURE 5.3 Path diagram for the causal model describing the effects of race (R), education (E), employment status (S), income (I), home ownership (O), and membership in voluntary associations (M) on the odds pertaining to the use of lawyers (L) in one's lifetime.

race. In other words, the college-educated are likely to use legal services because they have relatively high incomes, are self-employed, and therefore are likely to own property and participate in voluntary associations. It is not that college education increases knowledge about legal rights (an aspect of legal culture) that makes the difference, but that college education puts an individual in a more structurally advantageous position regarding wealth and property (stratification) and networks of social interaction (morphology). Were it the case that knowledge about legal rights had an effect on the use of lawyers, we would expect a direct effect of education on legal contacts, assuming, of course, that the educated know more about their legal rights than the uneducated. Since there is no such direct effect, it is clear from the evidence presented in Figure 5.3 that education (as an indicator of cultural life) does not produce a greater quantity of law than its absence (cf. Black, 1976:65).

Employment status is a weak link in the causal chain. The self-employed are more likely to own their homes than those who are employed by others (or were employed by others in their last job). It appears that the private ownership of property in general links the individual to the legal system, not merely the ownership of productive property such as a business. In fact, home ownership is the only variable that mediates the effect of business ownership on the use of lawyers. This finding demonstrates the appropriateness of using home ownership as an indicator of participation in the institution of private property. It measures the broadest level of such participation, and is thus the best indicator of the effects of ownership on the use of lawyers.

Morphological and Organizational Aspects of Membership

Morphology, the unequal distribution of social involvement, varies along several different dimensions, including differentiation, intimacy, and integration (Black, 1976:37). The last of these is indicated by the degree of participation in the life of the community. Marginality implies little participation; integration implies some degree of participation. In contemporary industrial society, or at least the American version, voluntary associations are an integral part of community life. Those who are members of such associations are more socially integrated, that is, they have higher social status, than those who do not participate. For the purposes of this study, those who belong to at least three community organizations or associations are considered *integrated,* those who belong to two or fewer are *marginal.* These associations include churches, unions, veterans' groups, fraternal orders, business associations, and nationality, professional, political, neighborhood, and civil rights groups.

The socially integrated are more likely to use legal services than the more marginal members of society (see Black, 1976:48). Those who belong to at least three community organizations contact attorneys more often than those with fewer memberships (see Table 5.2). In the multivariate path analysis (Figure 5.3), the effect of participation in voluntary associations on the use of lawyers is clearly independent of the effects of social-class indicators on lawyer use. This suggests that morphology is as important a dimension as stratification in explaining the civil legal process.

It could be argued that membership in organizations is an indication of the organizational aspect of social life rather than its morphological aspect (Black, 1976:91). Organization is the "capacity for collective action" (Black, 1976:85). Participation in organizational life increases the probability that one's actions will represent such participation, and, consequently, members of organizations, acting as representatives of those organizations, are more likely to use legal services than nonmembers (see Black, 1976:91). Undoubtedly, some legal contacts reflect specific collective issues. However, Mayhew (1975:413) has shown that it is rare for American citizens to act altruistically when dealing with grievances. Even for relatively serious matters, few seek remedies that reflect the interests of the members of some specific group or the public at large. Only in cases of discrimination did a meaningful proportion of the Detroit area sample (31%) seek action to right the wrongs experienced by their membership group. It is clear that the organizational (collective) aspect of life plays a very small part in disputes, legal or otherwise, experienced by most American citizens.

Religion and Politics: Unexpected Results

Neither religion nor political identification affect the use of legal services directly or indirectly. Protestants and Catholics are virtually identical in their rates of legal involvement; Jews in the sample are more likely to go to lawyers, but their numbers in the sample are too small to draw adequate generalizations. Since Jews appear to have more wealth and property on the average, that is, to be upper-middle class, and to be more socially integrated than the average, Jewish litigiousness appears to be an artifact of stratification and morphology effects.

Republicans are not more likely than Democrats to use legal services. However, those who are more politically *alienated* use legal services more than those who identify with either one of the two major parties. Only 67.4% of those who identify strongly with a major (or minor) political party have actually used legal services as compared with 79.7% of those who are independent or identify weakly with either of the two major parties ($\beta = -.32$, $p < .05$). In the log-linear regression model controlling for the effects of the structural variables on the civil legal process, political alienation remains a predictor of legal action.

THE MOBILIZATION OF LAWYERS FOR SERIOUS DISPUTES

In the preceding section, we examined the structural aspects of legal relations. We saw how legal contacts are shaped primarily by the stratification and morphology of social life. The preservation, transmission, and control of privately owned property frequently necessitates legal counsel. In general, social class and social integration create access to legal resources. Those who have more wealth or own property and those who participate in the organizational life of the community have greater access to attorneys than those who have less wealth, do not own property, or are socially marginal. Cultural variables do not play a direct role in the mobilization of lawyers. The better educated are likely to contact a lawyer because they are likely to be self-employed, own their own homes, and be active in the community. Blacks are less likely than whites to contact an attorney because they are less likely to own their own homes, and they have lower incomes. Once income and home ownership have been taken into account, there are no differences between blacks and whites in their litigiousness.

In this section, I demonstrate how the structure of legal relations, rooted as it is in economic life, plays an important role in shaping the dispute process. Since cultural factors do not play a role in the mobilization of law in general, they do not play a role here. Nor, as it turns out, does participation in the organizational life of the community affect the way in which disputes are settled. Only social class, indicated by wealth and the ownership of property, forms the structural context that shapes the transformation of serious everyday disputes into legal claims. Lawyers are most frequently asked to handle more or less routine property-related transactions. Once attorneys have been contacted in routine property matters, access to legal resources thus established facilitates the mobilization of lawyers for ordinary disputes that do not involve property.

The Importance of Social Class

Only home ownership and income affect the use of lawyers for serious everyday disputes (see Table 5.6).[8] Neither race, education, nor membership in voluntary associations affects the use of lawyers for such disputes. It is evident from this analysis that social-class variables play a central role in shaping the dispute process.

In developing a path model to describe the process by which structural variables affect the decision to seek legal assistance for serious everyday disputes, only race and education were retained as antecedent because they were part of the causal sequence established previously. Employment status was not included because of its limited role in the general model. Participation in voluntary associations was excluded because it has neither direct nor indirect effects in this context; it is neither correlated with the dependent variable nor is it antecedent in the causal model. Membership in voluntary

[8]Limiting the analysis to *serious* matters is less problematic in the study of civil disputes than criminal victimizations (see the Gottfredson–Hindelang and Black debate on the latter; *American Sociological Review*, 1979). The evaluation of disputes as serious is merely an indication of a threshold of public recognition or definition of the nontrivial nature of the dispute. It represents an evaluation that *something* ought to be done, but rarely does this involve legal action (about 1 in 11 disputants ends up seeing an attorney). In fact, as I have demonstrated in the previous chapter, with the proper statistical techniques, it is possible to treat the definition of an event as serious independent of the decision to go to law. In this section, I am interested in determining the extent to which structural variables affect the transformation of disputes from those that are defined as serious in general, warranting some sort of *social* control, into legally serious matters, warranting some sort of *legal* control.

TABLE 5.6
The Use of Lawyers for Serious Disputes

Variable	Saw a lawyer %	(N)	Odds	β effects
Home ownership				
Owns	9.78	(849)	.1084	+.32*
Rents	5.38	(353)	.0569	−.32
Income[a]				
≥$7000	9.92	(837)	.1101	+.35*
<$7000	5.21	(365)	.0549	−.35
Race				
White	8.55	(1006)	.0935	+.03
Black	8.16	(196)	.0889	−.03
Education				
Some college	11.03	(263)	.1239	+.19
High school or less	7.77	(939)	.0843	−.19
Memberships				
Three or more	8.56	(327)	.0936	+.01
Two or less	8.46	(875)	.0924	−.01
	8.49	(1202)	.0927	

[a] Total family income in 1966.
* $p < .05$ (adjusted for weight factor).

associations, an indicator of social integration, plays a role in establishing access to law for routine property transactions and for less bothersome disputes (see Chapter 4). But social integration does not play a role in explaining access to lawyers for the more serious disputes experienced by residents of the Detroit area.

The conditional effect of participation in the organizational life of the community requires some explanation. In the previous chapter, we saw how the decomposition of the alternatives variable reveals that such participation increases the use of lawyers for those who have in the past sought legal help from voluntary associations. This indicates that membership in such associations facilitates access to attorneys for the kinds of disputes studied here. But it is also the case that the availability of such help *indirectly* reduces the likelihood of legal contacts by reducing the perceived seriousness of the dispute. Thus, the effect of social integration, indicated by membership in voluntary associations, is to differentiate between serious and nonserious disputes. Nonserious disputes are those for which alternative dispute-settling mechanisms are available. In the present analysis, disputes are likely to go to attorneys regardless of the level of organizational involvement of the

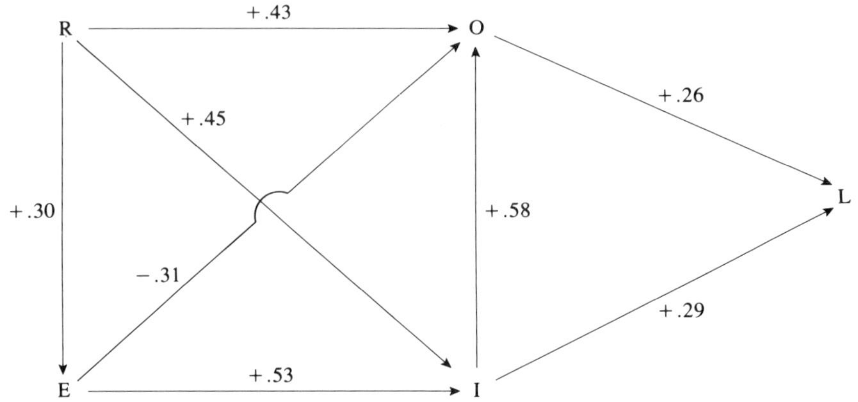

FIGURE 5.4 Path diagram for the causal model describing the effects of race (R), education (E), home ownership (O), and income (I) on the odds pertaining to the use of lawyers (L) for serious everyday disputes.

disputants because the analysis is limited to those disputes already defined as relatively serious.

Access to law, even for noneconomic matters, is determined by structural location in the economic system, that is, by wealth and property. In the best-fitting log-linear regression (logit) model controlling for race, education, income, and home ownership, only the main effects of income and home ownership on the odds pertaining to the use of lawyers for serious disputes are significant (see Figure 5.4 for the log-linear path model describing the causal relations among these variables).[9] This model assumes that the effects of income and home ownership on access to, and use of, lawyers are independent and additive. This analysis demonstrates that class position per se, independent of the effect of income on property ownership and the legal constraints that derive from property relations, accounts for differential access to legal services. When compared with lower-class individuals, a middle-class person is in a structurally advantageous position with respect to his or her ability to mobilize the coercive power of the state.

Cultural location in American society affects economic location, but being culturally privileged (white) or well informed (educated) has no direct effect on access to the legal profession. Whites are more likely than blacks to have high incomes and to own their homes, but it is their relative prosperity that gives whites greater access to lawyers, not ethnically derived cultural dif-

[9]The path model consists of the intersection of the three best-fitting logit models [(RE)(RI)(EI) ∩ (IRE)(IO)(RO)(EO) ∩ (IORE)(IL)(OL)], $\chi^2 = 11.22$ (adjusted for weight factor), df = 18, $p > .80$. The effect (RE) is derived from the saturated model [RE] where df = 0 and $\chi^2 = 0$. There are no significant interaction effects.

ferences. Similarly, those who have more education tend, on the average, to have higher incomes than the less-educated, but it is their income, not their educational attainment, that gives them the resources to afford legal services. Property ownership also plays a major role in mediating the relationship between culture and law. It is not cultural differences between whites and blacks that account for differences in their rates of lawyer use, but differential access to lawyers generated by different rates of home ownership. Education is inversely related to home ownership in the multivariate analysis (see Figure 5.4). This relationship is explained by the fact that young Detroiters, especially young blacks, are better educated than their older counterparts. Since young people are unlikely to own their own homes, most homeowners, especially older blacks, are less well educated than relatively young renters. But it is the older, less well educated homeowner who is more likely to contact an attorney than the younger, better-educated renter, even in matters unrelated to property. In conclusion, cultural variation does not play a direct role in the mobilization of lawyers for serious everyday disputes.

SOME THEORETICAL IMPLICATIONS

The resource theory of law has dominated the literature on the mobilization of lawyers since the mid-1960s. Resource theory is derived from the commonsense notion that the more wealth, power, prestige, or knowledge we have, the more likely it is that we will use these resources to acquire what we need or want. The theory also presumes that law is desirable, something that potentially benefits us all. Although the social organization of legal services may help to shape and define legal needs, those parties who benefit most are those who recognize their needs and translate their resources into advantages in the legal arena (Galanter, 1976:246). In so doing, they increase their ability to use the law to their advantage.

At the heart of the resource theory of law is the notion of legal competence (see Carlin, Howard, and Messinger, 1966:69–89), the ability to recognize and act upon the opportunity to use the legal system to secure some benefit or prevent some loss. According to Mayhew and Reiss (1969:311), "Those who have resources such as income, and to a lesser extent other resources such as education, confidence and social connections, are more likely to perceive the need for, afford, and gain access to legal services." The essence of this approach is that resources, especially economic resources, increase the capacity to engage in effective legal action. Conversely, poverty and other forms of resource deprivation create legal incompetence, the inability to pursue one's interests effectively.

Poverty has two distinct kinds of effects. First, the poor are rendered incapable by virtue of their ignorance, loss of will, passivity, feelings of powerlessness, and insecurity (Carlin, Howard, and Messinger, 1966:69–78). Thus, a major component of legal competence is psychological. Second, even when psychologically capable, the poor are rendered unable to be effective in pursuing their goals because of reduced access to legal representation, especially qualified representation. Poor people are unable to pay for adequate legal services, and when they do hire a lawyer, they are likely to be exploited (Carlin and Howard, 1965:426–429).

There are several analytical problems with the resource theory of law. The economic, political, cultural, educational, and organizational correlates of legal action are reduced to the psychological consequences of the absence of wealth, feelings of powerlessness, unwillingness to take action, ignorance of the law, and insecurity, respectively. In other words, all resources are reduced to a psychological level. Moreover, the argument that legal competence explains the use of legal services is circular. Evidence for the relationships between wealth and legal competence is offered in terms of the correlation between income, occupation, or some other measure of socioeconomic status and the actual use of legal services. This begs the question, since legal competence is itself indicated by the actual use of legal services. Legal competence is an hypothetical construct that adds little to our understanding of why the poor are less effective in securing their legal rights.

The resource theory makes two specific predictions that are not supported by the data. First, it predicts that education, representing increased knowledge of one's legal rights, increases willingness to take legal action (Mayhew and Reiss, 1969:111). Education increases one's opportunity for gainful employment, which, in turn, increases one's opportunity to contact an attorney, but education does not have a direct effect on the use of legal services. Second, resource theory predicts that politically active citizens will be more likely to assert themselves by legal means (Carlin, Howard, and Messinger, 1966:79). In fact, the reverse is true; as a form of social control, political involvement is an alternative to participation in the legal process (see Black, 1976:6).

In summary, the resource theory of law is of limited utility. It correctly predicts that wealth is a correlate of the use of legal services. But the use of lawyers by the wealthy is to a large degree constrained by the fact that the law is the fundamental institution of social control that regulates property rights. In other words, disputes involving property rights usually make the use of legal services necessary. Thus, contacting an attorney has little to do with legal competence. At best, the resource theory of law provides a quasi-psychological explanation of the residual effects of economic resources (income) on the likelihood of legal mobilization in matters involving the transmission of private property. Those with more income are assumed to be more capable of purchasing legal services because they need them in order to protect, preserve, or secure their property rights.

CONCLUSION

This chapter lends support to some of the major propositions in Donald Black's theory of legal behavior. Stratification, the unequal distribution of resources, and morphology, the unequal distribution of social involvement, play a significant role in the dispute-transformation process. Although the effect of stratification on legal behavior is linear for property matters, it is curvilinear for everyday disputes that do not involve the transmission of or control over private property. (The former, but not the latter, finding was anticipated by Black, 1976:13). Going to law is an upper-middle-class phenomenon. Neither the very rich nor the poor rely on attorneys to solve their everyday problems.

Participation in the organizational life of the community, an indicator of social integration, generates access to legal resources for everyday disputes in general, but there are no differences between the socially integrated and the socially marginal in the likelihood of contacting an attorney for serious problems.

There is some evidence to support Black's (1976:107) proposition that "law varies inversely with other social control," in that the politically alienated rely on legal counsel to handle their affairs more frequently than those who are more politically active. But there is little evidence to support the notion that cultural variables affect the civil dispute process. There may be cultural differences in the way in which different groups experience disputes, but these differences do not play a role in the transformation of disputes into legal matters. The apparent effects of education and ethnicity on the use of lawyers are completely explained by socioeconomic status and involvement in the community. The poorly educated and racial minorities do not seek legal remedies in ordinary matters, because they generally own little property, have little wealth, and do not participate in the organizational life of the community. Wealth, property, and participation generate access to legal resources, which creates a framework for defining everyday disputes in legal terms.

6

OPPORTUNITY STRUCTURES AND ACCESS TO LAW

OPPORTUNITY THEORY

The theoretical proposition that opportunities to engage in criminal activities are organized on the basis of structurally determined access to illicit resources has its origins in Sutherland's (1947) theory of differential association. According to Sutherland, all social conduct, including criminal behavior, is learned in close association with others who teach both the techniques (actions or means) necessary for the successful performance of a particular role and rationalizations (ideals, goals, or values) that explain or justify the behavior expressed in the role. From Merton (1957:185–214) comes the idea that techniques (means) and rationalizations (goals) may be acquired, but the opportunity to implement or realize them may or may not be available. Anomie is the state of normlessness that results when there is a disjunction between culturally prescribed goals and institutionalized means (opportunities) to achieve these goals. Consequently, the distribution of opportunities to pursue culturally prescribed goals depends on differential access to legitimate and illegitimate resources. As a result, opportunities to engage in legitimate and illegitimate activities are distributed unequally in society.

Building on the work of Sutherland and Merton, Cloward and Ohlin (1960:150–151) incorporate the principle of "differential opportunity structures" as a central component of their explanation of the production of delinquency in the lower class. To the extent that legitimate opportunities are more frequently available in the middle class, middle-class youth have little incentive to engage in delinquency. Illegitimate opportunities, however, are more frequently available in lower-class neighborhoods, increasing the incentive for lower-class youth to engage in delinquent acts. The notion that the distribution of delinquent behavior depends on differential opportunity structures in middle-class and lower-class communities is a useful tool for the present research since it captures the essential idea that access to opportunities to learn and engage in specific conduct is variable and *structurally* determined.

Opportunity structures have three distinct components (Cloward and Ohlin, 1960:148): (1) the opportunity to learn or acquire the techniques and rationalizations essential to the performance of a specific role, (2) the opportunity to define the role favorably, and (3) the opportunity to perform the role. In the present study, we are interested in the attorney–client relationship, the opportunity to learn the role of client, the opportunity to define the client role as desirable, and the opportunity to contact an attorney. Opportunities to learn the client role occur when potential clients associate with others who have already experienced the attorney–client relationship. Those whose experiences with attorneys have been favorable will encourage their relatives, friends, and acquaintances to follow suit. Just as juveniles learn to engage in delinquency through close association with others who define such conduct favorably, citizens learn when to contact an attorney through close association with those who know something about what to expect from such a contact.

Of those in our sample of Detroit area residents who have contacted an attorney at some time in their lives, most (74%) were referred initially by their relatives, neighbors, or friends. Of those who had never employed the services of a lawyer, most (72%) would seek advice from a relative, neighbor, or friend about how to go about getting one. Ladinsky (1976:218–222) describes "information networks" as informal systems of communication relying on personal contacts between overlapping sets of interpersonal associations. In the legal arena, information networks are equally extensive in urban and suburban communities. Legal culture is so deeply embedded in our society that there is little variation in access to information about legal services by type of community. Three-fourths of those who have contacted an attorney in the Detroit area, suburbanites and city dwellers alike, have done so upon referral by someone with whom they have a close personal relationship.

Income is a correlate of the way in which Detroiters gain access to information about attorneys. Lower-income residents of the Detroit area are significantly less likely to rely on close relationships for information about attorneys than middle- or upper-income individuals (see Table 6.1). On the other hand, residents of lower-income *neighborhoods* (including slums) are *more* likely to rely on relatives, friends, and neighbors for information about attorneys than residents of either middle- or upper-income communities. Moreover, residents of middle-class communities are most likely to rely on impersonal sources for attorney referrals. The effects of family income and the social-class composition of the community are additive (see note, Table 6.1). Consequently, lower-class residents of middle-income communities are least likely (only 63%) to rely on close relationships for information about attorneys. In contrast, upper-income residents of low-income communities are most likely (91%) to do so.

TABLE 6.1
Source of Attorney Referrals by Income and Social Class of the Community[a]

	Close relationships[b]			
	%	(*N*)	Odds	β effects
Income				
High	81.2	(101)	4.32	+.36°
Middle	75.2	(371)	3.03	+.01
Low	67.4	(175)	2.07	−.37*
Social class of the community				
Upper	75.4	(240)	3.07	+.03
Middle	70.3	(256)	2.37	−.22°
Lower	78.2	(165)	3.58	+.19

[a] The formula for the log-linear regression model in the three-way analysis that fits the marginals for both income and social class of the community is (IC)(IR)(CR); $\chi^2 = 4.04$ (adjusted), $df = 4$, $p > .40$; where the amount of variance in referral source (R) explained by income (I) is $\chi^2 = 7.49$, $df = 2$, $p < .05$ and by social class of the community (C) is $\chi^2 = 4.57$, $df = 2$, $p < .10$ (approx.). This model is additive.
[b] Close personal relationships include relatives, friends, or neighbors who are lawyers or who acted as a source of referral. Formal and impersonal contacts were through organizations, professional referrals, the yellow pages, or by "chance."
° $p < .10$; * $p < .05$ (adjusted).

Differential access to information networks by social class can be explained by the distribution of attorneys in the social-class structure of America. Upper- and middle-class residents of the Detroit area are about twice as likely as lower-income individuals to know someone personally who is an attorney (30%, 25%, and 15% for upper, middle, and lower income, respectively). Once we control for those who know attorneys, the effect of social class (income) on access to information networks disappears. In other words, among those who do not know someone personally who is an attorney, there are no class differences in the way in which they receive information about attorneys. Roughly half the respondents rely on individuals who are closely related for such information, regardless of their social-class position.

These findings suggest that legal culture is so pervasive in America that information about the client role is equally available to all social classes, regardless of whether they live in the city or suburbs (for a similar argument, see Sarat, 1977). On the other hand, the type of community one lives in plays a central role in transforming that information into action, the decision to contact an attorney. Many lower-class neighborhoods in the Detroit area are distinct communities, each with their own identity. Important decisions such as contacting an attorney involve seeking advice from relatives and friends, and these same close relationships provide alternative networks for dispute resolution. But residents of middle-class communities are relatively isolated from one another. Thus, they are more likely to rely on impersonal business or professional contacts for information about attorneys. It is in this atmosphere of impersonal relationships embedded in the formally organized structures of society that litigation is born. The middle class is more likely to have the opportunity to be in situations in which the performance of the client role is defined favorably.

The third component of opportunity structures, in addition to the opportunity to learn and to acquire definitions favorable to certain role behavior, consists of what Cloward and Ohlin (1960:148) refer to as "performance structures." Role performances occur in the context of organized social structures that provide opportunities to perform roles and receive the benefits of such performances. Opportunity structures often compete for the loyalty of potential role occupants. One explanation of delinquency is based on the assumption that legitimate and illegitimate opportunity structures provide competing incentives to juveniles to engage in lawful or unlawful conduct. Similarly, citizens are exposed, more or less, to opportunities to contact lawyers or seek alternative means of dispute resolution. Once going to law has been defined favorably, the decision to contact an attorney will depend on the opportunity to do so and the advantages associated with it in comparison with alternatives.

ACCESS TO LAW

Access is a relational concept that describes the situations that facilitate contact between those who do and do not occupy positions of power. Subordinates have access to power when they are able to communicate effectively with their superiors and influence their actions in ways that reflect the interests of the subordinates (Kornhauser, 1959:34,51,53). Attorneys have power to the extent that they have access to the coercive power of the state, and it is through them that citizens themselves gain access to state power. By becoming *clients*, citizens establish contact with someone, an attorney, who is able to mobilize state power on their behalf.

Access to law exists when citizens are able to become clients because they are part of the communication network that facilitates contact with attorneys (Carlin and Howard, 1965:430–431). Differential access to attorneys reflects the variable nature of structurally determined opportunities to enter into the client role.

Access to attorneys is a type of political mobilization, defined as the ability to gain access to government by organizing the means to do so (see Wrong, 1979:148). The mobilization of law in general, and lawyers in particular, generates access to the coercive power of the state. In this context, access to attorneys represents merely one of many different ways in which individual citizens or groups of citizens gain access to state power.

Political mobilization has been defined by political sociologists as the activation of citizens by those who have the ability to do so, in order to achieve their political goals (see Kornhauser, 1959:51; Wrong, 1979:148). In a democratically organized society, interest groups attempt to mobilize voters through political parties and direct mass appeals in order to influence the legislative process. At the same time, individuals and groups attempt to mobilize those who occupy legal and political roles in order to protect or enhance their interests. The former, downward mobilization, is usually labeled *proactive;* the latter, upward mobilization, is labeled *reactive.* Whenever citizens ask third parties who have the ability to interpret, enforce, or create laws, they are mobilizing state power (see H. L. A. Hart, 1961:91, for a discussion of these three fundamental legal activities). The capacity to mobilize law in these different ways depends on access to a variety of legal roles, including attorneys, the police, and legislators.

At the time of this survey, the American Bar Association's Canons of Professional Ethics prohibited advertising by attorneys. Organizations, however, were able to facilitate access to legal roles in a variety of ways. Civil-rights groups were able to mobilize law enforcement by producing complaints to the Massachusetts Commission Against Discrimination for acts of discrimination in housing and employment (see Mayhew, 1968). Similarly, activist legal organizations initiated class-action suits that effectively increased access to law through a broadening of legal rights (see Carlin, 1970; Finman, 1971; Brill, 1973). However, the fundamental structure of legal representation in America was, and still is, based on citizen-initiated, reactive mobilization of lawyers (Mayhew, 1975). Consequently, the mobilization of lawyers depends greatly on access to the legal profession for those who define legal action favorably.

Problems of Measurement

The notion of "access" has little currency in the sociological literature. It has been used in political sociology to describe the relationship between the rulers and the ruled, the state and its citizens, and the way in which each may influence the other. Nevertheless, the concept is vague because it has never been operationalized in a clear and consistent manner. Mayhew (1975:414) defines legal access in terms of rights "represented only when there are channels linking the representor and the represented." But this definition of legal access does not make clear the distinction between the potential use and actual use of legal services. This problem is not unique to the discussion of access to legal services, but appears as well in the literature on access to medical services (see Aday *et al.*, 1980; Lasker, 1981). The problem in the assessment of access to both legal and medical services is to distinguish the conditions that increase the availability of such services from the actual delivery of such services. To implicitly or explicitly identify conditions facilitating access to services in terms of the actual distribution of such services is to argue tautologically. What is needed is a method for clearly identifying and measuring the conditions of access independent of the actual distribution of services. Consequently, the best indicator of access to lawyers is one that measures the potential use of legal services.

Medical Services

The analogy between the process by which medical services and legal services are delivered has been made elsewhere (Carlson, 1976). Consequently, I will draw from the more extensive conceptualization and measurement of access in the medical sociology literature (see Aday and Andersen, 1975; Andersen, 1978). In addressing the issues involved in measuring the various aspects of medical and legal services, the models are essentially the same. Three distinctive components can be identified. First, there are those factors that are clearly external to the "delivery system." In the health area, these are represented as various aspects of "health policy" and "population-at-risk" (Aday and Andersen, 1975: pp. 6–7). Public health policies affect the level of funding for health services and public information about the kinds of services available. Population-at-risk variables reflect the perceived need for medical services, measured either in terms of public definitions or those of independent investigators. Measures of health policy and risk factors are difficult to construct in an objective fashion. They usually reflect the values of the subjects observed or the observer. Policy measures reflect the evaluations of policy makers with regard to what ought to increase access, but do not measure access itself. Given cultural and other sources of variation in perceived health problems, the subjective assessment of "unmet needs" becomes meaningless in an attempt to measure "true" disease rates. To the extent that physicians are used to assess the needs of patients, there are obvious biases in the evaluation of needs in relation to the services rendered (see Aday *et al.*, 1980:192–197). There is great variability by physician and by identifiable disease in the recognition–definition of need for physical as well as for so-called mental diseases (Scheff, 1966).

In the search for an objective measure of need, Aday *et al.* (1980:187) refer to the periodic survey of "disability days" by the National Center for Health

Statistics as an indicator, albeit approximate, of the presence of relatively serious physical illness. From these data, Aday *et al.* (1980) construct a "use-disability ratio" to measure access to medical services. This is analogous to the use-dispute index suggested by Sarat and Grossman (1975:1208) in their discussion of the mobilization of adjudication. Such a measure may provide an interesting description of differential access to legal institutions, but has little analytic value, since a correlation between the use-dispute index and actual use of services would be an artifact of the measurement process itself.

The second component of the medical delivery system used to indicate access is the structure through which medical services are processed (Aday and Andersen, 1975:15). Proximity to medical services, the number of physicians available, and type of physicians available are indicators of medical structures that facilitate access to medical services. The problem with these kinds of measures is that the presence of a resource, say a hospital, does not in and of itself indicate access. There may be a variety of obstacles to the receipt of services, even for those who are physically proximate. For example, many private hospitals refuse admission to those who cannot afford to pay. Moreover, the existence of new technology and the resources to acquire this technology help to structure how diseases are defined as well as their appropriate treatment. In effect, citizens define their medical needs in terms of those services that are accessible to them. Marks (1976:192) has shown that perceived legal needs correspond to preexisting patterns in the delivery of legal services. Nader (1980:46) has described the process by which the lack of access to legal remedies produces a restructuring of a dispute in nonlegal terms. The very existence of social barriers to access effectively convinces complainants of the futility of seeking legal remedies.

The third component of the medical-services delivery system involves the actual services received, that is, output. Usually measured in terms of consumer satisfaction, this is one of the least adequate measures of access. Satisfied consumers are assumed to have had greater access since their perceived needs have been met. There is some evidence that those with greater access to legal services may actually be dissatisfied and discouraged from further contact. This is especially so in the case of personal injury lawsuits (see Hunting and Neuwirth, 1962).

The quality (specialist versus general practitioner) and quantity (number of visits) of physician contacts are frequently used to indicate access. But since the central research question is to assess the effect of differential access to medical services on their actual use, the conceptualization and operationalization of both of these variables in the same terms is clearly a tautologous procedure. The same problem arises in assessing the effect of access to lawyers on the quality and quantity of legal services. Access as a theoretically useful concept implies that there exists the *opportunity* to seek the assistance of an attorney should the need (a dispute) arise. It does not imply, nor can it be measured by, the actual distribution of legal services.

Legal Services

Unlike the literature on access to medicine, the literature on access to law does not frame the issue explicitly in terms of the availability of services. Rather, the literature in the sociology of law reflects a commitment to justice, made possible when access to law does not depend on privilege (see Silverstein, 1968; Maddi and Merrill, 1971; Meeks, 1976; Plenningstorf and Kimball, 1976a, 1976b; Cappelletti and Garth, 1978). Nader (1980:3–6) makes this especially clear in the introductory sections of her work on nonlegal alternatives to dispute resolution. According to Nader (1980:64), barriers to access violate the fundamental principle of our legal system that each citizen be guaranteed equality before the law. Unequal access to the legal system exacerbates the "little injustices" produced by the economic and social arrangements of contemporary society. On the other hand, Mayhew (1975) expresses his concern for the injustices created by unequal access to the "institution of representation" itself. The unequal distribution of legal services by social class denies equal justice to those who cannot afford an attorney. The reformist efforts of the Office of Economic Opportunity of the Johnson administration to create government-sponsored legal services for the poor was an attempt to remedy this situation.

In order to develop objective, nonevaluative criteria for the measurement of legal access, we must divest ourselves of the ideological bases of our thinking about the matter (see D. Black, 1979, for a discussion of the merits of this approach to the scientific study of law). Equal access to law may be a desirable political goal, but this notion is difficult to operationalize. One's social position affects one's interests and, consequently, the kinds of so-called legal needs (routine matters, minor disputes, or major calamities) that one has. A comparison of the legal needs of the poor and the rich is in a sense like comparing apples and oranges. Disputes with landlords are a lower-class phenomenon; the acquisition, transfer, and maintenance of property is, by definition, a concern of the middle class; those in the highest economic positions are interested in corporate law and the economic relations it is designed to maintain. When disputes occur across class lines, formal equality of representation and access to legal institutions does not imply true equality. Many legal-services agencies for the poor have been co-opted by dominant interests, leading to ineffective representation and in some cases politically motivated policies that deny effective representation to the poor (see Finman, 1971). This is not unique in the history of legal aid. In fact, the co-optation of legal institutions designed to serve the poor has been an unfortunate part of the history of reform efforts since they began in the late nineteenth century. Pipkin (1979) describes the co-optation of the early legal-aid societies by elite interests. Small-claims courts, too, no longer facilitate access to law for those who cannot afford an attorney. These courts have become the vehicle for organized or wealthy interests to enforce small legal claims against the poor (Students of the Columbia Law School, 1969).

Measures of legal access must be free of ideological bias. But they also must be free of tautology. The resources approach to the measurement of access fails to distinguish between access to law and conditions associated with access to law. For example, Mayhew and Reiss (1969:311), argue that resources such as income and education make it possible for individuals to gain access to legal services, yet differential access to law is indicated by the unequal distribution of economic and other resources. "Nevertheless, the resources theory fails to account for the extent of legal services" (Mayhew and Reiss, 1969:311). This point is made even more strongly in the medical-services literature. Although there is a considerable amount of evidence in support of the hypothesis that income increases access to medical services (Andersen, 1978), Berkanovic and Reeder (1974) point out that socioeconomic status explains less of the variance in use of medical services than do other factors. Moreover, the relationship between socioeconomic status and receiving specialized treatment is curvilinear, with the middle class most likely to be referred by professionals to specialized facilities (Miller, 1973:180). In conclusion, it appears that the possession of resources per se is not an adequate indicator of access to law. It is, however, a factor that facilitates such access.

Certain kinds of legal problems make going to law unavoidable, regardless of social-class position (see Carlin and Howard, 1965:387). This is especially true of the transfer of property matters, which are routinely handled by attorneys, such as settling estates or purchasing homes. These matters are defined in terms of the way in which the legal system is organized to handle them. Home ownership, a variable that reflects the legal constraints imposed by property relations, is not, therefore, expected to be an indicator of access to legal services. The private ownership of property in this context is not a resource, but reflects a demand for legal services that is more or less created by the social organization of law in an economic system based on private ownership.

Contextual Effects

The discussion of access to both medical and legal services suggests that social class is an important component of the social context that facilitates access to opportunities for legal services. A useful way to conceptualize and operationalize the distinction between individual and contextual effects of social class is to distinguish between the individual's family status and the social-class characteristics of the neighborhood or the community in which the individual lives.

In their study of court referrals for juvenile delinquents, Reiss and Rhodes (1961) distinguish clearly between the effects of socioeconomic status per se and the community in which one lives. Slums, for example, create greater opportunities for illegal conduct for all social groups. At the same time, poor people who live in relatively affluent communities are relatively unlikely to engage in illegal conduct. Somehow, lower-class juveniles in these areas are not hooked into those networks that provide opportunities for delinquency among those of middle- and upper-class status. Elliot (1966) has demonstrated that lower-class juveniles who are not in an environment that provides opportunities to be delinquent are less delinquent than middle-class youth in a similar environment.

The individual and contextual effects of social class on legal services are empirically as well as analytically distinct, just as they are with respect to the mobilization of law for juvenile delinquency. The density of lawyers appears to increase with the social class of the community, since the likelihood of close personal associations with attorneys (e.g., neighbors) increases with class position. In a study of an upper-income suburban community whose residents include "high-ranking officers in major American corporations," a large number of attorneys, and other professionals, Baumgartner (1980) finds that the probability of going to law varies inversely with social status. Baumgartner explains her findings in terms of the loss of community in affluent suburbia, leading to dispute avoidance for personal problems. This contradicts Galanter's (1974:103) notion that the "haves," by virtue of their power, wealth, or status are "repeat players" in the legal system. Those who reside in upper-income communities are more likely to have access to networks of individuals who routinely avail themselves of legal counsel. With more attorneys available and more repeat players in upper-income communities, we should expect a positive correlation between social class of the community and going to law. On the other hand, in certain communities, upper-status individuals avail themselves of the privilege that status brings; they use informal networks to solve problems as an alternative to formal mechanisms of dispute resolution.

The objective of the present chapter is to analyze differential access to opportunities to seek legal assistance by evaluating the contextual effect of social class on the likelihood of contacting an attorney. The literature provides little guidance with respect to specific predictions regarding this effect. The following analysis lends support to Baumgartner's observation that those who reside in affluent suburbs are less likely to seek legal remedies for their disputes than one would otherwise expect given their economic and personal resources.

COMMUNITIES IN THE DETROIT AREA

Since 1951, United Community Services (UCS) of metropolitan Detroit has identified a set of subcommunities in Detroit for the purpose of planning the administration and allocation of funds and services (see "Subcommunities in the City of Detroit," UCS, 1970). In 1967, there were 49 such communities identified, ranging in population between approximately 20,000 and 50,000. This corresponds more or less to the criterion of a minimum of 25,000 inhabitants for suburban cities described in the 1972 *County and City Data Book* (U.S. Bureau of the Census, 1973). Consequently, suburban cities and Detroit subcommunities are roughly comparable units of analysis. The two cities that are incorporated independently within the city limits of Detroit, Hamtramck and Highland Park, had populations of 27,000 and 35,000 respectively. The average population for subcommunities was approximately 30,000.

Detroit has been described as a predominantly working-class city with many of its middle-class people living in lower-class communities (Miller and Swanson, 1958:153). At the same time, there is a high degree of ethnic and religious homogeneity within census tracts, across adjacent census tracts, and in residential patterns for the city as a whole. United Community Services identifies communities according to their natural boundaries in order to facilitate the allocation of funds to a variety of community organizations and programs.

Class Composition

The subcommunities identified by UCS include between 3 and 13 adjacent census tracts described in the *Census of Population and Housing: 1970 Census Tracts* for the Detroit SMSA (U.S. Bureau of the Census, 1972b). The percentage of families in each community with less than $3000 annual income in 1969 and the percentage with $25,000 or more were calculated. In the present study, communities that had more people in the lowest-income category than in the state of Michigan as a whole (7.5%) and fewer in the highest-income category (5.3%) were labeled "lower class." Communities that had fewer than 7.5% of their residents in the lowest-income category and more than 5.3% in the highest-income category were labeled "upper class." All the rest were considered "middle class." With this procedure, 34 communities were considered to be lower class, 11 were middle class, and 4 were upper class. Only 1 of the upper-class communities had a substantial proportion of high-income residents (about 20%).

Of the 22 remaining cities in the metropolitan area, 9 were upper class, 2 (Hamtramck and Highland Park) were lower class, and the rest were middle class. Only 2 of the upper-class suburban communities had a substantial number of high-income residents. Residents of smaller cities, towns, and unincorporated areas were excluded from the analysis because it was difficult to identify the appropriate community boundaries.

Racial Composition

Ethnic composition of the Detroit communities was determined by the proportion of black residents in each community. "Homogeneous black" communities were those in which 90% or more of the residents were black; "majority black" communities had between 50 and 89.9% black residents; "majority white" communities had between 10 and 49.9% black residents; and, finally, "homogeneous white" communities were less than 10% black. About half (25) of the communities were predominantly black (at least 50% black). Only 32% of the predominantly black communities were racially homogeneous, whereas 58% of the predominantly white communities were homogeneous. Racially homogeneous white and black communities were homogeneous across all adjacent census tracts, indicating a high degree of racial homogeneity in about half the communities. The more heterogeneous communities also varied greatly across census tracts, with variation from racially homogeneous to heterogeneous census tracts. Communities ranged from homogeneous black to majority white census tracts and from majority black to homogeneous white census tracts, never from homogeneous black to homogeneous white. Many of the communities appeared to be in transition. Between 1960 and 1970, the black population increased by 37% in the city of Detroit, whereas the overall population declined by 9% (U.S. Bureau of the Census, 1972a:702). This represents a relative increase of 51.2% in the black population. The white population declined from 71% of the total to only 56% of the total. An earlier DAS study, in 1958, described Detroit as a racially segregated city (see Lenski, 1961:69–73). This remained true for about half the city in 1967, but a large number of the remaining communities appeared to be in transition from predominantly white to black.

In 1967, the proportion of blacks in the city of Detroit in the DAS sample was 33%, somewhat lower than what one might expect given the census results a few years later. This can be explained by the fact that the DAS samples households, not individuals. Blacks, whose households were larger than whites, had proportionately fewer adults. The object of this survey was to randomly sample both male and females 18 years of age or older.

The contextual effects of the racial composition of Detroit communities are examined later in this chapter. The class composition of a community affects access to legal services independent of its racial or ethnic composition. Moreover, the effect of racial composition is explained by the effect of social class on the use of lawyers. Once again, we see that it is class, not race, that determines access to law.

Semi-Autonomous Social Fields

Sally Falk Moore (1978:54–81) defines the community as a "semi-autonomous social field." A community is a self-regulating entity that enforces rules that emerge in the course of interaction among its constituents and interprets legal rules in light of the common experiences of those who make up the community. Communities are semi-autonomous because they are independent of the "coercive force of government," yet affect and are affected by the legal rules that represent the coercive power of the state (Moore, 1978:79).

In her study of the Chagga of Tanzania, Moore describes the neighborhood and patrilineal kin networks as the basis of the local community. The Chagga do not live in clearly defined villages, but in a continuous line of small, adjacent farming units, much like the metropolitan sprawl found in contemporary American cities. Of course, the Chagga community or "lineage-neighborhood complex" is much smaller than the type of community described in Detroit, and it is organized on different social bases. Moore (1978:76) writes that power "comes from the *informal* accretion of economic, educational advantages, and network contacts" that enhance both the "capacity of persons inside the social field to mobilize the state on their behalf" (1978:64) and the capacity of those persons to resist external attempts by the state to control actions within. Social position, based on traditional sources of prestige, becomes an autonomous source of power. Those in more favorable positions are better able to mobilize the law in their own behalf or on behalf of the community. Power derives not only directly from the resources one may possess, but from one's proximity to those who control the community's resources. Consequently, the son of a former chief is in a better position to mobilize state power than someone else because he is closer to the center of power. This is true despite attempts by the socialist government to promote egalitarian values and equal access to state power.

In the modern urban community, it is the *distribution* of economic resources that defines its boundaries more than its cultural traditions or history.

Unlike the traditional societies that Moore studies, communities in metropolitan Detroit do not have boundaries clearly delineated by custom and territory. Nevertheless, traveling through the unbroken miles of residential structures in the Detroit area, we find sharp contrasts in residential modalities consistent with changes in the social-class composition of each community. Even today, in the 1980s, with the migration of many blacks into residential, social, and economic positions formerly occupied by whites, most of the communities have retained their earlier social-class characteristics.

The central thesis of this chapter is that economic and legal resources are differentially distributed in modern urban communities, and the distribution of these resources provides a context that shapes the transformation of disputes into legal claims. The distribution of wealth and the differential availability of attorneys across communities are the variables expected to affect the likelihood of legal contacts for everyday disputes and legal claims. The greater the concentration of wealth and legal resources, the more likely this transformation will occur.

FINDINGS

Residents of upper-income communities are more likely than residents of middle- or lower-income communities to contact an attorney at some time during their lives (see Table 6.2). But they are no more or less likely than residents of middle-income communities to contact attorneys for everyday disputes (see Table 6.3). It seems that the affluent are less likely than expected to rely on legal remedies for disputes unrelated to property. On the other hand, residents of lower-income communities contact attorneys less frequently than those from middle- or upper-income communities no matter what kinds of problems they are facing (see Tables 6.2 and 6.3).

Residents of suburbia are somewhat more likely than city dwellers to contact an attorney at some time in their lives (see Table 6.2), but they are almost twice as likely to do so for everyday disputes (Table 6.3). It is conceivable that there is something distinctive about a suburban life-style that increases litigiousness in comparison with living in cities. But given our previous discussion, we should expect the opposite to be the case; the opportunity to create informal communication networks in suburbia should yield a lower-than-expected ratio between lawyer use and disputes (the "use-dispute" index).

In the multivariate analysis, we discover in fact that the residents of affluent suburban communities are indeed significantly less likely to contact an attorney than one would expect given the independent (main) effects of income and the class composition of the community on the use of lawyers

TABLE 6.2
The Use of Lawyers in One's Lifetime by Income, Social Class of the Community, and Location

	Ever see a lawyer			
	%	(N)	Odds	β effects
Income[a]				
High	83.9	(93)	5.20	+.64**
Middle	75.0	(448)	3.00	+.09
Low	56.6	(320)	1.30	−.74***
Social class of the community[b]				
Upper	77.6	(232)	3.46	+.38**
Middle	73.9	(326)	2.84	+.18
Lower	57.4	(303)	1.35	−.56***
Location				
Suburban cities	74.5	(376)	2.92	+.23**
Detroit	64.9	(485)	1.85	−.23**
	69.1	(861)	2.24	

[a] High ≥ $15,000 total family income in 1966; Middle = $7000–$14,999 total family income in 1966; Low ≤ $7000 total family income in 1966. $\chi^2 = 30.45$, $df = 2$, $p < .001$. Among the 14 highest-income families (≥$25,000 total annual family income), the odds were 2.50, indicating curvilinearity at the highest range. For the 20 remaining upper-income individuals who live in small towns, the odds = 2.33. The overall odds for all 34 upper-income individuals in the weighted sample is 2.40.

[b] Community social class applies to suburban cities of 25,000 or more in the Detroit SMSA (1970 U.S. Census) and communities of approximately 25,000 each within the city of Detroit identified by United Community Services of Detroit. High = the proportion of families in each community with incomes in 1969 that exceeds the proportion of families in the state with incomes in 1969 equal to or greater than $25,000 and that is less than the proportion of families in the state with incomes in 1969 below $3000. Low = the proportion of families in each community with incomes in 1969 that exceeds the proportion of families in the state with incomes in 1969 below $3000 and that is less than the proportion of families in the state with incomes in 1969 equal to or greater than $25,000. Middle = all remaining communities.

** $p < .01$; *** $p < .001$ (adjusted for weight factor).

(see Table 6.4). In other words, suburbanites are more likely to use lawyers than city dwellers to the extent that, on the average, they are more affluent. But once we have taken into account the effects of wealth, the quality of social life in suburbia tends to reduce the degree of litigiousness among its residents.

From Table 6.4, it is evident that the social-class composition of the

TABLE 6.3
The Use of Lawyers for Everyday Disputes

	Saw a lawyer			
	%	(*N*)	Odds	β effects
Income[a]				
High	19.4	(93)	.240	+.62**
Middle	10.7	(447)	.120	−.07
Low	6.9	(319)	.074	−.55**
Home ownership				
Owns	12.0	(619)	.136	+.39*
Rents	5.8	(240)	.062	−.39*
Race				
White	10.7	(694)	.119	+.13
Black	8.5	(165)	.093	−.13
Social class of the community[b]				
Upper	12.9	(232)	.149	+.33°
Middle	12.9	(326)	.148	+.32°
Lower	5.3	(301)	.056	−.65**
Racial composition of the community[c]				
Predominantly white	10.6	(640)	.119	+.08
Predominantly black	9.1	(219)	.101	−.08
Location				
Suburban cities	13.6	(375)	.157	+.32*
Detroit	7.6	(484)	.083	−.32*
	10.2	(859)	.114	

[a] See n. a, Table 6.2.
[b] See n. b, Table 6.2.
[c] Predominantly white = at least 50% white; predominantly black = at least 50% black.
° $p < .10$; * $p < .05$; ** $p < .01$ (adjusted for weight factor).

community has an independent contextual effect on the use of lawyers that cannot be reduced to the effect of income itself. In other words, lower-income citizens who live in middle-income communities have a greater opportunity to contact a lawyer than those who live in lower-income communities (see Table 6.5). Similarly, middle-income Detroiters suffer a diminished opportunity to contact an attorney if they live in a low-income area.

From Table 6.5, it is apparent that the contextual effect of the class composition of the community on access to attorneys is curvilinear. Upper-income residents of *middle*-income communities contact attorneys far more frequently than upper-income residents of either more or less affluent communities. Moreover, these individuals are among the most litigious. Similarly, residents of *middle*-income suburbs contact attorneys more frequently than those who live in either more- or less-affluent suburbs.

TABLE 6.4
The Main and Interaction Effects on the Odds Pertaining to the Use of Lawyers in One's Lifetime (L) in the Best-Fitting Log-Linear Regression Model

Variable	β effects	p^a
Income (I)		
High	+.56	< .05
Middle	+.09	NS
Low	−.66	< .01
Class composition (C)[b]		
Upper	+.33	< .05
Middle/Lower	−.33	< .05
Location (A)		
Suburban cities	−.14	NS
Detroit	+.14	NS
Class composition × Location		
Upper-class suburbs	−.37	< .05
Other cities	+.37	< .05

[a] Adjusted for weight factor.
[b] Class composition is dichotomized here in order to eliminate the zero-cell problem and thereby make approximation unnecessary, and to test for interaction between class composition and location. The best-fitting log-linear regression model is [(ICA)(IL)(CAL)], $\chi^2 = 4.67$ (adjusted), $df = 6$, $p > .50$.

The contextual effects of social class are even more important in the explanation of the transformation of everyday disputes into legal claims than the use of lawyers in general. When it comes to the decision to contact an attorney for everyday disputes, neither income, nor property ownership, nor location play a direct role. The effects of these variables are mediated completely by the intervening effect of the class composition of the community on the use of lawyers. In the best-fitting log-linear path analysis, controlling for income, home ownership, location, and class composition, only the latter remains effective (see Table 6.6 and Figure 6.1). Wealth and property play a direct role in the use of lawyers for matters concerning wealth and property. But when it comes to non-property-related disputes, wealth and property play an indirect role in the mobilization of lawyers by increasing access to attorneys in more affluent communities and in suburbia. Yet, once again, the effects of wealth and location interact to reduce the probability of legal contacts for everyday disputes among affluent suburbanites (see Table 6.7).

In summary, access to legal services is a function of the distribution of economic and legal resources in communities. The social-class composition of the community, measured in terms of income distribution, provides a

TABLE 6.5

Conditional Odds Pertaining to the Use of Lawyers in One's Lifetime

	Community social class	Odds	(*N*)
Family income			
High	Upper	4.43	(38)
	Middle	7.60	(43)
	Lower	3.00	(12)
Middle	Upper	4.00	(135)
	Middle	3.52	(190)
	Lower	1.86	(123)
Low	Upper	2.28	(59)
	Middle	1.45	(93)
	Lower	1.02	(168)
Location			
Suburbs	Upper	2.87	(178)
	Middle	3.14	(182)
	Lower	1.67	(16)
Detroit	Upper	8.00	(54)
	Middle	2.51	(144)
	Lower	1.33	(287)
Overall odds		2.24	(861)

TABLE 6.6

Estimates of Main Effects in the Best-Fitting Log-Linear Path Model with the Odds Pertaining to the Use of Lawyers for Everyday Disputes (L) Dependent[a]

	β effects
Income × Ownership (IO)	+.57***
Income × Location (IA)	+.26**
Ownership × Location (OA)	+.48***
Income × Class composition (IC)	+.48**
Ownership × Class composition (OC)	+.64***
Location × Class composition (AC)	+1.74***
Class composition × Lawyer (CL)	+.49**

[a] The formula for the best-fitting log-linear path model is [(IO) ∩ (IO)(IA)(OA) ∩ (IOA)(IC)(OC)(AC) ∩ (IOAC)(CL)], $\chi^2 = 13.18$ (adjusted), $df = 19$, $p > .75$.
** $p < .01$; *** $p < .001$ (adjusted for weight factor).

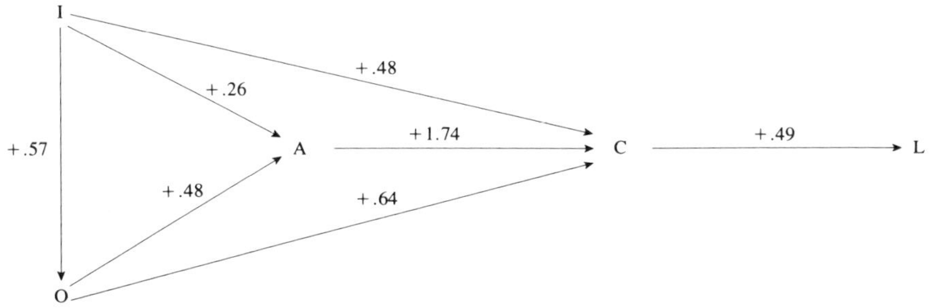

FIGURE 6.1 Path diagram for the best-fitting log-linear model describing the effects of home ownership (O), income (I), location (A), and the social-class composition of the community (C) on the use of lawyers (L) for everyday disputes.

context that shapes the transformation of disputes into legal claims. The effect of the community on the use of lawyers is independent of the ability to purchase legal services or constraints imposed by the ownership of property. In the case of legal contacts for all types of matters, the effects of annual family income and the social class of the community are independent, linear, and additive. In the case of legal contacts for everyday disputes, only the social-class composition of the community plays a direct role. The apparent effects of income and property ownership on the use of lawyers for ordinary, everyday matters can be explained by the way in which they facilitate access to attorneys. Wealth and property increase access to the opportunity structures that define legal remedies favorably and increase the opportunity to play the client role. Although it is generally the case that the opportunity to contact an attorney increases with the increasing prosperity of the community, the existence of informal information networks regarding legal services and alternatives serves to mitigate the effects of opportunity structures on the actual use of lawyers. This is apparently the case in relatively affluent

TABLE 6.7
The Use of Lawyers for Everyday Disputes by Social Class of the Community and Location

Location	Social class of the community	Saw a lawyer %	(*N*)	Odds
Suburbs	Upper	12.4	(178)	.141
	Middle	15.4	(182)	.182
	Lower	6.7	(15)	.071
Detroit	Upper	14.8	(54)	.174
	Middle	9.7	(144)	.108
	Lower	5.2	(286)	.055

suburbs where affluent residents are less likely to contact an attorney than one would otherwise expect.

The effects of race on the use of lawyers for everyday disputes in the Detroit metropolitan area are negligible (see Table 6.3), but the racial composition of subcommunities within the city of Detroit does appear to have a weak effect on access to lawyers (see Table 6.8). Residents of subcommunities that are predominantly white are more likely to contact a lawyer than those who reside in predominantly black subcommunities. In the best-fitting regression model, controlling for the race of the individual and the racial composition of the community, only the social-class composition of the community explains a significant amount of the variance in the odds pertaining to the use of lawyers (see Table 6.9). In other words, once we have taken into account the effects of the social-class composition of the community, all the apparent effects of race on access to law disappear. To the extent that blacks are more likely to live in black communities, and to the extent that these communities tend to be poor, blacks are less likely than whites to have access to attorneys.

Of additional interest is the effect of racial homogeneity on access to law. As it turns out, residents of relatively segregated (homogeneous) communities, both white and black, are significantly more likely to contact an

TABLE 6.8
The Use of Lawyers in One's Lifetime by Race and Racial Composition of the Community in Detroit[a]

	Ever see a lawyer			
	%	(*N*)	Odds	β effects
Race				
White	66.4	(324)	1.97	+.09
Black	62.1	(161)	1.64	−.09
Racial composition				
Predominantly white[b]	68.2	(274)	2.15	+.17°
Predominantly black	60.7	(211)	1.54	−.17°
Racial composition				
Homogeneous[c]	69.6	(240)	2.29	+.20*
Heterogeneous	60.4	(245)	1.53	−.20*
	64.9	(485)	1.85	

[a] Suburbs excluded; there are no homogeneous black communities and few blacks in general.
[b] ≥ 50% white.
[c] ≥ 90% white or black.
° $p < .10$; * $p < .05$.

TABLE 6.9

Analysis of the Variation in the Odds Pertaining to the Use of Lawyers by Class and Racial Composition

Variation due to	Likelihood ratio χ^2	*df*	p^a
Class composition (C)	26.63	2	< .001
Race (R)	0.47	1	NS
Racial composition[b] (Q)	0.13	1	NS

[a] Significant effects reflect the differences between the best-fitting log-linear regression model [(CRQ)(CL)], $\chi^2 = 10.63$, $df = 9$, $p > .30$, and the model excluding the specified effect. Non-significant effects reflect the differences between the best-fitting log-linear regression model and the model including the specified effect. There are no significant interaction effects.

[b] Refers to the distinction between predominantly white and predominantly black communities.

attorney than those who live in relatively integrated (heterogeneous) neighborhoods (see Table 6.8). Furthermore, this relationship is not explained by social-class differences in these communities. Moreover, these results are counterintuitive, since we would expect more conflict and litigiousness in heterogeneous communities. In fact, homogeneous communities are more stable in the sense that there is greater continuity in their institutional life, and stable communities generate more opportunities to contact attorneys (Lieberman, 1981:7).

THE ECONOMIC NATURE OF OPPORTUNITY STRUCTURES

The effect of the social-class composition of the community on access to law supports the notion that legal opportunity structures in modern industrial urban settings are essentially economic in origin. Individual wealth affects the ability to purchase legal services, whereas the concentration of wealth in the community affects access to legal services. As semi-autonomous social fields, modern urban communities are economic entities whose effects cannot be reduced to their constituent elements.

The concentration of economic and legal resources in modern urban communities provides a context that shapes the transformation of disputes into legal claims. In more affluent communities, the availability of legal resources creates the opportunity to define problems in legal terms. Once this occurs, the existence of informal information networks regarding the use of legal services reduces the probability that Detroit area residents will pursue legal remedies for their problems. This is especially the case in more affluent suburban communities. Upper-middle-class residents of middle-income communities are especially likely to rely on impersonal referral mechanisms when it comes to choosing an attorney, a process that contributes to the litigiousness of the upper-middle-class urbanite.

To summarize, the effects of wealth and property on the use of lawyers are mediated by the economic and legal characteristics of the community. Ethnicity, measured in terms of race and the racial composition of the community, does not directly affect the opportunity to contact an attorney. Racially homogeneous communities are more likely to provide opportunities for legal contacts than more integrated areas. The existence of informal information networks about legal services reduces the effect of the social-class composition of the community on the use of lawyers. Despite the increased opportunity to use legal services in affluent suburban communities, the residents of these communities are less likely to do so than their urban counterparts. Detroiters who are most likely to have the opportunity to use legal services and avail themselves of that opportunity are upper-middle-class residents of middle-class suburban communities and residents of upper-income communities within the city of Detroit.

7

DISPUTES AS SOCIAL ACTS

Fundamental to a sociological theory of social control is the notion that norms regulate conduct through sanctions imposed on individuals whose actions occur within the context of organized social relationships. From the interactionist perspective, normative regulation defines situations and gives behavior meaning. Without consequences (i.e., sanctions), social behavior is meaningless. To the extent that sanctions occur within the context of existing social relationships, these relationships are given meaning. Through normative regulation, unorganized social behaviors become meaningful social acts with implications for participation in, and the social control of, complex social relationships (Swanson, 1965:106).

Laws are norms that regulate social behavior within the political context of society. To the extent that there is some probability that legal norms are backed by official sanctions, they give behavior meaning, define situations, and impose structure on social acts. For example, an act is defined as theft to the extent that there is a law prohibiting specific conduct backed by the reasonable probability that a person who engages in such conduct will be arrested. There is considerable historical and comparative evidence that the regulation of such conduct varies over time and space. The existence of a legal category such as "grand larceny" gives certain behavior meaning in the larger sociopolitical context of society as a whole. Substantive criminal law structures social behavior; it gives meaning to social acts.

DISPUTES AS LEGAL CATEGORIES

In their study of disputing in five federal judicial districts, Miller and Sarat (1981) report that they were unable to explain variation in prelegal disputing in terms of institutional variables. They conclude that variation in disputing is explained primarily in terms of differences in dispute categories, most of which they define in their study in civil legal terms, such as torts. To explain variation in disputing in terms of legal differences between types of disputes is tautologous. To the extent that disputes as social acts have meaning within the context of legal rules, the structure of the dispute process depends on the legality of the dispute. Consequently, the objective of studying differences among dispute categories in the way in which disputes are processed should be to explain these differences, not to accept them as given.

Miller and Sarat also treat the individual dispute as the unit of analysis, yet interpret the data and make inferences in terms of the aggregate unit, the type of dispute (see Robinson, 1950, for a discussion of this analytic problem). Disputes as meaningful social acts are defined, more or less, within normative frameworks, both societal and legal. On the individual level (social behaviors), noninstitutional factors play a role in the dispute process, whereas on the aggregate level (social acts), institutional factors play such a role. When disputes are treated as social acts, we can begin to make predictions regarding the relationships between disputes and the political, economic, and social institutions of society.

An act is criminal to the extent that there is some risk of detection and punishment by the police (Black, 1979). Similarly, an act is immoral to the extent that it is regulated in accord with the mores of society. In other words, legal regulation and moral regulation are variable qualities of social acts. When there is risk of loss of liberty, a social act is defined as a crime. A civil dispute is often subject to normative or moral regulation before a lawyer is contacted. To the extent that there is some risk, however small, of advice given or legal action taken by an attorney, a civil dispute becomes a legal matter. Just as criminal acts are defined in terms of the probability of detection by law enforcement officials, civil legal disputes are defined in terms of the probability of the mobilization of lawyers.

Legality is a variable quality of criminal offenses and civil legal disputes. In the aggregate, criminal offenses can be measured in terms of the certainty of punishment by law enforcement officials (Silberman, 1976). In the aggregate, civil disputes can be measured in terms of the proportion of individual disputes that involve attorneys. An assault is more criminal than smoking marijuana because there is a greater risk of detection and punishment for the former than for the latter. Civil disputes, too, vary in their degree of legal regulation. In the present study, civil disputes are measured in terms of the probability of contacting an attorney, the probability of an attorney taking specific action, and the final outcome of the dispute. The purpose of this chapter is to analyze the institutional determinants of 23 aggregate civil disputes.

EXPLAINING THE MOBILIZATION OF LAW

INTERCORRELATIONS AMONG THE PROCESS VARIABLES

Table 7.1 summarizes the findings regarding the intercorrelations among the endogenous (process) variables measuring the seven stages of the dispute process for 23 civil disputes. Aggregate measures were obtained for each variable, first by coding each stage of the dispute process "1" or "0" to indicate whether or not a given dispute had passed through that stage, then by calculating the proportion that scored "1" for each of the seven endogenous variables: (1) something should be done, (2) third-party help, (3) legal norms invoked, (4) saw a lawyer, (5) legal action taken (e.g., went to court), (6) outcome (favorable or unfavorable), and (7) satisfaction (subjective evaluation of the outcome).

The correlation matrix (reported in Table 7.1) reveals that the first stage of the process is not correlated with any of the others, except for an unexpected negative correlation between the first, "Something should be done," and the last, "Satisfaction." When disputants try to do something about a dispute, they are likely to become frustrated. One route to contentment is, apparently, to do nothing at all. As social acts, the definition of disputes as "not worth the bother" reduces the personal costs associated with them (e.g., negative feelings such as anger; see Tavris, 1982). A dispute is more likely to yield dissatisfaction if it is something society defines as problematic than if it is trivialized. If a leaky faucet has not been fixed properly, is this important? Is this the sort of thing one ought to fight about, even if there is

TABLE 7.1

Correlation Matrix for the Endogenous (Process) Variables[a]

	Something should be done	Third-party help	Legal norms invoked	Saw lawyer	Legal action	Outcome
Third-party help	−.06					
Legal norms invoked	+.35	+.24				
Saw lawyer	+.20	+.60***	+.64***			
Legal action	+.05	+.41*	+.29	+.60***		
Outcome	−.28	+.39*	−.17	+.19	+.38*	
Satisfaction	−.43*	+.19	−.04	+.09	+.37*	+.82***

[a] $N = 23$ civil disputes.
* $p < .05$; ** $p < .01$; *** $p < .001$.

some risk of failure? Or should it be ignored, since the costs associated with trying to get it fixed may outweigh the annoyance of the occasional drip?

Seeking third-party help is correlated with two critical secondary stages of the mobilization process: contacting a lawyer and legal action (see Table 7.1). But the effect of third parties on the decision to seek legal assistance explains the apparent effect of third-party help on the type of legal action taken (see the path diagram in Figure 7.1). Attorneys decide whether to take legal action and what kind of action to take independent of the input from third parties. Third parties do play a role, however, in determining the outcome of the dispute. When third parties are involved in the dispute process, the results are typically more favorable to the respondent. Third parties are an important resource in the settlement of disputes.

The kinds of disputes that are more likely to invoke legal norms are also more likely to mobilize attorneys (see Table 7.1 and Figure 7.1). That the invocation of legal norms remains correlated with contacting attorneys suggests that these are not truly independent stages of the mobilization process. By definition, whenever legal contacts occur, legal norms have been or are invoked. Nevertheless, there are instances in which people feel that they should see a lawyer but do not, and where solutions to problems are worked

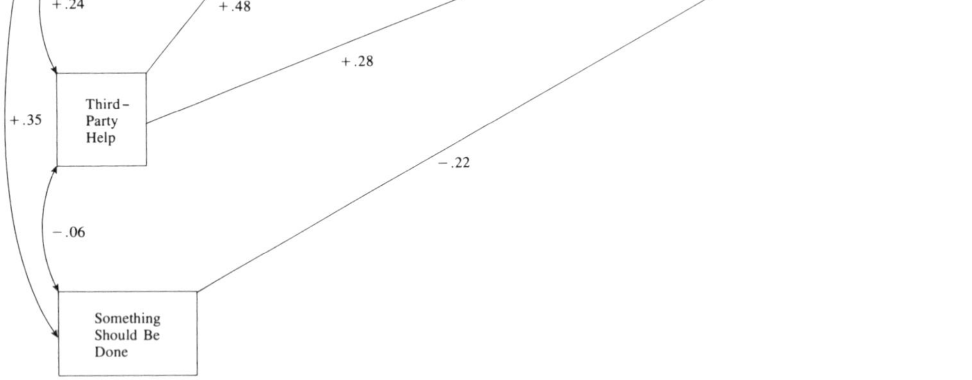

FIGURE 7.1 Path diagram for the best-fitting linear model describing the sequential process among the endogenous variables.

out in anticipation of potential legal remedies without actual contact with an attorney. The more likely it is that a dispute is the kind for which legal remedies exist, the more likely it is that lawyers are contacted, and vice versa.

Seeing a lawyer increases the probability that some sort of legal action is taken. Disputes for which legal remedies exist are also the sort that generate more contacts with attorneys. But it is the kind of dispute that is more likely to generate a favorable outcome that is more likely to generate specific legal actions by attorneys. Legal process appears to have a teleological structure in which disputes are more likely to move through the process if succeeding stages are more likely to produce satisfactory results. At the end of the process, there is a very strong positive correlation between the extent to which disputes yield objectively favorable outcomes and the level of satisfaction among claimants.

The path analysis for the seven original endogenous variables reveals that, in the aggregate, it may be more useful to treat secondary legal process variables as endogenous, and prelegal variables as exogenous. It is the *legal* character of the dispute that gives it special meaning. The initial decision to do something about a problem is explained in terms of the situational context of the individual dispute. Third parties act as referral sources for attorneys and affect the outcomes of civil legal disputes.

Correlates of the Mobilization Process

The mobilization of lawyers and succeeding stages of the mobilization process are explained by factors that are both internal and external to the process. The transformation of disputes from nonlegal to legal is explained, in part, by prelegal aspects of the transformation process. The explanation of each transformation is a necessary condition for the explanation of the next. But those variables that are exogenous to the mobilization process account for most of the variance in the mobilization of lawyers.

Table 7.2 and Figure 7.2 describe the results of a path analysis that takes into account both the situational and structural correlates of the mobilization process. Prelegal stages of the dispute process, including the invocation of legal norms, are treated as exogenous in order to isolate the determinants of legal mobilization per se. Once the different stages of the mobilization process have been explained, we can determine whether their explanations are independent of one another. This is accomplished by examining the residual correlations among the endogenous variables. The absence of a relationship between two adjacent endogenous variables indicates that the explanations of each are, in fact, independent.

TABLE 7.2
Coefficients in the Best-Fitting Linear Path Model[a]

Endogenous variables	Exogenous variables	Path coefficients (β effects)
Saw lawyer	Church membership	−.37***
	Business association	+.22*
	Politically involved	+.25*
	Contact Better Business Bureau	+.31**
	Third party	+.23*
Legal action	Politically involved	+.61***
	Discuss with friends	−.34**
	Contact public and/or private organization	+.34**
	Income	+.24*
Outcome	Visibility	−.41**
	Male	+.38*
	Strong political identification	+.53**
	Frequency of dispute	+.58***
	Third party	+.32*
Satisfaction	Politically involved	+.22*
	Contact police	+.24*
	Male	+.32**

[a] N = 23 civil disputes.
* $p < .05$; ** $p < .01$; *** $p < .001$.

The path coefficients reported in Table 7.2 are derived from a recursive system of equations (see Duncan, 1966) that represents a sequential model of legal process. The path diagram in Figure 7.2 is the best-fitting linear, recursive model describing the mobilization of law. The path coefficients describing the effects of each endogenous variable on successive endogenous legal variables disappear except for the effect of "Outcome" on "Satisfaction" ($\beta = +.56$, $p < .001$). The effect of the invocation of legal norms on contacting an attorney is reduced considerably, but remains statistically significant ($\beta = +.29$, $p < .05$). In other words, the explanation of legal contacts is independent of the explanation of the kind of legal action taken by attorneys once contacted and whether outcomes are favorable or not. The subjective evaluation of outcomes as satisfactory remains dependent on their objective result. And the invocation of legal norms affects the decision to seek the assistance of legal counsel independent of its structural determinants.

The three stages of the mobilization process in which 12 exogenous variables play a role are (1) saw a lawyer, (2) the lawyer took action, and (3) the actual outcome of the dispute (see Figure 7.2). Five of the variables are significantly correlated with the decision to contact a lawyer, four with the

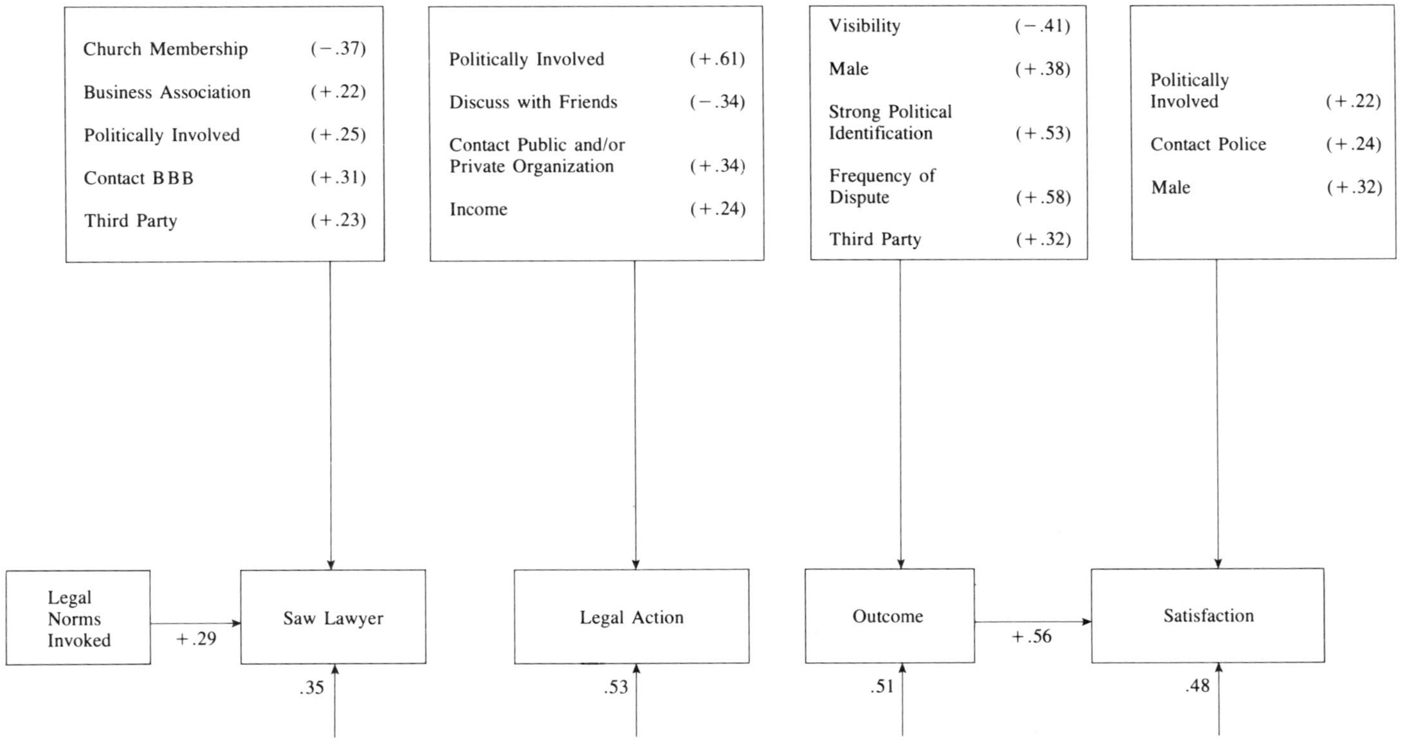

FIGURE 7.2 Path diagram for the best-fitting linear model describing the sequential model of legal process.

lawyer's decision to take some kind of formal legal action, and five with the actual outcome of the dispute. Only two of these variables, political involvement and third-party help, are activated more than once. Two of these variables and another (police contact) are associated with the subjective evaluation of the outcome as satisfactory, independent of the actual outcome itself.

Political, economic, and social activity are associated with the initial mobilization of law—contacting an attorney. The kinds of disputes that occur among the more politically active and among those who are active members of business associations or who seek assistance from such associations are more likely to go to law. The legality of disputes also depends on third-party involvement. Disputes that are embedded in political and economic institutions are more likely to become embedded in legal institutions as well. To the extent that third parties act as representatives of community interests and standards (in W. I. Thomas' (1923) terminology, third parties are "defining agents"), they are embedded in the social institutions of society. Disputes that are so embedded are also more likely to become embedded in legal institutions. In contrast, however, we find that the more disputes are embedded in religous institutions, indicated by church membership, the less likely they are to become embedded in legal institutions. This is consistent with Black's proposition (1976:107) that law varies inversely with other social control. In Black's terms, church membership is more "respectable" than nonmembership. Consequently, disputes among the less respectable are more likely to be subject to legal regulation.

Although the level of political activity among claimants is also associated with the likelihood that attorneys will take some sort of formal legal action on their behalf, the amount and kind of resources available to disputants play an important role as well. Income is an important determinant of whether or not the attorney will do something on behalf of the client. Organizational resources, public and private, provide an important stimulus to action on the part of attorneys. In contrast, the opportunity to discuss matters with close personal friends tends to reduce the demand for legal action. Whereas impersonal third parties activate initial contact with an attorney, further discussion among friends leads to a redefinition of the dispute as not worth the bother of further pursuit. Disputes among those with economic and organizational resources are more likely to be litigated in some form, whereas disputes among those with social and personal resources are more likely to be dealt with outside the courts.

Status variables play a role in determining whether outcomes are favorable or not. Disputes that are more likely to involve men are more likely to yield favorable outcomes for the claimant. For example, men are generally more likely to report consumer problems than women, whereas women are more likely to report experiencing disputes with landlords. Men are often defined as the purchasers of expensive goods; women, more frequently responsible for problems centered around the home, handle matters with landlords. To the extent that a dispute is defined as a "man's" problem, it is more likely to produce a successful result. Similarly, disputes among those who identify strongly with either of the two major political parties, Republican or Democratic, are more likely to yield favorable outcomes.

Third-party help increases the likelihood of a successful claim, whereas the visibility of the dispute reduces the chance of success. Visibility is the only situational variable that is significantly associated with any of the secondary legal variables. Once disputes become visible, it becomes more difficult to successfully resolve them in the face of intransigence among disputants. Less visible disputes imply less public commitment to a certain point of view, making attempts at reconciliation by third parties more apt to succeed. Once an attorney becomes involved and a claim has been filed, disputants become committed to battle within our adversarial legal system.

The frequency of the dispute has a stronger effect on the outcome of the dispute process than any other variable. Frequent disputes produce more institutionalized responses within the legal system, increasing the probability of their successful resolution. Conversely, the successful resolution of disputes encourages the further institutionalization of dispute-resolution mechanisms. In other words, the existence of legal remedies increases the frequency with which legal definitions are imposed on conflict situations, thus generating more disputes.

That claimants obtain favorable outcomes does not necessarily imply that their putative adversaries lost the case. The vast majority of disputes are resolved favorably, and most of these yield some sort of compromise designed to mollify both sides. Only in the very few cases that go to court do we end up with a clear cut winner-take-all situation.

The single greatest determinant of the level of satisfaction for disputes is their successful resolution. Disputes that are more likely to produce successful outcomes, for whatever reasons, are also more likely to yield satisfied citizens. Factors that play a direct role in increasing the probability of success play an indirect role in increasing the level of satisfaction. Outcomes of disputes involving the politically active and males are more likely to be labeled as satisfactory than outcomes of disputes involving the politically alienated and women. Contacting the police also increases a citizen's subjective evaluation that a dispute has ended in a satisfactory conclusion. The act of calling the police (a common occurrence in neighborhood disputes) increases a citizen's feeling that something has been accomplished, independent of whether the police have been able to help resolve the dispute. Since the act of calling the police is itself a way of punishing a neighbor who has caused a disturbance, citizens continue to call the police in such situations despite the fact that there is little they can actually accomplish.

CONCLUSION

The aggregate data support the strong version of the value-added model of the mobilization of law. The quantitative explanation of each stage of the mobilization process is independent of the preceding one. The endogenous variables, as indicators of the sequentially ordered stages of the mobilization process, are not explanatory in the statistical sense even though each is a necessary condition for the next. The mobilization process is a closed system activated by external structural mechanisms.

Although there is some overlap among the variables that activate the different stages of the legal-mobilization process, for the most part, the kinds of variables that enter into the explanation of each stage are qualitatively different. This implies that the explanation of each is qualitatively distinct. The rate of legal contacts is determined by the embeddedness of disputes in political, economic, and social institutions. The rate of legal action depends on the economic, organizational, and personal resources available to disputants. And the rate of success across dispute categories depends on the social status of the typical claimant for each kind of dispute. Political activity plays a role at virtually every stage of the mobilization process, affecting the subjective evaluation of the outcome rather than its objective result. Nevertheless, this variable is reactivated independently at each stage. In value-added terms, it contributes to the amount of law by explaining some of the variance in each endogenous variable.

The strong version of the value-added model does not hold for the prelegal or primary stages of the dispute process. These definitional aspects of disputing are not sequentially ordered in the aggregate, nor are their explanations independent. Despite controls for relevant situational and structural variables, the correlation between the invocation of legal norms and the decision to contact an attorney does not disappear. In the aggregate, the situational variables that pertain to primary process have little or no predictive value, and the structural variables that pertain to secondary legal process have no predictive value for the primary, prelegal aspects of disputing.

There is an apparent contradiction between the definitional aspects of the value-added model on the individual level and the findings derived from the aggregate analysis of dispute categories as social acts. By definition, each stage of the dispute process is a necessary condition for the next. By definition, contacting an attorney implies the invocation of legal norms, including legal norms that define the situation to be without remedy. On the other hand, there are some situations in which legal norms are invoked without further contact with an attorney. Thus, on the individual level, once we know the distribution of disputes at each stage of the process, the degree of association between any two dichotomous measures of these stages is positive, yet indeterminate (see Chapter 4). On the aggregate level, the probability distribution of each endogenous variable does not determine the probability distribution of the next. A dispute that has a relatively high *rate* of invocation of legal norms may have a relatively low *rate* of legal contacts. For example, in personal injury cases, insurance claims are frequently settled without legal intervention in light of existing remedies.

There is a tendency toward artifactual positive correlations between adjacent endogenous variables in the aggregate analysis of social process. As the proportion of cases attaining a given stage of a process approaches that of the preceding stage, the correlation between the two rates approaches +1.00. In essence, they become equivalent. It is this underlying inherent association among endogenous variables that makes social processes appear to be unitary phenomena. Since the rate of attrition in the dispute process is relatively great, correlations between adjacent variables in the sequential model are expected to be weak.

For example, since the proportion of cases that go to court is extremely small, even in relation to those that are handled by attorneys, variation in court rates are affected very little by variation in lawyer rates. Generally speaking, the empirical correlations between adjacent stages of the dispute process reflect real, rather than definitional, associations.

The strong intercorrelations among the endogenous variables (see Table 7.1) and their path coefficients (see Figure 7.1) describe the sequentially ordered linkage among the stages of the mobilization process. Thus the mobilization process appears to be a closed system. But when we take into account the effects of the exogenous variables on each stage of the process, we find that most of the endogenous effects disappear. Once we account for the variance in one endogenous variable, its apparent effect on the next disappears. In only one instance do we find a residual effect of one endogenous variable on another in the regression analysis; the effect of "Outcome" on "Satisfaction" cannot be explained in terms of the effects of the exogenous variables on the remaining endogenous variables. This indicates that the effects of the actual outcomes of disputes on their subjective evaluation are real.

To summarize, these findings establish support for the strong version of the value-added model of the mobilization of law. Explanations of the sequentially ordered stages of the mobilization process are independent of one another. Moreover, the transformation of disputes into legal claims is determined by structural factors that are exogenous to the mobilization process. Definitional processes prior to the actual mobilization of attorneys also play a role in the transformation of disputes into legal claims.

8

CONCLUSION

SUMMARY OF FINDINGS

In the preceding chapters, we found a considerable amount of evidence supporting the strong version of the value-added model of legal process (see Figure 1.1). Figures 4.3 and 7.2 summarize the individual and aggregate data, respectively. On the individual level, each stage of the dispute process is explained by a distinct set of situational variables. As disputes are transformed into legal claims, structural factors begin to play a role, with economic and organizational variables especially important in explaining the mobilization of attorneys. Since its determinants have both primary and secondary characteristics, third-party involvement becomes a critical point in the transition from prelegal dispute to legal matter. Third-party involvement is affected by two situational characteristics of disputes: persistence and visibility. Persistent, visible disputes eventually come to the attention of third parties who may attempt to mediate or who may recommend courses of action to one or other of the disputants. In addition, property ownership plays a role in mobilizing third parties as representatives of community norms or standards. Third parties are part of the situation, but they often become more than this. As intermediaries in the dispute process, they may evoke legal or nonlegal standards of conduct when trying to settle disputes. If alternative mechanisms of dispute resolution are available, disputes are less likely to be defined as serious and are less likely to become legal matters. On the other hand, third parties frequently encourage disputants to seek legal remedies when disputes are defined as too serious to be handled by alternative means.

In the aggregate, disputes are legally defined, structurally determined, social acts. Each stage of the mobilization of law is explained independently of the next in the sequence. Moreover, the kinds of exogenous variables associated with each stage are qualitatively different. Embeddedness in political and economic institutions is critical in determining the initial mobilization of lawyers, but economic and organizational resources play an important role in determining the legal action attorneys take. The social status of the claimant affects the actual outcome of the dispute; higher-status persons are more likely to achieve what they initially expected. The mobilization of police in civil legal matters only affects the subjective evaluation of the outcome; claimants are more likely to be satisfied with the outcome of disputes in matters involving the police than in other matters, regardless of their actual outcome.

One variable, the situational visibility of the dispute, consistently violates the principle of independence central to the value-added model. Visibility interacts with relational distance to reduce the latter's effect on the seriousness of disputes. Similarly, the effects of property ownership on third-party involvement and contacting a lawyer are reduced when disputes are relatively visible. And finally, visible disputes are less likely to produce favorable outcomes than those processed with less public visibility. This suggests that visible disputes are embedded in and subject to the definition of the situation, regardless of the factors that otherwise affect the transformation of disputes into legal claims. The visibility of disputes reduces the impact of other situational and structural variables in both the primary (dispute) and secondary (mobilization) phases of legal process.

Figure 8.1 summarizes the research pertaining to the value-added model of legal process. Situational variables principally affect the dispute process, the primary or prelegal phase of the dispute transformation process, whereas structural variables principally affect the mobilization of law, the secondary or legal phase of the process. Prior to the mobilization of lawyers, the dispute process cannot be explained by institutional or structural factors. Only third-party involvement is affected by the structural location of the dispute. Once everyday disputes have been transformed into legal claims, their situational characteristics no longer play a role in the way in which they are processed. Economic, political, and organizational variables affect the mobilization of lawyers, legal action taken, and the outcome of disputes, but these effects are mitigated by their public visibility. The public visibility of disputes determines the way in which they are defined, the way in which they are processed, and their outcomes.

The Situational Context of Disputing

In general, the social control of everyday disputes can be understood in terms of the characteristics of the social situations that determine how they are evaluated and, consequently, processed. Relational distance between disputants and the availability of alternative dispute-resolution mechanisms affect the evaluation of the seriousness of the problem as part of the process by which citizens decide to seek legal assistance for everyday disputes. The visibility of a dispute plays a large role in determining the way it is processed; visibility entails its own constraints. The absence of visibility intensifies the effect of relational distance on seriousness. Visibility, along with persistence,

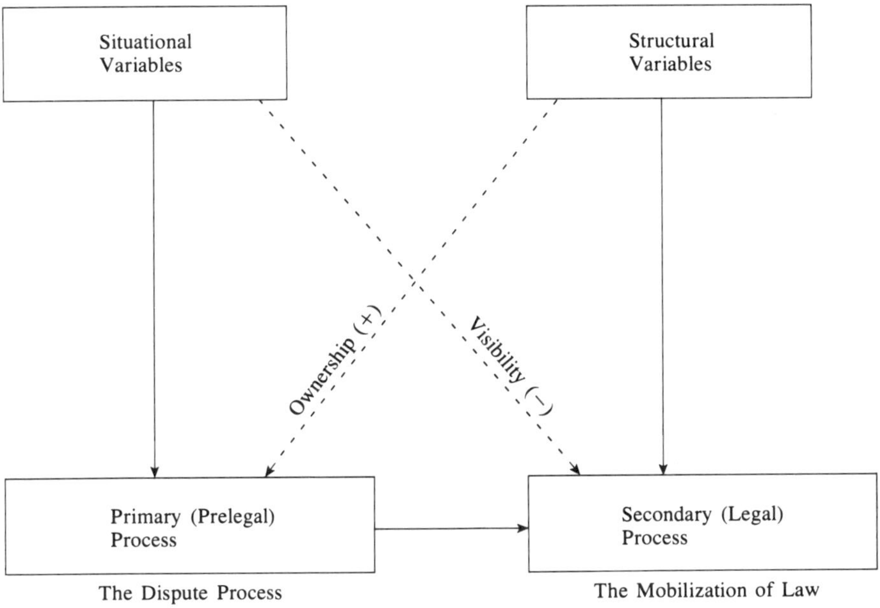

FIGURE 8.1 A value-added model of legal process.

increases the likelihood of third-party involvement in the mobilization process. The availability of alternatives is a situational factor to the extent that the very existence of alternatives affects how disputes are evaluated and processed. However, the direct positive effect of this variable on the mobilization of law suggests that it represents structured access to legality by providing institutionalized roles whose occupants act as authority figures in recommending that someone see a lawyer.

Disputes between distant parties are more likely to produce a legal response than those involving closely related parties. Moreover, the evaluation of disputes as serious fully explains this relationship between relational distance and law. Variations in the way in which disputes are evaluated are a direct function of relational distance; disputes between distant parties are relatively serious, especially when they are not readily observable. And serious disputes are the sort that, according to those involved, ought to be the subject of legal control.

By incorporating seriousness as a variable in the model, we know something more about the process by which citizens decide to mobilize the law. The objective nature of the relationships between disputing parties affects the likelihood that disputes will be evaluated subjectively as serious. In other words, the subjective evaluation of disputes as serious can be explained in objective, quantitative terms. It should be noted that the relative persistence of the dispute does not directly affect its evaluation as serious, despite the fact that persistence appears to be an objective indicator of seriousness.

The transformation of disputes from everyday problems to legal matters follows a sequentially ordered, value-added process that is relatively strong (see Figure 4.3). In the strong version of the value-added model of social process, each stage of the process is explained independently. In the weak version, it is assumed that the exogenous variables affect each stage of the process equally. Each prelegal stage of the process is uniquely explained by particular situational factors. Seriousness is explained by the availability of alternatives and relational distance; third-party involvement is explained by the persistence and visibility of the dispute. At the point of transition to legal mobilization, the model weakens. Situational and structural properties, represented by visibility and ownership, respectively, interact with third-party involvement and the use of lawyers as if to connect two otherwise distinct processes: social control and legal control. Third-party involvement is truly a transitional stage that transforms the social control of everyday disputes, which varies according to the situational context of the dispute, into the legal control of disputes between parties whose access to lawyers depends on their relative position in the social structures of society. It is precisely because third parties bring interests other than their own into the situation that the structural properties surrounding the dispute become relevant. Since law is enforceable through third parties who represent the interests of the community (however those interests are defined), third parties are crucial intermediaries in the mobilization of law in general, and of lawyers in particular.

The Structural Context of Disputing

Structural factors play an important role in the mobilization of lawyers for everyday disputes. In general, increases in wealth and the ownership of property increase the likelihood of legal contacts. But among the wealthiest individuals, there is a tendency to avoid legal confrontation when involved in disputes that do not involve property. Participation in the organizational life of the community also increases the likelihood that disputants will contact an attorney. The effects of education and ethnicity disappear, however, once economic and organizational factors are taken into account. To some extent, blacks are denied access to the law because of their class position. Once the effects of income and ownership are taken into account, the association between race and the use of lawyers disappears. In other words, cultural differences in the way in which whites and blacks experience life's daily problems do not affect what they do about them. Similarly, the well educated are more likely to have access to attorneys because of their income, employment status, ownership of property, and participation in organizations, not because they are more aware of their legal rights than those who are less educated.

Had cultural factors, instead of or in addition to structural factors, played a role in the dispute process, there would have been residual effects in the causal analysis that incorporated these variables. But there were none. If we assume that, on the average, the better educated are more aware of their legal rights than those with less education, and knowing one's rights increases the probability that one will pursue legal remedies, we should expect education to affect the use of lawyers, independent of the effects of wealth and property. But there is no such effect. Were we to assume that cultural differences between blacks and whites play a role in the dispute process, we should find race and legal contacts correlated once the effects of wealth and property were taken into account. But they are not.

There are cultural differences in how blacks and whites define their experiences with *legal* matters. For example, blacks tend to treat buying a home as a relatively serious matter. For many, theirs is the first generation to have such an experience. But these differences do not translate into differences in the propensity to contact attorneys. To the extent that whites are more likely to have access to attorneys because of their economic status, they are more likely to contact attorneys for matters unrelated to property.

Although there may be individual differences in knowledge of legal rights, they do not appear to be a function of cultural factors, including formal schooling. On the other hand, those who have had prior legal experience may be more aware of their legal rights than those who have not. But then a correlation between legal knowledge and the use of lawyers would be a spurious function of the structural context that generated access in the first place. In the United States, the standards and expectations that are part of its legal culture are so widespread that there is little variation in legal knowledge by class, race, or other social category. Legal knowledge is a constant, not a variable, in American society. America is, after all, a litigious society (Lieberman, 1981).

The Community Context of Disputing

The contextual effect of the social-class composition of the community on the use of lawyers is especially important for understanding how everyday disputes between citizens and their neighbors, landlords, employers, or government agencies are processed by the civil justice system. The effects of wealth and property on the use of lawyers are mediated entirely by the contextual effect of the distribution of wealth in the community. In the modern urban context, the distribution of wealth and legal resources, not cultural tradition, determine how everyday disputes are defined and whether or not they are transformed into legal claims. The class composition of the community is affected by the wealth of its residents, the ownership of property, and its location in suburbia. But it is only the class composition of the community that directly affects the mobilization of lawyers for everyday disputes. Residents of low-income communities are relatively unlikely to contact a lawyer when faced with disputes. They are even less likely to contact a lawyer than one would expect given their income and property status. Residents of upper-income communities in the city of Detroit and residents of middle-income communities in the suburbs are among those most likely to contact a lawyer to handle such matters.

Since residents of upper-income communities are especially likely to know someone personally who is an attorney, or to have a close personal relationship with someone who can refer them to an attorney, the opportunity to contact an attorney increases with the aggregate wealth of the community. Residents of low-income communities also rely on close relations for information about attorneys, but poor people rarely know someone personally who is an attorney. Among those who live within the city limits of Detroit, the odds pertaining to the use of lawyers increase with the wealth of the community. But residents of upper-income suburban communities are less likely than their urban counterparts to pursue legal remedies for their everyday problems.

The use of legal services is largely an upper-middle-class phenomenon. Those who are most likely to contact a lawyer are upper-middle-class residents of middle-income suburban communities and the residents of upper-income communities within the city.

In summary, the dispute process occurs in the context of specific communities. How disputes are defined and whether they are transformed into legal claims depends on the distribution of economic and legal resources in the community. The mobilization of lawyers depends on opportunity structures that are defined in economic and legal terms. The effects of structural variables on secondary legal process for property matters and other institutionalized legal relations are direct, but the effects of social structure on the mobilization of lawyers for everyday disputes are indirect. When legal remedies are less clearly available, the decision to contact a lawyer is affected by the structure of opportunities to do so. This structure is affected by the distribution of wealth in the community, that is, on its class composition. Consequently, the transformation of disputes into legal claims is shaped by the social class context in which they occur.

THEORETICAL IMPLICATIONS

A great deal has been written on theories of social control. It is not my intention in this chapter to present a new theory, but rather to show where the present work fits in the general scheme of things. I have developed a framework for the analysis of social process that facilitates the testing of specific theoretical propositions within a single, multivariate model. I have demonstrated how to quantify process models that have been treated previously in a descriptive, qualitative manner. Not only does this new method facilitate rigorous hypothesis testing, but it also makes it possible to evaluate the assumption that social process is value-added. In particular, I have shown that the explanation of each stage in the value-added model of the dispute process is independent of the next, and vice versa.

This finding is especially important because it implies that the results of previous research on social process may be quite misleading. Both qualitative and quantitative studies that attempt to identify the correlates of a particular stage of a given process, say receiving the death penalty in the criminal justice system, often misidentify the correlates of preceding stages of the process. So, for example, blacks may receive the death penalty more frequently than whites, not because of racial discrimination during court proceedings, but because they are more likely to be indicted for first-degree homicide (see Radelet, 1981). Only when we control for preceding stages in a given process, recognizing its sequential nature, can we properly identify the correlates of any given stage. When doing so, it is also necessary to take into account the empty cells generated by the conditional relationships between the different stages in the process. When one stage is a necessary condition for the next, there can be no cases in which events pass through the second stage, but not the first. Thus, an analysis of process variables relying on contingency tables must, theoretically speaking, have empty cells.

The value-added model of social process has its roots in structural-functionalist approaches to social theory. The basic theoretical concern is whether given structural conditions are conducive to particular outcomes. Smelser (1962:1–22) argues that dysfunctional conditions such as structural strain, hostile beliefs, and tension between groups precipitate episodes of collective behavior. By implication, functional relations between structural components of society produce rational behavior and stable social relationships.

Critics of this approach consider the study of dispute resolution fundamentally conservative in its implications (see Cain and Kulscár, 1982). To identify the situational and structural conditions conducive to that resolution is to determine how best to maintain the status quo. If we see disputes as expressions of underlying conflicts of interest between social classes or groups in society (e.g., landlords and tenants) then strategies designed to resolve disputes do not address the fundamental sources of conflict that generate disputes in the first place.

I recognize that disputes frequently originate in the conflicting interests of different classes and other strata within society. But it is not the purpose of the present research to address this issue, the proper concern of some conflict theorists and Marxists. Rather, its purpose is to provide a framework for testing theoretical predictions derived from a variety of approaches to the study of law and society. The research describes how class position plays a role in the mobilization of lawyers. But it also specifies the conditions under which lower-class citizens can and do mobilize legal resources to protect their interests in a democratic society. I do not take as given either the proposition that law only reflects the interests of elites, nor that it only reflects the will of the people. What the value-added approach makes problematic is the extent to which legal process reflects the ability of the average citizen to mobilize state power to protect his or her individual interests or those of the group or groups he or she represents.

The model presented in this book describes objectively the process by which disputes are transformed into legal claims. No matter what the origin of the initial normative violation that gave rise to the dispute, the course of its resolution (or lack of resolution) is determined by the situational and structural location of the dispute in the community. The obverse of explaining how a dispute moves from one stage to another is explaining why a dispute does not do so, or why it exits from the process at a given stage. Just as economic resources explain the use of lawyers for certain disputes, the absence of such resources explains why lawyers are not contacted in many cases. Thus, the structure of the environment in which disputes occur determines whether they remain unresolved or become resolved to the satisfaction of the disputants. Many cases exit from the system before they end in a satisfactory legal solution. Moreover, I do not assume, as some apparently do (Galanter, 1975:69; 1976) that going to see a lawyer is a good thing to do, that law is inherently beneficial. I agree with Turk (1976) that law frequently intensifies conflicts between parties; it is a weapon that can be used to increase one party's position to the detriment of another.

The value-added model of legal process integrates macro- and microlevels of analysis, a major objective in the development of scientific sociology (see Collins, 1975:14, for a more complete discussion of this matter). The model accomplishes this by integrating primary (situational or microlevel) and secondary (structural or macrolevel) legal processes within a single framework. Moreover, the dispute process is analyzed on the microlevel within a social constructionist, phenomenologically oriented, symbolic interactionist framework, one that is consistent with the conflict approach to macrolevel analysis

(Collins, 1975:91). This is reinforced further by John Lofland's work on value-added models of microprocesses (see Lofland and Stark, 1965) and his contention that conflict and power play a major role in determining how events are defined and labeled (Lofland, 1969:13–24).

I conclude, therefore, that there is nothing inherently conservative or progressive, structural-functionalist or conflict oriented, in the value-added model of legal process. It is an analytic framework within which a variety of theoretical propositions can be tested, regardless of their origins.

Primary and Secondary Legal Process

The distinction between primary and secondary legal process is built principally on the work of H. L. A. Hart (1961:77–96) and Edwin Lemert (1951:75–78). Hart distinguishes between primary and secondary rules of law, whereas Lemert distinguishes between primary and secondary deviance, actions that violate rules, including violations of substantive law. Primary rules are those for which there is a moral obligation to obey. This obligation is manifest in terms of some probability ("prediction" in Hart's terms) of obedience to norms supported and enforced by the community. Secondary rules of law are procedural rules supported and enforced by the legal community. The enforcement of and moral support for substantive criminal laws are correlated, but variable, qualities of legal rules (Silberman, 1976). In this sense, both legality and morality can be seen as variable characteristics of legal rules. Whereas Hart argues that social support is necessary for legal regulation, there is evidence (Silberman, 1976; 1979) that legal regulation affects moral regulation and conformity to legal rules. Primary and secondary legal process (moral and legal regulation) are mutually embedded phases of a single social process, the social control of conduct through the resolution of disputes.

Secondary legal process reflects attempts by citizens to mobilize state power to protect their collective or individual interests. Since the mobilization of law in democratically organized societies is primarily reactive in nature, calling the police and contacting an attorney are attempts to use state power on behalf of the victim or claimant. Primary process implies the use of informal mechanisms of social control in the prelegal processing of disputes, whereas secondary process implies the use of formal mechanisms of legal control in settling disputes that have been transformed into legal claims.

Primary Process and Symbolic Interactionism

Empirical work on the dispute process has largely been uninformed by a systematic theoretical framework. As I indicated earlier, the interactionist perspective guides the present work. One of the few scholars to understand the significance of this perspective for the explanation of the civil legal process is Neil Shover (1973) who, in his article "The Civil Justice Process as Societal Reactions," recognizes that the definitional process is central to our understanding of civil legal problems; definitions of legal problems shape and are shaped by the objective features of the situations in which these problems arise. Shover (1973:255) adds, "The civil justice process is a reality-defining one in which interactional processes at several stages shape the emergent problem definition." Unfortunately, Shover's discussion is too general, providing little direction with respect to the specification of variables for research purposes. This is a common complaint about interactionism, which is often presented as a perspective, rather than a well-articulated theory.

Edwin Lemert's (1951:37–44) work on societal reactions to deviance provides a rich framework from which to derive an explanation of the dispute process. Lemert distinguishes between individual, situational, and systemic sources of deviation. Individual variables result "from the special way in which social and cultural influences impinge upon and interact with normal [biological and psychological] qualities of the person" (Lemert, 1951:37). For example, some individuals may be more disputatious or litigious than others. Systemic variables reflect more or less organized patterns of activity and communication about such activity (Lemert, 1951:44). Disputes are shaped by the informal network of associations that define them in legal terms. Friends who have already played the client role in similar situations convey to others the costs and benefits of occupying such a role.

But it is the situational context of the dispute process that is of greatest interest here. According to Lemert (1951:37), situational variables reflect "forces in the situation external to the person." Lemert adds that "situations have a compelling force" that cannot be reduced to the idiosyncratic characteristics of the individuals who are an integral part of these situations. The very structure of the situations in which disputes occur may transform such disputes into legal claims, regardless of the disputatiousness of the participants or their familiarity with the attorney–client relationship.

According to Lemert (1951:38), time and space are important dimensions of the social situation. In the present study, the time dimension of the social situation is operationalized in terms of the relative persistence of disputes. Some disputes last longer than others, and the longer they last, the more difficult it is to ignore them. In other words, we can expect persistent disputes to be transformed into legal claims more frequently than those that are less persistent. The relational distance between disputants is a spatial dimension of the social situation, one that affects the perceived seriousness of the dispute. Disputes between distant parties are, in general, defined as more serious than those between intimates. And these are more likely to involve attorneys.

Lemert (1951:51) also treats social visibility as an important dimension of the social situation. In general, we expect more frequent societal reactions when events are publicly visible. In the case of disputing, third parties are more likely to become involved, and when they do, they tend to refer difficult cases to attorneys. When high visibility is due to the nature of the situation itself, societal reactions become standardized (Lemert, 1951:52). In other words, the visibility of disputes constrains certain responses by third parties, regardless of the status of the individuals involved. But when disputes are less visible, the characteristics of the social situation no longer determine the course of action taken by the disputing parties. In the present study, we have discovered that the social status of the individual plays a role in the transformation process for disputes with a low degree of visibility.

In many cases, "the situation is so structured as to reduce the limits of possible responses" (Lemert, 1951:38). In other situations, alternative responses may be readily available to disputants. By increasing options, the availability of alternatives should reduce the likelihood of legal contacts for everyday disputes. As a situational variable, culture shapes the dispute process by supporting mechanisms of social control embedded in the situation (see Lemert, 1951:40, for a discussion of aspects of American culture that facilitate social deviance). According to Lemert (1951:40), urban location yields less frequent use of mechanisms of social control than suburban or rural areas because of a "breakdown" in traditional forms of social regulation. This should result in increased legal intervention in urban areas.

The interactionist framework has proved to be extremely helpful in generating hypotheses in the study of the transformation of disputes into legal claims. The transformation process is explained by the situational context in which disputes occur. This context shapes the dispute process more or less as expected, but it is a complicated process that takes a complex, multivariate statistical analysis to disentangle.

Secondary Process and Mobilization Theory

The mobilization of law is a special category of political mobilization, one that reflects the legitimate use of state power. The use of state power is lawful to the extent that it is regulated by a set of explicit procedural rules, the violation of which is routinely sanctioned. The mobilization of law is the mobilization of legal officials who create and enforce legal rules when using the legitimate coercive power of the state to support certain acts and prohibit others. Legal mobilization in a modern state enforces the interests of one party against those of another (see Chambliss and Seidman, 1971:28–35). The very process by which disputes are resolved on a winner-take-all basis serves to cast the norm-enforcing agency in a norm-creating role (Chambliss and Seidman; 1971:35). Although law enforcement and law creation are analytically distinct conceptualizations, they are often empirically indistinguishable. The study of the mobilization of law, properly conceived, is the study of both its enforcement and its creation.

Legal process in the United States is predominantly reactive in nature, initiated by citizens as complainants in civil suits or as victims of crime (see Reiss, 1971; Black, 1973). Albert J. Reiss, Jr. (1971:88) defines police dependency on citizen complaints as reactive mobilization and the policy of actively seeking out criminal violations as proactive mobilization. Many studies of police behavior focus on initiatives taken by the police when enforcing the law through devices such as entrapment and selective enforcement (see Skolnick, 1966; Chevigny, 1969), but there is ample evidence that most police action depends on citizen initiative (see Reiss and Bordua, 1967; Reiss, 1971; Lundman, 1980). Reiss argues that the mobilization of police by individual citizens is the predominant way in which events come to be defined as crimes. He attributes the predominance of reactive mobilization to the technological problems associated with the institutionalized protections of procedural rights limiting access to places identified as private (also, see Stinchcombe, 1963:158). Reiss (1971:118) also recognizes that the police respond to political pressure from powerful interest groups.

The proactive mobilization of law by attorneys is prohibited in the United States, although this does occur from time to time in the form of ambulance chasing. Moreover, many law firms employ less overt proactive strategies for generating business. In principle, the enforcement of contracts, torts, and property law cannot be initiated by attorneys or other officials (Black, 1973:128), but in reality this does occur. Nevertheless, citizens initiate the vast majority of lawyer–client contacts (Mayhew and Reiss, 1969; Mayhew, 1975).

Hart (1961:85) defines criminal law in terms of a coercive order maintained by public officials and civil law as rights and responsibilities delegated to private individuals or groups "who may choose whether or not to insist on performance or exact the penalty." On the other hand, Weber (1978:643) argues, "The delimitation of the spheres of public and private law is *even today* not entirely free from difficulty" (italics added). Zemans (1983:691) points out that "The very nature of the judicial process blurs the private-public distinction." The public or private nature of law does not depend on substantive differences, but on the relationship between the state and the individual. When officials mobilize the law to achieve some policy objective, law is proactive and public. When citizens mobilize the law because of interpersonal or group conflicts, law is reactive and private. But the actions of private individuals may in the long run produce changes in public policy (Zemans, 1983:692). And changes in public policy may alter incentives for private parties to litigate disputes. In this study, we are interested in citizen mobilization of lawyers with regard to civil legal disputes; in other words, this is a study of private law.

The fact that this is a study of the use of coercive state power by subordinates is consistent with a theory of law that admits that moral obligations may become legal ones. The study of citizen mobilization is the study of the reactive process by which socially defined rights and obligations are transformed into legal rights and obligations. Two sources of proactive mobilization of legal agents are (1) organized groups who, by virtue of their political or economic power, are able to shape the policies and practices of police departments, law firms, legal departments, legal-services agencies, and (2) state agencies that act to protect their own organizational interests. In democratically organized societies, the mobilization of law is primarily reactive, whereas in totalitarian societies, legal mobilization is predominantly proactive (see Wrong, 1979:158–179).

Law as an Economic, Political, and Organizational Phenomenon

In his book *The Behavior of Law*, Black (1976) presents a theory of law that is composed of a number of propositions concerning the effects of economic, political, and organizational variables on legal behavior, several of which have been evaluated in the present study (see, especially, Chapter 5). Law is an economic, political, and organizational phenomenon. Legal rules regulate economic activity, and, in fact, it is difficult at times to distinguish between these rules and the relations of production they regulate. Private property is a legal concept that, along with other principles of capitalism, has become institutionalized in the mores and law-ways of capitalist societies. Similarly, law is an integral part of the governmental process. And, finally, law is organizational (Mayhew and Reiss, 1969; Galanter 1974). Since law is part of the bureaucratic apparatus of the state (Lenin, 1965), much of what has been written about complex organizations applies to legal process. Research on courts in particular (e.g., Blumberg, 1967) has focused on the effects of the bureaucratic features of the legal system on the way in which criminal cases are processed. Galanter's (1974) work on the role of repeat players in the judicial system is consistent with this principle, although this conceptualization is outside the mainstream of organizational theory.

The way in which law behaves in relation to its external concomitants depends on the embeddedness of each in the law itself. Thus, economic variables affect the mobilization of law differently for economic matters that are in themselves institutionalized parts of the legal system than for matters that are not. When disputes concern property rights, there is a direct, linear effect of the economy on law. When disputes occur between neighbors or between landlords and tenants, when services are inadequate, when consumer items do not work properly, or when other everyday problems occur, the effect of economic variables on the mobilization of law is curvilinear.

Political activity does not play a direct role in the mobilization of law for individual disputes, but, in the aggregate, the polity is a correlate of the legality of different types of civil legal disputes. The link between polity and legality is especially evident in disputes between citizens and government agencies. In general, the kinds of disputes that are most likely to involve an attorney are those with government agencies, especially when they are relatively serious. Disputes with public welfare agencies and with the police are the two kinds of disputes with governmental agencies that are most likely to involve legal counsel. This is the case despite the absence of readily available free legal services for the poor at the time of the study. Disputes that are embedded in the political process are most likely to lead to the mobilization of attorneys, independent of the economic resources of the individual disputant.

And, finally, organizational life plays an indirect role in the mobilization of law by affecting the way in which disputes are defined and processed. Alternative dispute-resolution mechanisms are part of the organizational life of the community. Their presence in the community reduces the seriousness of disputes and, thus, the need to seek legal remedies. The organizational life of the community plays an indirect role through the development of personal and impersonal networks that increase or decrease access to legally oriented definitions of situations and, ultimately, access to attorneys themselves. Class-linked opportunity structures, too, affect the probability that a lawyer will be contacted in a given matter. But the most direct effect of organization on law is the result of participation in the organizational life of the community. Not only are organizations more likely to be "repeat players," using the legal system to their advantage more frequently than individuals (Galanter, 1974), but individuals who participate in organizational life are more likely to play the game of law, and to do so successfully.

To conclude, it is difficult to separate law from its economic, political, and organizational components. The economy, the polity, and social organization are both part of law and part of its determinants.

Urban Communities as Semi-Autonomous Social Fields

Disputes are transformed within the context of the communities in which they occur. Communities vary in the way in which disputes are defined and processed. They constitute semi-autonomous social fields in the sense that they provide independent normative frameworks within which daily routines are given meaning. Modern urban communities differ from traditional societies because the conditions associated with legality depend not on custom, but on the distribution of economic, organizational, and legal resources.

The single most important contextual property of communities that affects the legality of disputes in the Detroit metropolitan area is the social-class composition of the community; the *distribution* of wealth determines the way in which disputes are processed. The location of the community interacts with the distribution of wealth so that disputes in affluent suburban communities are less likely to become legal matters than one would otherwise expect.

Wealth is a correlate of intimate contact with persons who are attorneys, but relying on impersonal referral networks in selecting attorneys is a characteristic of those who reside in *middle*-class communities. The resident of the middle-class suburban community is more likely than any other to rely on such networks, readily defining disputes in legal terms, whereas the urban middle class is more likely to rely on direct self-help and informal mediation (see Buckle and Thomas-Buckle, 1982). Residents of urban middle-class communities are less likely than their suburban counterparts to rely on formal mediation, lawyers, or courts in resolving disputes.

In her review of the research on the neighborhood justice movement, Merry (1982) reports that the existence of alternative mechanisms for dispute resolution does not decrease the amount of formal litigation. If anything, there is evidence that disputes that would otherwise have been avoided, negotiated, or mediated informally are referred to neighborhood justice centers. Moreover, most cases are referred to mediation at neighborhood justice centers by the courts themselves. Thus, it is evident that these centers have not become the alternative that they were intended to be. The evidence presented here is consistent with these findings; third-party intervention increases rather than decreases the probability of disputes being transformed into legal claims. Paradoxically, however, the existence of alternative mechanisms of dispute resolution indirectly decreases the probability of legal intervention by reducing the relative seriousness of the dispute. Residents of communities in which alternative mechanisms of dispute resolution are available are more likely to rely on some sort of self-help approach first, then seek the assistance of intermediaries, and should this fail, seek legal counsel. In the absence of alternatives, disputants are more likely to be litigious. As Buckle and Thomas-Buckle and Merry have argued, neighborhood justice centers have not adapted to existing community patterns of dispute settlement, but have superimposed another layer of bureaucracy on the court system.

The social organization of community life creates opportunities to learn how to handle disputes. These opportunity structures include "coping networks," which offer emotional support and, at the same time, shape the process by which a dispute will be conducted (Buckle and Thomas-Buckle, 1982:88). Impersonal attorney referral networks also play an important role in shaping the conduct of disputants. Whereas coping networks facilitate self-help among disputants, referral networks encourage disputants to seek legal remedies. The nature of these opportunity structures, or networks, is determined by the distribution of economic, organizational, and legal resources that provide the context within which community expectations are formed. The absence of community and the availability of alternative mechanisms of dispute resolution are two conditions of legality that affect the transformation of disputes into legal claims. The atomization of life in some suburban communities encourages the avoidance of confrontation, since residents have no stake in maintaining continuing relationships (see Baumgartner, 1980:95). On the other hand, the existence of alternative mechanisms of dispute resolution implies greater social solidarity in the community. With more avenues for handling them, everyday problems seem to be less serious, and disputants are less likely to jump to the most extreme, often legal, remedies available.

IMPLICATIONS FOR FUTURE RESEARCH

Social surveys are ideally suited to the systematic study of all aspects of the dispute process. Although the dispute is the unit of analysis, the disputant is the basic object of our sampling procedure. Since disputants are located in the situations and social structures in which disputes emerge, they act as informants, albeit not neutral ones, by providing case histories of the disputes that they have experienced. Sampling disputes in this way is similar to cluster or area sampling where the sampling unit is the household. All disputes encountered in each household constitute a random sample of the universe of disputes. Some households may generate no disputes in the sample, some only one, and still others may generate several. Any subset of disputes defined substantively, geographically, or temporally constitutes a random sample of that subset of the universe of disputes.

The survey method has several advantages over other approaches (see Chapter 2 for a more complete discussion of the pros and cons of this methodology). The most important consideration is that it represents an attempt to map the entire dispute process from beginning to end. Strategies that select among cases that have gone to court, or some other later point in the process, are subject to sample selection bias. This is especially true when they attempt to reconstruct case histories retrospectively. The problem of biased reporting of past events is problematic in all social research, but even more so in retrospective studies of legal events. It is not possible to obtain valid estimates of the correlates of earlier stages in the civil dispute process when a study only incorporates cases that have gone through a later stage.

The high rate of attrition of cases as they move from one stage of the dispute process to the next is one disadvantage of the survey method. Fortunately, statistical techniques that are suited to the analysis of highly skewed frequency distributions have been developed (see Goodman, 1978) and are employed in the present research. When properly conceived, process models generate theoretically empty cells in contingency tables involving relationships between endogenous variables. This problem is solved theoretically and empirically once we realize that each variable is a necessary condition for the next (see Appendix A).

The sequential model of legal process can be adapted to the study of legal change. Use of the survey method to collect case histories at several points in time makes it possible to integrate cohort analysis and the log-linear method employed in the present research (see Glenn, 1977; Silberman, 1978). The "period" effect (time) in cohort analysis can be incorporated in the value-added model of legal process as an exogenous variable. The question becomes: To what extent is the transformation of disputes into legal claims affected by external events linked to certain periods of time, such as changing legislation? Similarly, the "cohort" effect can be treated as exogenous to the dispute process. Certain events may affect some age-cohorts differently from others. For example, persons who grew up during the Vietnam War era may respond differently to disputes than those who grew up before or after that period. Aging, too, is a correlate of disputing. In order to assess accurately the effect of time (period) on the dispute process, we must control for differences among cohorts in the way in which disputes are defined and processed. The effect of time (if there is one) on the dispute process is manifest as change in the rate of transformation from one stage of the dispute to the next.

Time is an exogenous variable, but its effects are manifest as changes in the causal structure defining the relationships among the endogenous variables. In other words, if time affects the dispute process, it does so by changing the underlying structure of relations among components of the legal system. One manifestation of such change would be an increase in litigiousness brought about by an increase in the supply of attorneys, changing community standards, or expanding legal rights. Of further interest is change in legal process that reflects increases or decreases in differential opportunities to seek legal redress. This sort of change is indicated by the interaction effect of time and social structure on the rate of transformation of disputes from one stage of the dispute process to the next. A significant negative interaction involving the effect of time and income on legal contacts would indicate a reduction in the degree of inequality between the "haves" and "have-nots" in access to legal resources. In summary, the survey of disputes, if repeated systematically over time, is ideally suited to the study of legal change.

The Study of Social Process

Sequential models of social process historically have been qualitative and descriptive. Quantification of process models in some contemporary work has been limited to the analysis of one stage, or step, at a time or to retrospective studies of selected cases. In this book, I have quantified a sequential model of legal process within a framework that makes it possible to incorporate the entire process within a single, multivariate causal model.

The value-added approach specifies a particular causal structure in which the explanation of each stage of the process is independent of the explanation of the next. The value-added model holds, more or less, for the dispute process, but it need not do so for other social processes. In the case of the dispute process, there are two distinct phases, primary and secondary, that are explained by situational and structural variables, respectively. Various specific stages within each phase are also explained by different subsets of exogenous variables.

The sequential model of social process has numerous applications. One of the most obvious is in the analysis of cases processed by the criminal justice system. Victimization surveys are ideally suited to the process analysis of criminal cases. By studying criminal victimizations, we are turning our attention away from the study of defendants to the study of criminal acts. Moreover, this avoids the problem of sample selection bias inherent in research that relies on the analysis of official data, that is, on cases that have been reported to the police. Since many crimes go unreported, the analysis of criminal acts should begin with the experiences of the victims of crime in order to achieve a complete understanding of how criminal acts are defined and processed. The experiences of the victims of crime, after all, constitute the first stage of the criminal justice process.

Another application of the sequential model is in medical sociology. Here, the model addresses several questions: How do physical ailments come to be recognized and defined as medical problems? When are doctors mobilized in the treatment of physical disease? What role do alternatives such as traditional medicine or new self-help approaches play in reducing or increasing the incidence of medical problems? What are the conditions under which some cases are referred for surgery whereas others are not?

Although the application of a value-added model to the study of physical illness should prove fruitful, its application to the so-called mental illness process should be even more productive. In fact, the study of any sort of social deviance can be organized within the framework developed here. Primary and secondary deviance are analogous to primary and secondary process. Lemert (1951:75–77; 1967:17–18) conceptualized the distinction between primary and secondary deviance in terms of situational and structural contingencies, respectively. But his evidence was qualitative and descriptive. By distinguishing between primary and secondary *process*, I have made it possible to quantify the propositions of labeling theory and to evaluate them empirically.

The Quest for Explanation in Sociological Research

The quest for universals in sociological research has been replaced by the quest for scientific, quantitative explanation. Ralph Turner played an important, albeit symbolic, role in signaling this change when he argued (1953:610), "Empirical prediction always requires some statistical or probability statements." Turner adds that the method of analytic induction is useful for describing the essential elements of a closed system, but these elements are activated by external factors correlated with them. The explanation of a given social process, then, lies in a quantitative strategy designed to predict how that process operates. The scientific study of social process depends on its quantification.

In the sociology of law, there has been little integration of theory and research, especially in the study of the dispute process. Theoretical speculation, illustrated with anecdotes and analogies, exists side-by-side with narrow empirical studies. Social processes are described in depth by ethnographers trained in a variety of disciplines. Or, the findings of research describing the correlates of some particular phenomenon are reported in articles published in scientific journals. In the present work, I have taken Turner's dictum seriously. By constructing an explanation of one particular social process, I have demonstrated how to go about constructing explanations of social process in general.

The scientific study of law and society requires that our theories be well grounded in the real world (see Glaser and Strauss, 1967:35–43). But we must also recognize that our models of the world are themselves social constructs. Theory and research are inseparable. The explanation of legal phenomena cannot be separated from its empirical analysis. And, finally, the empirical explanation of legal process depends on our ability to distinguish between elements of systems that are intrinsic and those that are extrinsic in origin. The scientific study of legal process entails the quantitative explanation of the intrinsic aspects of legal process in terms of their external correlates. The quantity of civil law is a function of the situations and social structures that transform disputes into legal claims.

APPENDIX A

THE LOG-LINEAR APPROACH TO THE ANALYSIS OF LEGAL PROCESS

ADVANTAGES OF THE LOG-LINEAR APPROACH

This book relies heavily upon the log-linear method for the analysis of survey data, a method especially suited to the analysis of dichotomous dependent variables (see Goodman, 1972a, 1972b). Causal models are constructed using a modified path-analysis approach designed to analyze multidimensional contingency tables when there is a clear ordering among the variables (see Goodman, 1973b). Path coefficients are derived from a set of sequentially ordered log-linear regression equations or *logit* models.

The dependent variable in the log-linear model is the *odds*, the ratio of cases in the "yes" category to those in the "no" category for a given dichotomous variable. For example, if 75% of the problems involve lawyers, the odds are 3:1 (3.00) that a given problem involved an attorney. At issue, then, is the extent to which membership in one category or another of a given independent variable affects the likelihood (odds) that a lawyer has been contacted.

The effect parameters (β's) reported in this volume are derived from log transformations of the multiplicative model (see Goodman, 1972a). In the transformed log-linear model, the dependent variable becomes the *log-odds* and the effect parameters are the natural logarithms of the multiplicative effects. Consequently, the log-linear regression model (logit) takes the form of the usual linear regression model:

$$\Omega_{ijk} = \gamma_i \gamma_j \gamma_k \gamma_{ij} \gamma_{ik} \gamma_{jk} \gamma_{ijk}$$

(the saturated multiplicative model)

where Ω = odds and γ = multiplicative parameter or

$$\Phi_{ijk} = \beta + \beta_i + \beta_j + \beta_k + \beta_{ij} + \beta_{ik} + \beta_{jk} + \beta_{ijk}$$

(the saturated log-linear model)

where $\Phi = \log \Omega$ or log-odds, and $\beta = \log \gamma$ or effect parameter. In the saturated log-linear model, all the main and interaction effects are included. This is one of the greatest advantages over traditional regression approaches that assume linear additive effects with few, if any, interactions (Goodman, 1978:2).

The main advantage of the log-linear approach over the linear approach to regression analysis is that there is no need to make inappropriate assumptions regarding levels of measurement and their distributions. At this stage in the development of the sociology of law, we do not have the capability to measure the quantity of law with any degree of precision (see Greenberg, 1983, for a discussion of the problems associated with the quantification of law). Black, (1980:209–217) argues that, in principle, law is quantifiable in interval or even ratio scales, but recognizes that such scales have yet to be constructed. Fortunately, sophisticated mathematical tools for the analysis of nominal variables have been developed (Greenberg, 1983:250); Goodman's log-linear approach is one of them.

Since the variables in log-linear analysis are nominal, either dichotomous or polytomous, assumptions regarding the relative magnitude of categorical variables are not necessary. But the log-linear method does enable us to assume ordering between categories and indicate directionality in relationships between variables. Furthermore, nominal variables are closer to the reality of social data. It is usually the social scientist who imposes higher-order scales on fundamentally categorical data through index construction and other artificial devices. The log-linear method is especially suited to the analysis of social process since the dependent variables are, by definition, dichotomous.

The log-linear method has the further advantage of being based on dependent variables that do not require the assumption that they are normally distributed (Goodman, 1978:2). In fact, the maximum-likelihood estimation procedure used in log-linear analysis is quite sensitive to the highly skewed distributions obtained in the analysis of process data, where there may be a considerable amount of attrition from one stage to the next.

There are two additional advantages to the log-linear method over other approaches. First, it offers a technique for selecting parsimonious explanations of dependent variables by identifying the best-fitting logit models. Second, the log-linear method is analogous to the analysis of variance. As in traditional analysis of variance, it is possible to evaluate the extent to which each independent variable, or interaction between or among independent variables, explains the variation in the odds pertaining to the dependent variable.

Goodman (1973b) has developed a modified path analysis approach analogous to more established techniques (see Duncan, 1966). Just like the older methods, the log-linear path model joins theoretical assumptions regarding the temporal order of the endogenous variables with an empirical analysis of the effects of the exogenous variables on those considered endogenous in the model. According to Goodman (1973:179), earlier approaches "are not suited to the case where the variables are polytomous or dichotomous, but the models proposed herein are." The log-linear path model is equivalent to the sum of the best-fitting logit models for each of the dependent (endogenous) variables in the general model. Just as it is possible to evaluate the goodness-of-fit between the logit model and the data, the path model itself can be evaluated to test whether it does or does not fit the data reasonably well.

THE TREATMENT OF STRUCTURAL ZEROS IN PROCESS MODELS

Path analysis for process data often includes structural zeros, that is, theoretically defined empty cells. This is the case in the relationship between the seriousness of the dispute (S) and contacting an attorney (L). Disputes that involve legal assistance are, by definition, more serious than those that do not. Consequentially, there were no cases in which disputes were not serious and a lawyer was contacted (see the table presented on page 70). From Goodman (1972a), we derive the following:

$$\beta_s = \frac{\text{log-odds } (S) - \text{log-odds } (\bar{S})}{2}$$

$$= \frac{\log .0894 - \log 0.0}{2}$$

$$= \frac{-2.41 - (-\infty)}{2}$$

$$= +\infty$$

In the above equation, the effect of seriousness on legal contacts is positive ($\beta_s = +\infty$). On the other hand, log-linear equations are unsolvable when $+\infty$ is included as a term. There are no remaining degrees of freedom once the corresponding marginals are determined. Consequently, β_s has no meaningful value; it is indeterminate.

In the multiway contingency table, fitting the marginals governed by the cross-tabulation of seriousness (S) and seeing a lawyer (L) creates structural zeros. For example, in the three-way table (*XSL*, where *X* is any variable):

		L	not-L
X	S	√	√
	not-S	0	√
not-X	S	√	√
	not-S	0	√

In the above case there are two structural zeros. Structural zeros reduce the number of degrees of freedom since the expected values in these cells are always zero and correspond to the observed frequency. The "starting table" option in Goodman's ECTA program corrects for this problem. The BMDP statistical package (Dixon, 1981) has incorporated a structural zero option that should facilitate the kind of analysis described here. The formula for calculating the degrees of freedom, correcting for structural zeros, is (see Bishop *et al.*, 1975:217–218)

$$df = V - Z_e + Z_p$$

where V = the number of *df* associated with the complete model, Z_e = the number of cells with zero expected values, and Z_p = the number of zero cells in the expected marginal configurations.

The inclusion of the [seriousness × lawyer] effect in the log-linear regression model adds nothing to its explanatory power in a statistical sense. Goodness-of-fit chi-square values are equivalent in models with and without the [seriousness × lawyer] effect. Yet, as I have shown above, the [seriousness × lawyer] relationship can be represented in terms of a positive effect ($\beta = +\infty$). Seriousness is logically prior to lawyer contact and its effect is positive; contacting attorneys depends on the perception of disputes as serious enough to warrant their assistance.

APPENDIX B

INCIDENT SCHEDULES

MAIN INCIDENTS: NEIGHBORHOOD PROBLEMS

23. We've talked so far about how you might handle possible problems. But here are some actual problems that may have come up for you at one time or another while living in the Detroit area. First, many people run into problems with their neighbors at one time or another. In the past ten years, which of these have ever happened to you? [HAND CARD 1 AND READ EACH ONE]

23a.	Problems with neighborhood children or teenagers?	___1. YES	___5. NO
23b.	Problems with noisy, disorderly, or undesirable neighbors?	___1. YES	___5. NO
23c.	Neighbors that don't mind their own business?	___1. YES	___5. NO
23d.	Someone who tried to sell or rent to undesirable people?	___1. YES	___5. NO
23e.	A neighbor who failed to keep up his property?	___1. YES	___5. NO
23f.	Any other problems or disagreements that you may have had with a neighbor?	___1. YES ________________ ________________	___5. NO

24. IF MORE THAN ONE PROBLEM CHECKED, ASK: Which of these problems you mentioned bothered you most within the last 10 years? Would you please circle the number of that one on your card. BE SURE THAT R CIRCLES ONE, AND CIRCLE THAT ONE BELOW AND ENTER IT ON PAGE 16, QUESTION 35. (IF ONLY ONE PROBLEM TO Q. 23, CIRCLE ITS NUMBER.)

23a 23b 23c 23d 23e 23f

MAIN INCIDENTS: RENTAL

25. Do you own your own home, or are you renting?

____1. OWNS (OR BUYING) ____2. RENTS

GO TO Q. 26

IF OWN, ASK:

25a. Have you rented in Detroit during the last ten years?

____1. YES, RENTED ____5. NO, DID NOT

SKIP TO Q. 28

26. Many people who rent run into problems at one time or another with the landlord or his agent. Would you tell me which of these problems have happened to you when renting in the Detroit area? [HAND CARD 2 TO R AND READ EACH ONE]

26a.	The landlord did not make repairs or provide services.	___1. YES	___5. NO
26b.	The landlord does not keep undesirable tenants or people out of the building.	___1. YES	___5. NO
26c.	The landlord claimed that you damaged the property.	___1. YES	___5. NO
26d.	The landlord claimed that you owed him money.	___1. YES	___5. NO
26e.	Any other problems that you may have had with your landlord?	___1. YES ___5. NO ________________ ________________ ________________	

27. IF MORE THAN ONE PROBLEM CHECKED, ASK: Which of these problems you mentioned bothered you most during the last 10 years? Would you please circle the number of that one on your card. BE SURE THAT R CIRCLES ONE, AND CIRCLE THAT ONE BELOW AND ENTER ON PAGE 16, QUESTION 35. (IF ONLY ONE PROBLEM TO Q. 26, CIRCLE ITS NUMBER.)

26a 26b 26c 26d 26e

MAIN INCIDENTS: EXPENSIVE PURCHASE

28. Often when people pay a lot of money for a car, furniture, or appliances, or repairs to any of these, they run into a problem. Would you tell me which of these have happened to you while living in the Detroit area? [HAND CARD 3 AND READ EACH ONE FOR R TO ANSWER]

28a.	Badly overcharged for a car, furniture, or something else expensive.	___1. YES	___5. NO
28b.	What I got was broken or didn't work as it should.	___1. YES	___5. NO
28c.	Trouble with a guarantee, contract, service policy, or repairs.	___1. YES	___5. NO
28d.	Trouble with credit, or with a collection agency.	___1. YES	___5. NO
28e.	Other problems.	___1. YES (SPECIFY)___________	___5. NO

29. IF MORE THAN ONE PROBLEM CHECKED, ASK: Which of these problems you mentioned bothered you most within the last 10 years? Would you please circle the number of that one on your card? BE SURE THAT R CIRCLES ONE, AND CIRCLE THAT ONE BELOW AND ENTER ON PAGE 16, QUESTION 35. (IF ONLY ONE PROBLEM TO Q. 28, CIRCLE ITS NUMBER.)

28a 28b 28c 28d 28e

30. Very briefly, what was the object or service involved in this problem?

MAIN INCIDENTS: PUBLIC ORGANIZATIONS

31. Now I'd like to find out if you have had any problems in dealing with federal, state, or local government agencies? [HAND CARD 4 AND READ EACH ONE FOR R TO ANSWER]

31a. The Social Security and Veterans Administrations give people several kinds of benefits. Have you ever had a problem in getting benefits you deserved, like pensions, medical care, loans, or anything else of that sort?

____1. YES ____5. NO

31b. Have you had troubles with social workers or welfare officials?

____1. YES ____5. NO

31c. Have you had a problem with the government over your federal income tax return?

____1. YES ____5. NO

31d. Have you ever had a problem with property taxes, or with inspections of your property?

____1. YES ____5. NO

31e. What about problems because the city ignored your complaints about such services, as street cleaning or repair, garbage collection, or water service?

____1. YES ____5. NO

31f. Have you ever had problems with the police department or policemen?

1. YES ____5. NO

31g. Have you had any other problems with local, state or federal government officials? (SPECIFY) IF NONE, WRITE NONE.

____

____

32. IF MORE THAN ONE PROBLEM CHECKED, ASK: Looking back on the problems you had with these government agencies, which of these gave you the most trouble in the last 10 years? Would you please circle the number of that one on your card? BE SURE THAT R CIRCLES ONE, AND CIRCLE THAT ONE BELOW AND ENTER ON PAGE 16, QUESTION 35. (IF ONLY ONE PROBLEM TO Q. 31, CIRCLE ITS NUMBER.)

31a 31b 31c 31d 31e 31f 31g

MAIN INCIDENTS: DISCRIMINATION

33. Some people feel that they have been treated unfairly because of their age, sex, race, religion, nationality, or beliefs. Since living in the Detroit area, have you been treated unfairly in any of the following ways? [HAND CARD 5 AND READ EACH ONE FOR R TO ANSWER] FOR EACH Q (33a, b, c, d, AND e), IF YES, SPECIFY IN ONE WORD THE TYPE OF DISCRIMINATION, i.e., WHETHER IT WAS BASED ON "AGE", "SEX", "RACE", "RELIGION", "NATIONALITY", OR "BELIEFS".

33a.	In getting a job or being promoted on a job? ____YES (SPECIFY ______________) ____7. NO
33b.	In joining a club or organization? ____YES (SPECIFY ______________) ____7. NO
33c.	In buying or renting a house or apartment? ____YES (SPECIFY ______________) ____7. NO
33d.	In getting some service you should get? ____YES (SPECIFY ______________) ____7. NO
33e.	Any other way you have been treated unfairly because of your age, sex, race, religion, nationality or beliefs. ____YES ____7. NO ↓ ASK: In what way was that? (SPECIFY TYPE ALSO) ______________________________

34. IF MORE THAN ONE PROBLEM CHECKED, ASK: Which of these cases bothered you most within the last 10 years? Would you please circle the number of that one on your card? BE SURE THAT R CIRCLES ONE, AND CIRCLE THAT ONE BELOW AND ENTER ON PAGE 16, QUESTION 35. (IF ONLY ONE PROBLEM GIVEN TO Q. 33, CIRCLE ITS NUMBER.)

33a 33b 33c 33d 33e

35. SUMMARY OF PROBLEMS

ENTER HERE THE MOST IMPORTANT PROBLEM NUMBER FROM EACH OF THE FIVE AREAS. WHERE NO PROBLEM IN AN AREA, WRITE "None".

PROBLEM NO.	AREA
________	35a. NEIGHBORHOOD (from Q. 24)
________	35b. RENTAL (from Q. 27)
________	35c. EXPENSIVE PURCHASE (from Q. 29)
________	35d. PUBLIC ORGANIZATION (from Q. 32)
________	35e. DISCRIMINATION (from Q. 34)

36. SELECTION OF SUPPLEMENTARY QUESTIONS FOR TWO PROBLEMS

IF R HAD PROBLEMS IN TWO OR MORE AREAS LISTED IN 35a-e, ASK:

Now please look over the problems that bothered you most in each of the areas we have talked about. Let's see...in the ________ area, it was a problem about ________; in the ________ area it was about ________. ETC. (READ MOST IMPORTANT OR ONLY PROBLEM IN EACH AREA INDICATED IN Q. 35a-e.)

Now which one of these gave you the most difficulty of all? (ENTER BELOW IN 36a) And which one would you put next? (ENTER BELOW IN 36b)

PROBLEM NO.

________ 36a. MOST DIFFICULT PROBLEM ⟶ ASK SUPPLEMENT I, Q's 37-48.

________ 36b. 2nd MOST DIFFICULT ⟶ ASK SUPPLEMENT II, Q's 49-60.

IF R HAD MOST IMPORTANT PROBLEM IN ONLY ONE AREA, ENTER ITS NUMBER IN 36a ABOVE, WRITE "None" IN 36b, AND ASK SUPPLEMENT I. SKIP SUPPLEMENT II, Q's 49-60.

IF R HAD NO PROBLEMS AT ALL, WRITE "None" IN 36a AND 36b ABOVE, AND SKIP TO Q. 61 ON PAGE 29.

CASE HISTORY FORM

CHECK BELOW THE APPROPRIATE AREA FROM Q. 36a AND ASK FOLLOWING QUESTION

37. ___a. NEIGHBORHOOD AREA: Thinking back now to the problem that bothered you (most) in the neighborhood, you said it had to do with ____________________, could you tell me what the problem was mainly about? ONE PROBE REQUIRED (P).

___b. LANDLORD-TENANT AREA: Thinking back now to the problem that bothered you (most) with your landlord, you said it had to do with ____________________, could you tell me what the problem was mainly about? ONE PROBE REQUIRED (P).

___c. EXPENSIVE PURCHASE AREA: Thinking back now to the problem that bothered you (most) with regard to buying things, you said that it had to do with ____________________, could you tell me what the problem was mainly about? ONE PROBE REQUIRED (P).

___d. PUBLIC ORGANIZATION AREA: Thinking back now to the problem with a government agency that bothered you (most), you said it had to do with ________________, could you tell me what the problem was mainly about? ONE PROBE REQUIRED (P).

___e. DISCRIMINATION AREA: Thinking back now to the unfair treatment that gave you the (most) problem, you said it had to do with ____________________, could you tell me what the problem was mainly about? ONE PROBE REQUIRED (P). SPECIAL ADDITIONAL PROBE FOR DISCRIMINATION: What was it about the situation that first made you see you were being treated unfairly?

____

____

____

____

____

____

____

____

38. Did anyone who caused you this problem act against some law?

____1. YES ↓ ____5. NO ↓

38a. What law was that?	38b. Was anyone who caused you the problem in the wrong in any way? ____1. YES ____5. NO

39. How did you (do you) want to see this problem settled?

____

____

____

____

40. Did you do (have you done) anything (more) to get it settled this way?

____1. YES ↓ ____5. NO

40a. What did you do?

41. Was (is) there any action you wanted to take on this problem but felt you couldn't for some reason?

____1. YES ↓ ____5. NO

41a. What was (is) it that you wanted (want) to do?

41b. Why did (do) you feel you couldn't (can't) do that?

42. IF NOT ENTIRELY CLEAR FROM PRECEDING ANSWERS, ASK THIS QUESTION. IF ALREADY ENTIRELY CLEAR, SKIP THIS QUESTION BUT INDICATE BY Q#'s WHERE INFORMATION IS LOCATED.

How did the problem finally come out? FOR CONTINUING PROBLEMS, ASK: How does the problem stand now?

____

____

____

____

43. On the whole, were you satisfied with the way that it finally came out? FOR CONTINUING PROBLEMS, ASK: On the whole, are you satisfied with the way the problem stands now?

____1. YES ↓

43a. Were (are) you satisfied mainly because you got your lawful rights, or because you got what you wanted, or because you got the best you could?

____1. LAWFUL RIGHTS

____2. GOT WHAT WANTED

____3. GOT BEST I COULD

____5. NO ↓

43b. Were you dissatisfied mainly because you felt you didn't get your lawful rights, or mainly because nothing was done?

____1. DIDN'T GET YOUR LAWFUL RIGHTS

____2. NOTHING WAS DONE

44. Now I'd like to know something about which people you may have talked to on this problem or who may have given you some help or advice on it. First, did you ever get advice from a lawyer on the problem?

____1. YES ↓

____5. NO

44a. What did he tell you to do, or what did he do?

Here are some other people you might have talked to at one time or another on the problem. [HAND CARD 6 AND READ ALL OF Q. 45; THEN ASK QUESTIONS 46 AND 47 FOR EACH OF THE PERSONS CHECKED "YES" IN Q. 45.]

45.	46. Why did you think this would be a good person to turn to on this problem?	47. Did this person say or do anything that made any difference in what you did or in what happened?
45a. Did you ever talk with a friend or neighbor? ____1. YES ____5. NO	46a.	47a. ___1. YES ___5. NO ↓ What was that?
45b. Someone who works where you do? ____1. YES ____5. NO	46b.	47b. ___1. YES ___5. NO ↓ What was that?
45c. A public official? ____1. YES, SPECIFY OCCUPATION ____________ ____5. NO	46c.	47c. ___1. YES ___5. NO ↓ What was that?
45d. Some organization or group? ____1. YES, SPECIFY ORGANIZATION ____________ ____5. NO	46d.	47d. ___1. YES ___5. NO ↓ What was that?

GO BACK TO Q. 46 AND 47.

48. ASK ONLY OF NEIGHBOR AND LANDLORD-TENANT AREAS: Finally, did you ever call the police on this problem?

____1. YES ____5. NO (SKIP TO Q. 49)

48a. What did they do?

48b. Did they give you any advice as to what you should do?

____1. YES ____5. NO→ GO TO Q. 48d

48c. What advice did they give you?

48d. Were you completely satisfied with the way the police handled the matter?

____1. YES ____5. NO

48e. Why weren't you satisfied?

REFERENCES

Aday, Lu Ann and Ronald Andersen
1975 Access to Medical Care. Ann Arbor: Health Administration Press.

Aday, Lu Ann, Ronald Andersen, and Gretchen V. Fleming
1980 Health Care in the U.S.: Equitable for Whom? Beverly Hills: Sage.

Akers, Ronald L.
1975 "Toward a comparative definition of law." Pp. 33–40 in R. L. Akers and R. Hawkins (eds.), Law and Control in Society. Englewood Cliffs, N.J.: Prentice-Hall.

Andersen, Ronald
1978 "Health status indices and access to medical care." American Journal of Public Health 68:458–463.

Baumgartner, M. P.
1980 "Law and the middle class: Some evidence from a suburban town." Presented at the annual meetings of the Law and Society Association, Madison, Wisc.
1981 "Social control in a suburban town: An ethnographic study." Unpublished doctoral dissertation, Yale University.

Becker, Howard S.
1960 "Notes on the concept of commitment." American Journal of Sociology 66:32–40.
1963 Outsiders: Studies in the Sociology of Deviance. New York: Free Press.

Berkanovic, Emil and Leo G. Reeder
1974 "Can money buy the appropriate use of service? Some notes on the meaning of utilization data." Journal of Health and Social Behavior 15:93–99.

Bernstein, Ilene N., William R. Kelley, and Patricia A. Doyle
1977 "Societal reaction to deviants: The case of criminal defendants." American Sociological Review 42:743–755.

Biderman, Albert D.
1975 "Victimology and victimization surveys." Pp. 153–169 in I. Drapkin and E. Viano (eds.), Victimology: A New Focus (Vol. 3). Lexington, Mass.: Lexington Books.

Bishop, Yvonne, Stephen E. Feinberg, and Paul W. Holland
1975 Discrete Multivariate Analysis: Theory and Practice. Cambridge, Mass.: MIT Press.

Black, Donald
1970 "Production of crime rates." American Sociological Review 35:733–748.
1972 "The boundaries of legal sociology." Yale Law Journal 81:1086–1100.
1973 "The mobilization of law." Journal of Legal Studies 2:125–149.
1976 The Behavior of Law. New York: Academic Press.
1979 "Common sense in the sociology of law." American Sociological Review 44:18–27.
1980 The Manners and Customs of the Police. New York: Academic Press.
1983 "Crime as social control." American Sociological Review 48:34–45.

Black, Henry C.
1979 Black's Law Dictionary. St. Paul: West Publishing.

Blumberg, Abraham S.
1967 Criminal Justice. Chicago: Quadrangle Books.
Bock, R. Darrell and George Yates
1973 Multiqual: Log-Linear Analysis of Nominal or Ordinal Qualitative Data by the Method of Maximum Likelihood. Ann Arbor: National Educational Resources.
Bohannan, Paul
1980 "Law and legal institutions." Pp. 3–11 in Wm. M Evan (ed.), The Sociology of Law. New York: Free Press.
Braun, Hugo E., Jr. and Daniel J. Page
1979 The Language of Real Estate in Michigan. Chicago: Real Estate Education Company.
Brill, Harry
1973 "The uses and abuses of legal assistance." The Public Interest 31:38–55.
Buckle, Leonard and Suzann R. Thomas-Buckle
1982 "Doing unto others: Dispute processing in an urban American neighborhood." Pp. 78–90 in R. Tomasic and M. M. Feeley (eds.), Neighborhood Justice: Assessment of an Emerging Idea. New York: Longman.
Bumiller, Kristin
1981 "Choice of forum in diversity cases: Analysis of a survey and implications for reform." Law and Society Review 15:749–774.
Cain, Maureen and Kálmán Kulcsár
1982 "Thinking disputes: An essay on the origins of the dispute industry." Law and Society Review 16:375–402.
Caplovitz, David
1963 The Poor Pay More. New York: Free Press.
Cappelletti, Mauro and Bryant Garth
1978 "Access to justice: The newest wave in the worldwide movement to make rights effective." Buffalo Law Review 27:181–292.
Carlin, Jerome E.
1970 "Store front lawyers in San Francisco." Transaction 7 No. 6:64–74.
Carlin, Jerome E. and Jan Howard
1965 "Legal representation and class justice." U.C.L.A. Law Review 12:381–437.
Carlin, Jerome E., Jan Howard, and Sheldon L. Messinger
1966 "Civil justice and the poor: Issues for sociological research." Law and Society Review 1:9–89.
Carlson, Rick J.
1976 "Measuring the quality of legal services: An idea whose time has not come." Law and Society Review 11:287–317.
Chambliss, William J.
1976 "The saints and the roughnecks." Pp. 148–161 in Wm. J. Chambliss and M. Mankoff (eds.), Whose Law? What Order? New York: Wiley.
Chambliss, William J. and Robert B. Seidman
1971 Law, Order, and Power. Reading, Mass.: Addison-Wesley.
Chevigny, Paul
1969 Police Power: Police Abuses in New York City. New York: Pantheon Books.
Cloward, Richard A. and Lloyd E. Ohlin
1960 Delinquency and Opportunity. New York: Free Press.
Coates, Dan and Steven Penrod
1981 "Social psychology and the emergence of disputes." Law and Society Review 15:655–680.

Cohen, Albert K.
1966 Deviance and Control. Englewood Cliffs, N.J.: Prentice-Hall.
Collins, Randall
1975 Conflict Sociology: Toward an Explanatory Science. New York: Academic Press.
Corbin, Arthur Linton
1952 Corbin on Contracts. St. Paul: West Publishing.
Costner, Herbert L. and Robert K. Leik
1964 "Deductions from 'axiomatic theory'." American Sociological Review 29:819–835.
Countryman, Vern and Ted Finman
1966 The Lawyer in Modern Society. Boston: Little, Brown.
Curran, Barbara A.
1977 The Legal Needs of the Public. Chicago: American Bar Foundation.
Curran, Barbara A. and Francis O. Spalding
1974 The Legal Needs of the Public: Preliminary Report. Chicago: Special Committee to Survey Legal Needs of the American Bar Association and the American Bar Foundation.
Detroit City Planning Department
1974 A Profile of Detroit—1970. Detroit: Detroit City Planning Department.
Dixon, W. J.
1977 BMDP-77 Biomedical Computer Programs: P-Series. Los Angeles: University of California Press.
1981 BMDP Statistical Software-1981. Los Angeles: University of California Press.
Duncan, Otis Dudley
1966 "Path analysis: Sociological examples." American Journal of Sociology 72:1–16.
Ehrlich, Thomas
1981 "Federal legal help for the poor: A debate over means and ends." New York Times. Interview, June 28: E5.
Elliot, Delbert S.
1966 "Delinquency, school attendance, and dropout." Social Problems 13:307–314.
Etzioni, Amitai
1975 A Comparative Analysis of Complex Organizations. New York: Free Press.
Feeley, Malcolm M.
1979 The Process is the Punishment: Handling Cases in a Lower Criminal Court. New York: Russell Sage.
Felstiner, William L. F.
1974 "Influences of social organization on dispute processing." Law and Society Review 9:63–94.
Felstiner, William L. F., Richard L. Abel, and Austin Sarat
1981 "The emergence and transformation of disputes: naming, blaming, claiming . . ." Law and Society Review 15:631–654.
Finman, Ted
1971 "O.E.O. legal services program and the pursuit of social change: The relationship between program ideology and program performance." Wisconsin Law Review 1971: 1001–1084.
Fitzgerald, Jeffrey and Richard Dickins
1981 "Disputing in legal and nonlegal contexts: Some questions for sociologists of law." Law and Society Review 15:681–706.
Galanter, Marc
1974 "Why the 'haves' come out ahead: Speculations on the limits of legal change." Law and Society Review 9:95–160.

1975 "Delivering legality: Some proposals for the direction of research." Pp. 67–96 in L. Brickman and R. Lempert (eds.), The Role of Research in the Delivery of Legal Services: Working Papers and Conference Proceedings. Washington, D.C.: The Resource Center for Consumers of Legal Services.

1976 "Delivering legality: Some proposals for the direction of research." Law and Society Review 11:225–246.

Gibbons, Don C.

1977 Society, Crime, and Criminal Careers. Englewood Cliffs, N.J.: Prentice-Hall.

Glaser, Barney G. and Anselm L. Strauss

1967 The Discovery of Grounded Theory: Strategies for Qualitative Research. Chicago: Aldine.

Glaser, Daniel

1971 Social Deviance. Chicago: Markham.

Glenn, Norval D.

1977 Cohort Analysis. Beverly Hills: Sage Publications.

Goodman, Leo A.

1972a "A modified multiple regression approach to the analysis of dichotomous variables." American Sociological Review 37:28–46.

1972b A general model for the analysis of surveys." American Journal of Sociology 77:1035–1086.

1973a "Causal analysis of data from panel studies and other kinds of surveys." American Journal of Sociology 78:1135–1191.

1973b "The analysis of multidimensional contingency tables when some variables are posterior to others: A modified path analysis approach." Biometrika 60:179–192.

1978 Analyzing Qualitative/Categorical Data: Log-Linear Models and Latent Structure Analysis. Cambridge, Mass.: Abt Books

Gottfredson, Michael R. and Michael J. Hindelang

1979 "A study of *The Behavior of Law*." American Sociological Review 44:3–18.

Greenberg, David F.

1983 "Donald Black's sociology of law: A critique." Law and Society Review 17:337–368.

Gulliver, P. H.

1979 Disputes and Negotiations: A Cross-Cultural Perspective. New York: Academic Press.

Hart, H. L. A.

1961 The Concept of Law. London: Oxford University Press.

Hoebel, E. Adamson

1954 The Law of Primitive Man: A Study in Comparative Legal Dynamics. Cambridge: Harvard University Press.

Horwitz, Allan V.

1983 "Resistance to innovation in the sociology of law: A response to Greenberg." Law and Society Review 17:369–384.

Hunting, Roger B. and Gloria S. Neuwirth

1962 Who Sues in New York City? New York: Columbia University Press.

Jacob, Herbert

1978 Justice in America: Courts, Lawyers, and the Judicial Process. Boston: Little, Brown.

Kaplan, John

1973 Criminal Justice: Introductory Cases and Materials. Mineola, New York: Foundation Press.

Kitsuse, John I.
1964 "Societal reaction to deviant behavior: Problems of theory and method." Pp. 87–102 in H. S. Becker, (ed.), The Other Side. New York: Free Press.

Kornhauser, William
1959 The Politics of Mass Society. Glencoe, Ill.: Free Press.

Kritzer, Herbert M.
1981 "Studying disputes: Learning from the CLRP experience." Law and Society Review 15:503–524.

Ladinsky, Jack
1976 "The traffic in legal services: Lawyer-seeking behavior and the channeling of clients." Law and Society Review 11:207–224.

Lasker, Judith N.
1981 "Choosing among therapies: Illness behavior in the Ivory Coast." Social Science and Medicine 15A:157–168.

Laumann, Edward O.
1966 Prestige and Association in an Urban Community: An Analysis of an Urban Stratification System. Indianapolis: Bobbs-Merrill.

Lee, Alfred McClung and Norman D. Humphrey
1943 Race Riot. New York: The Dryden Press.

Lemert, Edwin M.
1951 Social Pathology. New York: McGraw-Hill.
1967 Human Deviance, Social Problems, and Social Control. Englewood Cliffs, N.J.: Prentice-Hall.

Lempert, Richard O.
1972 "Norm-making in social exchange: A contract law model." Law and Society Review 7:1–32.
1976 "Mobilizing private law: An introductory essay." Law and Society Review 11:173–189.
1981 "Grievances and legitimacy: The beginnings and end of dispute settlement." Law and Society Review 15:707–716.

Lenin, V. I.
1965 The State. Peking: Foreign Languages Press.

Lenski, Gerhard
1961 The Religious Factor. Garden City, New York: Doubleday.

Lieberman, Jethro K.
1981 The Litigious Society. New York: Basic Books.

Lindesmith, Alfred R.
1947 Opiate Addiction. Bloomington, Ind.: Principia Press.

Lochner, Philip R., Jr.
1975 "The no fee and low fee legal practice of private attorneys." Law and Society Review 9:431–473

Locke, Hubert G.
1969 The Detroit Riot of 1967. Detroit: Wayne State University Press.

Lofland, John and Rodney Stark
1965 "Becoming a world-saver: A theory of conversion to a deviant perspective." American Sociological Review 30:862–875.

Lundman, Richard J.
1974 "Routine arrest procedures: A commonwealth perspective." Social Problems 22:128–141.

1979 "Organizational norms and police discretion: An observational study of police work with traffic law violations." Criminology 17:159–171.
1980 "Police patrol work: A comparative perspective." Pp. 52–65 in R. J. Lundman, Police Behavior: A Sociological Perspective. New York: Oxford University Press.
Macaulay, Stewart
1963 "Non-contractual relations in business: A preliminary study." American Sociological Review 28:55–67.
Maddi, Dorothy L. and Frederic R. Merrill
1971 The Private Practicing Bar and Legal Services for Low-Income People. Chicago: American Bar Foundation.
Marks, F. Raymond
1976 "Some research perspectives for looking at legal need and legal services delivery systems: Old forms or new?" Law and Society Review 11:191–205.
Marks, F. Raymond, Robert O. Hallauer, and Richard R. Clifton
1974 The Shreveport Plan: An Experiment in the Delivery of Legal Services. Chicago: American Bar Foundation.
Mather, Lynn and Barbara Yngvesson
1981 "Language, audience, and the transformation of disputes." Law and Society Review 15:755–822.
Matza, David
1964 Delinquency and Drift. New York: Wiley.
Mayhew, Leon
1975 "Institutions of representation: Civil justice and the public." Law and Society Review 9:401–429.
Mayhew, Leon and Albert J. Reiss, Jr.
1969 "The social organization of legal contacts." American Sociological Review 34:309–318.
McIntosh, Wayne
1981 "Language, audience, and the transformation of disputes." Law and Society Review 15:823–848.
Meeks, James E.
1976 Antitrust Aspects of Prepaid Legal Services Plans. Chicago: American Bar Foundation.
Meier, August and Elliott Rudwick
1979 Black Detroit and the Rise of the UAW. New York: Oxford University Press.
Merry, Sally E.
1979 "Going to court: Strategies of dispute management in an American urban neighborhood." Law and Society Review 13:891–925.
1982 "Defining 'success' in the neighborhood justice movement." Pp. 172–192 in R. Tomasic and M. M. Feeley (eds.), Neighborhood Justice: Assessment of an Emerging Idea. New York: Longman.
Merton, Robert K.
1957 Social Theory and Social Structure. New York: Free Press.
Michigan Law Review
1968 "The administration of justice in the wake of the Detroit civil disorder of July 1967." Michigan Law Review 66:1542–1630.
Miller, Daniel R. and Guy E. Swanson
1958 The Changing American Parent: A Study in the Detroit Area. New York: Wiley.

Miller, Michael H.
1973 "Who receives optional medical care?" Journal of Health and Social Behavior 14:176–182.
Miller, Richard E. and Austin Sarat
1981 "Grievances, claims, and disputes: Assessing the adversary culture." Law and Society 15:525–566.
Moore, Sally Falk
1978 Law as Process: An Anthropological Approach. Boston: Routledge.
Nader, Laura
1979 "Disputing without the use of force." Yale Law Journal 88:998–1021.
1980 No Access to Law. New York: Academic Press.
Nagel, Ilene H.
1980 "The behavior of formal law: A study of bail decisions." Presented at the annual meetings of the Law and Society Association, Madison, Wisc.
Nie, Norman H., C. Hadlai Hull, Jean G. Jenkins, Karin Steinbrenner, and Dale H. Bent
1975 SPSS: Statistical Package for the Social Sciences, (2nd ed.). New York: McGraw-Hill.
Pastor, Paul A., Jr.
1978 "Mobilization in public drunkenness control: A comparison of legal and medical approaches." Social Problems 25:373–384.
Pipkin, Ronald M.
1979 "Legal aid and elitism in the American legal profession." Pp. 185–192 in J. J. Bonsignore, E. Katsh, P. d'Errico, R. M. Pipkin, S. Arons, and J. Rifkin (eds.), Before the Law: An Introduction to Legal Process, (2nd ed.). Boston: Houghton-Mifflin.
Plenningstorf, Werner and Spencer L. Kimball
1976a Legal Services Plans: A Typology. Chicago: American Bar Foundation.
1976b Employee Legal Service Plans: Conflicts Between Federal and State Regulations. Chicago: American Bar Foundation.
Quinney, Richard
1970 The Social Reality of Crime. Boston: Little, Brown.
1974 Critique of Legal Order. Boston: Little, Brown.
Radelet, Michael L.
1981 "Racial characteristics and the death penalty." American Sociological Review 46:918–927.
Reiss, Albert J., Jr.
1971 The Police and the Public. New Haven: Yale University Press.
Reiss, Albert J., Jr. and David J. Bordua
1967 "Environment and organization: A perspective on the police." Pp. 29–32 in D. J. Bordua (ed.), The Police: Six Sociological Essays. New York: Wiley.
Reiss, Albert J., Jr. and Albert L. Rhodes
1961 "The distribution of juvenile delinquency in the social class structure." American Sociological Review 26:720–732.
Robinson, W. S.
1950 "Ecological correlations and the behavior of individuals." American Sociological Review 15:351–356.
Ross, H. Laurence
1971 Settled Out of Court: The Social Process of Insurance Claims Adjustments. Chicago: Aldine.

Sarat, Austin
1976 "Alternatives in dispute processing: Litigation in a small claims court." Law and Society Review 10:339–375.
1977 "Studying American legal culture: An assessment of survey evidence." Law and Society Review 11:427–488.
1983 Address to the annual meetings of the Law and Society Association, Denver, Colorado.

Sarat, Austin and Joel B. Grossman
1975 "Courts and conflict resolution: Problems in the mobilization of adjudication." American Political Science Review 69:1200–1217.

Scheff, Thomas J.
1966 Being Mentally Ill. Chicago: Aldine.

Shover, Neal
1973 "The civil justice process as societal reactions." Social Forces 52:253–258.

Silberman, Matthew
1976 "Toward a theory of criminal deterrence." American Sociological Review 41:442–461.
1978 "The study of legal change: The survey and related methods." Presented at the annual meetings of the Law and Society Association, Minneapolis, Minn.
1979 "Deterrence and social control: A reply to Grasmick and McLaughlin." American Sociological Review 44:872–879.

Silbey, Susan S.
1981 "Case processing: Consumer protection in an attorney general's office." Law and Society Review 15:849–882.

Silverstein, Lee
1968 "Waiver of court costs and appointment of counsel for poor persons in civil cases." Chicago: American Bar Foundation.

Skolnick, Jerome
1966 Justice Without Trial. New York: Wiley.

Smelser, Neil J.
1962 Theory of Collective Behavior. New York: Free Press.

Stinchcombe, Arthur
1963 "Institutions of privacy in the determination of police administrative practice." American Journal of Sociology 69:150–160.

Students of the Columbia Law School
1969 "Small claims court: Reform revisited." Columbia Journal of Law and Social Problems 5:47–68.

Sutherland, Edwin H.
1947 Principles of Criminology, (4th ed.). Philadelphia: Lippincott.

Swanson, Guy E.
1965 "On explanations of social interaction." Sociometry 28:101–123.

Tavris, Carol
1982 Anger: The Misunderstood Emotion. New York: Simon and Schuster.

Theodorson, George A. and Achilles G. Theodorson
1969 A Modern Dictionary of Sociology. New York: Crowell.

Thomas, W. I.
1923 The Unadjusted Girl. Boston: Little, Brown.

Turk, Austin T.
1976 "Law as a weapon in social conflict." Social Problems 23:276–291.

Turner, Ralph H.
1953 "The quest for universals in sociological research." American Sociological Review 18:604–611.
United Community Services (UCS)
1970 "Subcommunities in the city of Detroit." Detroit: United Community Services.
U.S. Bureau of the Census
1967 "Income in 1966 of families and persons in the United States." Current Population Reports, Series P-60, No. 53. Washington, D.C.: U.S. Government Printing Office.
1972a Statistical Abstracts of the United States: 1972. Washington, D.C.: U.S. Government Printing Office.
1972b Census of Population and Housing: 1970 Census Tracts. Final Report PHC(1)-58 Detroit, Michigan SMSA. Washington, D.C.: U.S. Government Printing Office.
1973 County and City Data Book, 1972. Washington, D.C.: U.S. Government Printing Office.
1975 "Money income in 1973 of families and persons in the United States." Current Population Reports, Series P-60, No. 97. Washington, D.C.: U.S. Government Printing Office.
1982 Statistical Abstracts of the United States: 1982–83. Washington, D.C.: U.S. Government Printing Office.
Waldo, Gordon and Theodore G. Chiricos
1972 "Perceived penal sanction and self-reported criminality: A neglected approach to deterrence research." Social Problems 19:522–40.
Weber, Max
1954 Max Weber on Law in Economy and Society. Translated by Edward Shils and Max Rheinstein. Cambridge: Harvard University Press.
1978 Economy and Society. Guenther Ross and Claus Wittich, (eds.). Berkeley: University of California Press.
Wolfgang, Marvin E.
1967 "Analytical categories for research on victimization." Pp. 165–185 in A. Mergen and H. Schafer (eds.), Kriminologische Wegzeichen, Festschrift fur Hans von Hertig, Band 29, Hamburg: Kriminalistik.
Wonnacott, Ronald J. and Thomas H. Wonnacott
1970 Econometrics. New York: Wiley.
Wrong, Dennis H.
1979 Power: Its Forms, Bases, and Uses. New York: Harper and Row.
Yale Law Journal
1973 "Legal services and landlord-tenant litigation: A critical analysis." Yale Law Journal 82:1495–1511.
1979 "Dispute resolution." Yale Law Journal 88:905–909.
Zemans, Frances K.
1983 "Legal mobilization: The neglected role of the law in the political system." American Political Science Review 77:690–703.
Znaniecki, Florian
1934 The Method of Sociology. New York: Farrar and Rinehart.

AUTHOR INDEX

For complete bibliographical information, see References, p. 179.

S

T

W

Y

Z

SUBJECT INDEX

D

S